POLAND'S SECRET ENVOY
1939-1945

*To unconquered women
of captive Warsaw*

POLAND'S SECRET ENVOY
1939-1945

George "Jur" Lerski

Bicentennial Publishing Corp., Inc.
New York

Designer—Krzysztof Winnicki
Composition—Mildred Brooks

Printed by Bicentennial Publishing Corp., Inc.
417 Manhattan Ave., New York, N.Y. 11222

PREFACE

In writing this preface I must overcome the temptation to turn it into a review. In my opinion, a preface should serve as an introduction to the book, and it may even be used to portend intellectual experiences and impressions, while a review would tend to close its pages after passing final judgment on its contents. In this foreword I promise the reader that the reminiscences of Jerzy Lerski, "Jur", as the emissary of the Commander-in-Chief and Prime Minister, who was parachuted into German-occupied Poland make fascinating reading.

The line of demarcation between the author's reminiscences and the actual historical event in which he participated has been effaced. The historical facts are like a steel structure built on a granite foundation, while memories resemble fireproof bricks which line its walls. This imperial edifice symbolizing Poland's thousand-year history which is proudly crowned by the "Polish Underground State" will contain one brick bearing the deeply engraved name "Jur" — Jerzy Lerski.

He who assumes the task of "emissary" of the Supreme Commander and Prime Minister must possess exceptional qualifications. The emissary's role is more than that of a recorder which repeats matters entrusted to it. Neither is he a courier who crosses forbidden borders with microfilms or secretly coded texts in order to deliver them at the end of his assigned mission. The emissary is a living individual whose background knowledge complements the microfilm texts with the understanding that his words outweigh the tramsmitted messages with which he is acquainted, and which he may be required to repeat in the event that the films entrusted to him must be destroyed. In a way the emissary is a sort of confessor to those who send him on his mission. Usually the officials see him for the first time as they examine him with great interest—in this case, it was a rosy-cheeked youth to whom they were to enrust great national secrets and personal confidences. It is essential that the emissary is prepared as an individual to undertake this important mission. He cannot be politicaly unsophisticated because he would be unable to comprehend instructions nor could he fulfill requirements. He must be an intelligent person, educated and above all well-informed and politically oriented. Finally, the role of emissary places upon the individual great moral and intellectual demands. He is forbidden to mix his personal views with those he is instructed to transmit. Only if he is asked for his personal opinion can he express his own convictions and sympathies. By nature, he must be truthful and possess a remarkable memory to which at times more information is entrusted than to the microfilm in this possession. Finally, the emissary must possess such courage that he is prepared to face death in the event of arrest.

All of the demands were completely fulfilled by "Jur." He came from a family with a tradition of participation in Polish uprisings against Russia in the 19th century. He possessed a political instinct and a social sense which encouraged him to take an active part in public activities. At the outbreak of the war, he was Chairman of the Polish Social-Democratic Youth and a member of the Supreme Council of the Democratic Party. Whenever condition allowed, he continued his studies throughout the war, and ultimately became a professor of history at the University of San Francisco. During the war years and the period of occupation of Poland by the enemy, he exemplified the twenty-odd year old youth who not only loved his country, but also one who was anxious to fight for it. This prompted him, following the failure of the September 1939 campaign and the defeat of the Polish Army, to illegally cross several unfriendly borders to the west where he eventually joined the re-established Polish Army in France. He left his army only to return to occupied Poland in order to participate actively in the underground struggle. His round-trip mission, to Poland and back to England, was successfully accomplished.

"Jur's" reminiscences may be divided into two parts — his sojourn in captured Poland, and as an emigre in England. These are tied into a whole by his dramatic nighttime parachute jump into his Nazi-occupied homeland and the death-defying return overland to England. The portraits of underground Poland described by "Jur" in this book prompt me to compare them with Matthew Brady's photographs of the United States Civil War, when he described Warsaw as seen by the occupying power and the Warsaw concealed from the eyes of the enemy. With unequaled patriotism, courage, and derision of the enemy, the residents crowded the streets of the capital in the presence of the invisible and anonymous leadership of Polish conspirators who were active while concealed in the underground. On one hand there were arrests, round-ups, and public executions, and on the other, country picnics in a quiet environment and flirtations with pretty girls to whose charms "Jur" succumbs willingly. At all times "Jur" not only plays the role of observer, but he is also a participant. Since he is sensitive and possesses good powers of observation, a remarkable memory, and a sense of humor, he is capable of effectively reflecting in these reminiscences the never to be forgotten atmosphere and scenes from the embattled country and its capital.

The portion of the book dealing with his sojourn in Great Britain deals with two areas. The first is the enthusiastic greeting of the elements of the Polish army which came to England after the French defeat, and the second is the rejection suffered after the war ended when the Poles did not succumb to the pressure of the British government to capitulate to the Soviets. In between, he describes the active political life pursued by Polish emigres, as well as how they faced the problems which grew out of the war and the occupation of Poland by the enemy.

"Jur's" book faithfully reflects the highlights and shadows of emigre life. In the section dealing with his stay in England, of special value are the chapters devoted to the life and political activities of Tomasz Arciszewski who served as Premier of the Polish government in exile. Officially, he was Arciszewski's

Private Secretary, but unofficially he was his interpreter, his constant companion and friend.

The language of his reminiscences is lively, expressive, and unpretentious. "Jur" makes no effort to attain an artificial literary style with which so many reminiscences are blessed. As a consequence, his pictures are painted in living colors with clearly delineated shapes. Moreover, this book is a genuine account of the war years and the German occupation, as well as a treasure house of names and an encyclopaedia of events which in many instances have been shrouded in secrecy until now. It shall constitute a priceless source of information for future historians. In reading "Jur's" account, I have gained the impression that I have just come to a meeting which is attended by many acquaintances whom I have not seen in forty years.

Altogether, there were less than thirty individuals who carried out missions as political couriers to Warsaw. Some of these have already published their memoirs. Of all of these, I place Lerski's book above all others because of his attitude of service to the public cause, a greater attention to the part played by others, the wealth of information that he furnishes, and the facinating atmosphere which emanates from these pages.

"Jur," the emissary, has served Poland well. Lerski, the scholar, has made a substantial contribution to his country's history.

Stefan Korboński
Last Chief of the Polish Underground
State in World War II

FOREWORD

My sincere prayers seem to have finally been heard, after eight years of unbelievable frustrations with American publishers. Of the ten books written or edited by me (eight of them in the English language), this one is personally the most important because it renders a somewhat delayed account of the six crucial formative years of my fullest involvement in the struggle for Poland's Democracy and Independence, and as a loaded appeal and message to Anglo-Saxon readers, especially those of my second Motherland—America. The delay was partly deliberate since, as a professional historian, I preferred to wait until more important *dramatic personae* publish their war memoirs, and most of the archives be opened for scholarly research. But this story of mine was first written and almost published eight years ago, long before the Polish text of *Emisariusz "Jur"* was accepted by the Polish Cultural Foundation in London as a less documented and less analytical version of the earlier English language manuscript. Though forbidden in Communist-controlled Poland, it already is, since 1984, in its third edition, with a couple of additional printings, mainly for the black-market needs in the captive country of my birth.

Why, then, such a delay in the free world? For very strange reasons, worth recording. First of all, some ten million Americans of Polish descent have failed to establish even one publishing company for Polish books in English. This explains why even classics of great literature, with the exception of Nobel Prize winners (Sienkiewicz, Reymont, Singer, Miłosz), are not available to the American or British public. Neither do the so-called "Ministers of Culture" of postwar Communist regimes care much for translations of exquisite novels by Wacław Berent, Maria Dąbrowska, Pola Gojawiczyńska, Eliza Orzeszkowa, Bolesław Prus, Andrzej Strug, Stefan Żeromski, *et alii.* Deeply regretting such a sad state of affairs, I am convinced that it shows clearer than any "Polish joke" the frightening intellectual poverty of our American Polonia and her amazing lack of self-esteemed alertness.

It is certainly not enough to brag about the high number of postwar Polish professors teaching in American schools of higher learning, of whom this writer was one before his 1982 retirement. One would have to read truly humiliating letters of refusal on the part of various University presses and other more famous publishers to realize what insurmountable obstacles those scholars often encounter in trying to be "heard," or rather read by the American public, mainly to document our Polish plight in a less and less friendly academic environment. Bitter as it may sound, I decided not to hide the truth about my own hard experiences, knowing that most of my learned colleagues have often been in similar unpleasant situations.

When the president of a local publishing company announced with pride at a 1980 Christmas party that *Poland's Secret Envoy* will soon be published in his series of World War II documentary stories, I was sure that as a gentleman with a West Point background he would keep his word. Little did I know, however, that he was financially dependent on his senior editor, a German-Jewish lady, who was on a round-the-world tour at the time. Evidently unhappy that the decision was reached in her absence, she rejected the manuscript without even reading it carefully, using the strange excuse that it did not sufficiently meet the "sex and violence" criteria to interest potential readers. Hm ... As far as violence is concerned, I speak about killed and wounded Poles already on pages 3 and 4 of my memoirs, including the description of Corporal Wiśniewski's head rolling towards me in the Żabinka battlefield. And the tragic death of my own father in a Nazi concentration camp, possibly caused to some extent by my activities, should suffice to any decent human being as the violent ingredient of this book. Humbly, I admit that there is little bragging about my sex conquests, but in the part of the world where we were brought up, one does not write about such intimate affairs.

One of the University presses was subsequently ready to publish the book, but its main reader demanded that I first share with him my primary sources to be used in his forthcoming book, which I chose to refuse. The other stressed that I should have written much more about the Jewish Holocaust. This argument was used again and again in my voluminous correspondence with alleged experts, unaware of the fact that for my wartime services recorded in these pages I was awarded the "Righteous Gentile" recognition by the Yad Vashem Institute in Israel, and that my tree to commemorate those deeds grows in that sacred place in Jerusalem, testifying to my lifelong philo-Semitism. However, let's be frank. Though the Jews indeed suffered more than any other nation from Hitler's Germany, World War II also had other aspects, for goodness sake! At least after the hecatomb they were able to establish their sovereign state in Southwest Asia, while the Polish nation, the first to offer armed resistance to the Nazis, and which fought 'till the last day of the European conflict, was sold down the river by her Allies at Teheran and Yalta, losing as many people as did the Jews. Though actively helping the latter, I was primarily involved in the Polish struggle, being in the special service of all wartime Premiers and Commanders-in-Chief. Don't I have, therefore, a primary duty to "tell the West" about our contributions to the final victory? Or is it to be a taboo according to certain anti-Polish pseudo-intellectuals? Come on ... this story of mine would be published by my wife in any case, from whatever money I am able to leave her, because some of us learned well how to be persevering against all odds. I can understand to some extent why one off the best known British publishing houses was reluctant to sponsor such a book, which illustrates how blatantly unfaithful to its commitments was the *perfide Albion.*

The most ridiculuous, however, was the reason of the last of ten rejections (some of those publishers, might I add, not even having the courtesy to return the manuscript!), when a not too bright New York publisher accused me of writing too Polish a story. And what the hell did they expect from me? — a French,

Jewish, or Hungarian war story?

After years of the above described gehenna, I decided to ask my wartime associates of the Polish Freedom Movement "Independence and Democracy" (NiD), Bolesław Wierzbiański and Bolesław Łaszewski of the Bicentennial Publishing Corporation in New York City, to help me in completing my most important life endeavor. Boldly they conceded to undertake the publication, for which I will remain truly grateful 'till my last days, hoping that they will not be disappointed with the result of facing a hostile academic book market. But, after all, it still is, thank God, a free country! Perhaps this risk, without sufficient distribution and publicity apparatus, will prove worthwhile as the beginning of a much needed Polish publishing enterprise in the English language.

Sincere thanks are due to the last surviving leader of the Polish Underground State, the fearless Stefan Korboński, whose precious support all the way is graciously verbalized in his Preface, also used in the Polish version of my memoirs. For editorial and secretarial assistance I am grateful to Mary Wielski, Gail Bondi, Sandra Gamble and last but not least, to untiring Ksenya Zavarin. But it is my loving wife Halinka who had encouraged me with her selfless help to overcome all obstacles to bring this very special project to successful fruition.

G.J.L., 1988

CHAPTER I

GENERAL SIKORSKI'S TOURIST
(1939 - 1941)

My crusade began late in August of 1939, when, mountaineering in the exquisite Tatra region of southern Poland with friends, we suddenly learned of the Nazi-Soviet pact directed against our country.

As chairman of the Social Democratic Youth (PMSD) in the cosmopolitan city of Lwów, I considered it a clarion call for an international struggle against all totalitarian systems.[1] I was twenty-two, a fourth year law student at Jan Kazimierz University and an economics student at the Foreign Trade Institute (A.H.Z.). having served earlier (for one year) in a reserve officers' school, I had just been commissioned with the rank of Second Lieutenant and assigned to the Ninth Squadron of anti-aircraft artillery in Trauguttowo near Brześć (Brest-Litovsk). In view of the deteriorating international situation, I had to turn down an appealing summer consular apprenticeship in North Africa. Instead, I toured the fascinating country with my family, visiting friends and relatives. Near the German frontier we noticed barbed wire fences and defiant detachments of Polish soldiers at various border sites.

The ominous tenor of our holiday heightened when my stepfather, Lieutenant Colonel Adam Sołtysik, a prominent surgeon in charge of the evacuation hospital in the event of a war, was called for duty in mid-August. My carefree youth ended with a memorable dinner-dance at the Palace of Arts in Lwów. Beneath me was the panorama of the glorious city, for which three generations of the Lerski family had fought.

Full mobilization of Poland was called the very next day,

9

August 30, after postponements due to pressure from anxious Western leaders who remembered the provocative effects of pre-World War I mobilization. I was to report to Trauguttowo on September 1, but nonetheless managed to call an emergency meeting of the Social Democratic Youth to discuss necessary measures in the face of war. Afterward, we went downtown to nearby Akademicka Street to bid farewell to the Lwów garrison which had been called up to the Western border. In their enthusiasm, the girls threw flowers on the marching men, among whom were our colleagues, who proudly continued on with flowers clinging to their helmets and rifles.

I had not yet fully grasped the gravity of the situation, and with great optimism packed my suitcases with textbooks so I could still prepare for my upcoming exams which had been temporarily postponed.

On August 31, 1939, with five other reserve officers I boarded the train at the imposing Lwów train station, where parents and friends had come to say their goodbyes. Our first night was uneventful, as we moved slowly behind other military transports. At dawn however, the train came to a sudden halt just outside the Kowel junction in Volhynia. Alongside the railway cars ran an excited worker who announced that German bombs had just been dropped on the station building and that there were dead and wounded.[2]

As we continued on our journey to the fortress town of Brześć, we passed through the marshy regions of Eastern Poland. The small railroad stations were filled with lamenting women bidding farewell to their men, perhaps intuitively sensing the gravity of this departure better than I and my companions. When we reached our destination we were taken to Trauguttowo, some 10 kilometers south of town, to a newly built officers' hotel, the center of anti-aircraft artillery training. Some units had already left to reinforce front-line formations, and I was assigned to serve in the 5th Battery under Captain Tadeusz Dobrzański, who was to become my good friend throughout the initial part of the war.

We had only one 40mm Bofos gun as opposed to the usual

four, the bulk production being sold to our prospective English ally. Our precious gun we named "Krzysia" (little Christine), and its barrel was frequently red hot from attempts to repel the German air raids on Brześć's railway junction and fortress. These stepped-up Nazi assaults on Brześć were a result of the transference of the Polish High Command from Warsaw. Mysterious nighttime torch signals also convinced us that the German spy network, nicknamed the "Fifth Column", was present nearby.

September 4th brought the great news that at last the British and French had declared war against Nazi Germany in fulfilment of their treaty obligations. We were no longer alone in our mortal struggle. While the political obligation was filled, military support was not forthcoming, and in lieu of decisive military action from either Western ally came propaganda leaflets strewn across the German landscape. Moreover, even though the bulk of the German armed forces was concentrated against Poland, no serious attempt to attack Germany's vulnerable Western border was made. Within one week Panzer armored units surrounded a central Polish Army Group near the holy city of Częstochowa. At this point it was obvious that our outdated infantry and brave cavalry divisions were no match for the modern Nazi armada.[3] By September 11th, when we were ordered to prepare for evacuation, the Polish Air Force had been nearly annihilated and the **Luftwaffe** planes had the skies to themselves.

On September 12th we were loaded on a train carrying ammunition and chemical weapons. At this time the heaviest bombardment yet was aimed at these transports. When the skies finally cleared, we began our journey to the East. A few hours later the train abruptly halted and we were told to run for cover in the surrounding fields as the air attacks continued with renewed vigor. German dive bombers were merciless in slaughtering cattle, hapless peasant women as they worked in their fields, and anything else in sight. As I watched from my hiding place, the head of Corporal Wiśniewski, one of the NCOs who had been hiding a few yards away, came rolling towards me. This was the first death in battle I had ever

11

witnessed.

When the attack ended, I was asked by three Polish policemen to help them in protecting about thirty disarmed German airmen from the vengeance of enraged local villagers; I obliged reluctantly by arranging their passage on the train. Although I acted in accordance with the international agreement on POWs, the elimination of such a group could possibly have shortened the war by a day or two—just a thought that crossed my mind at the time.

The prisoners were turned over to Polish authorities at the Sarny station, from which we headed south to the "defensive triangle" backed by supposedly allied Rumania, where Western help from across the Black Sea was expected.[4] In the next air attack we evidently damaged one of the German planes, which fell wavering from side to side like a wounded bird. We were thrilled, convinced that we were still doing something positive in our national defense; and our morale rose high as we sang beneath the starry sky of the eastern Borderlands.

Soon after, I was again placed in charge of anti-aircraft defense. A group of resolute cadet officers, a couple of gunners, and I were to stay on an open platform car with "Krzysia" to protect the chemical weapons and ammunition being transported to the planned south-eastern center of resistance. Early on the morning of September 14th, our train came to a halt near Radziwiłłów, south of Dubno in Volhynia. There was a back up of transport trains, a perfect target for an air attack. All but ten men of about five hundred left the cars to seek cover in the surrounding fields. We soon heard the awesome sounds of a German bomber squadron, Dorniers flying at an altitude far too high for "Krzysia" to reach. The first bomb came with the strident accompaniment of machine-gun fire and Second Lieutenant Zbigniew Małecki, on duty at the locomotive, was killed. Our crew tried to keep the bombers at bay, but they quickly returned hitting the ammunition cars, and, as the passenger car behind us began to burn, with it went my lecture notes and textbooks. An officer came running alongside the train yelling unintelligibly. To get him under control, I took my pistol, aimed it at him, and ordered him to pull himself together and set a better example for the others. This rather strange but effective version of psychology calmed him quickly and we later became friends.

When the attack was over we were pleased to notice one German bomber wavering—then utter silence. Just then, Captain Dobrzański came running out to tell us we all deserved the Cross of Valor for our perseverance in such a mismatched battle, but that we must abandon this transport and continue on foot in the direction of allied Rumania. Once there, we were to await French and British support from the Black Sea. A small crew of volunteers under Cadet Officer Stachiewicz stayed behind to guard the train. I never heard from any of them again, and can only assume they were killed either by the Nazis or the Soviets.

Through the second night we marched alongside cars and limousines carrying Polish and foreign dignitaries from Krzemieniec southward in retreat from the Nazi advance. Just before dawn we stopped in an Ukrainian village near Wiśniowiec to rest on hay in a barn. A few hours later, on September 17, 1939, Captain Dobrzański related the shocking radio message that said the Red Army had just crossed the entire eastern Polish border, with no warning or any official declaration of war. Not since the 18th-century partitions had Poland faced such a horrible situation...

Some optimists hoped that the Russians had come to aid us against the Nazis, and a few officers even welcomed them as brothers, only to be taken prisoners and deported into the depths of the Soviet Union. A couple of senior officers committed suicide in despair. As for my battery, however, none of the officers had any illusions as to Stalin's intent. In light of these events we radioed and learned that President Ignacy Mościcki, along with civil and military government leaders, was crossing into Rumania, with whom we had a treaty of mutual assistance.

On the other hand, there were still some centers of resistance against the Nazis; one of them was my native city of Lwów, some one hundred miles west. About three hundred of us marched on to join in Lwów's defense, and, being familiar with this area from previous explorations, I became their guide. Our journey took us through the border regions to Volhynia and Podolia, where the Ukrainian villagers looked upon us, the remnants of the Polish Army, with hostile suspicion. They did nothing to alleviate the burdens of our march, and even dispersed their horses into the fields so we could not have the aid of horse. Exhausted by our long march, occasionally spotting Soviet planes overhead, we finally reached the spectacular Dominican church of Podkamień on September 19, 1939.

The convent was full of refugees wanting us to help defend them from Soviet occupation and Ukrainian marauders. The Abbot, however, advised us against resisting the overwhelming onslaught of Soviet troops which was expected at any moment. For one night we settled in for a much needed rest in the monks' quarters, and before leaving the entire unit went to Confession and Holy Communion. We then continued our pilgrimage to Lwow, where we still hoped to be of some service to the national cause.

On the outskirts of Brody our group was approached by a Ukrainian official with a red armband claiming to represent the Soviets and demanding our surrender. He produced documents proving him to be a negotiator for the local Soviet authorities, and announced that we were surrounded by Soviet troops and had only one hour to lay down our arms and be delivered as prisoners to the Soviets. This was indeed a difficult decision to make. We could stay put and risk a surprise attack by either the Russians or the Ukrainians; we could march and fight in the open against co-citizens of the Polish state; or we could surrender to the Soviet troops. Captain Dobrzański finally advised that, "In order to continue the struggle we must survive; therefore, we should march to Brody rather than fight the local Ukrainians."

To this day the memory of that heap of abandoned weapons still haunts my conscience and makes me wonder if perhaps we should have chosen to die in honor instead of unheroically surrendering our arms to the seditious Ukrainians. However, to our knowledge we only were at war with Hitler's Germany, not with either the Soviets or the local non-Polish population.

When we reached the railroad station at Brody, the Soviet officers assured us that before long we would be fighting the Germans side by side. Meanwhile, we were escorted to a train and placed under guard. In the morning, from the train's windows we saw red flags displayed in most of the homes in that predominantly Jewish town, and other trains at the station carrying huge Soviet tanks and heavy military equipment.

The night of September 20th, our transport moved southward. The rank and file of our battery had been released and allowed to go home, so only twenty officers and cadets remained under Soviet guard. We were all determined to escape and return to Lwów, which was still fighting valiantly against the Germans. Our escape at dusk from the slow moving train was not too difficult because of the laxness of guards at that time. A Polish railroad worker near the Krasne-Busk station gave us shelter so we could rest for a few hours, and we were fed warm milk and scrambled eggs on tomatoes, which was grately appreciated.

After sunset we joined the stream of refugees and soldiers in the march westward to Lwów. As we approached the city the sound of heavy artillery, which we has heard before our forced detour to Brody, had stopped; we realized that Lwów must have been forced to surrender, not to the Germans with whom we were at war, but rather to the Soviets. We contined on amidst the motorized columns, and as I knew the territory well from past skiing trips, I led my companions away from the railroad tracks to the Łyczaków district, and suggested that the cadets split into several groups, giving each group two addresses where they would find food and shelter if they used my name.

After the groups parted, I walked to the downtown area with Captain Dobrzański and a few others, where we witnessed Soviet troops, a barrage of red flags, and huge posters of Stalin, Marx, and Lenin hanging from public buildings. Seeing my home town so transformed was emotionally too much for me to take, and for the first time in my life I fainted. I could not believe that this lovely city which had been loyal to Poland since the Middle Ages could not hold her own. Regaining consciousness, I recognized a woman in the crowd that had gathered, who informed me that my parents were safe and well, and fortified by these news, I walked to my house at Romanowicza Street.

My family was relieved and overjoyed at my arrival, and even though the apartment was full of distant relatives and other refugees, we were given a warm meal and a place to sleep on makeshift bedding spread on the floor. As my companions rested, I checked in by telephone with my friends to find where the rest of our detachment was lodged. They had all been received with traditional Lwów hospitality, which survived even though the population had doubled in just a few days.

Since our active duty terminated with the Soviet occupation, for the time being I went back to my studies. I borrowed text books and notes from friends and managed to pass my final examinations. I was asked by the Rector of the Trade Institute, Dr. Henryk Korowicz, to give a speech in Polish at the commencement ceremonies. Speeches in Russian, Ukrainian, and Yiddish had been provided for, but there was still a need for a Polish address.

The ceremony opened with a statement in Russian by an official representative of the NKVD. When my turn came, I began by stating that we were glad our city had resolutely and effectively resisted the Nazis; and continued by expressing the hope that the historic nation of Poland who had always fought for its freedom, and had produced such great minds as Nicholas Copernicus, Adam Mickiewicz, and Marie Curie-Skłodowska, all of whom had been mentioned with respect by the chief representative of the Soviet occupying authorities, surely had no lesser right to full freedom in its own territory than the Byelorussians and Ukrainians. As the crowd cheered wildly at these statements, I noticed the red-headed Mr. Joel Zang, a Jewish student, rushing up to the NKVD officers to translate my speech into Russian. They too, in accordance with Stalinist practice, had been automatically applauding without knowing the content of my argument. At this point I prudently left the ceremony.

The situation was equally serious at Lwów University where I was still attending classes. The revered professors continued with their regular lectures, but we were all required to participate in frequent meetings with Soviet overseers. Late in November, the Polish Rector of the University, Professor Edmund Bulanda, summoned the leaders of student organizations for an important meeting with the Vice-Rector of Moscow University and professor of Russian literature, Captain Edel of the NKVD. I was frightened at the prospect of meeting a distinguished academician in police uniform. He proved amicable and diabolically clever. In his opening statement he assured us that it was in the interest of the Soviets to learn why we, the young people of Lwów, were so uncooperative. He gave us his word of honor as a university professor and an officer that no notes would be taken and that we could talk freely with no fear of reprisal.

There were a few opportunists who asked, for example: "Why do Soviet authorities permit continued illumination of Our Lady's statue in the heart of town at Mariacki Square?" Commissar Edel pretended anger and scolded the questioner, "What the hell are you complaining about? The Revolution is long over and we are not afraid of any religious nonsense. We are a different type of Communists from the early Bolshevik hotheads." After an hour or so I asked about the long lines at retail stores. Edel stated matter of factly that the needs of the sixteen Soviet republics were as great as the length of time needed to go by train from Lwów to Vladivostok (twenty days in 1939). Moreover, he argued, we Poles should readily understand, having been technologically so ill-prepared to face the German blitz. Under Stalin the Soviet Union had become a strong military power so that no fascist aggressor would dare to attack. In other words, he was telling us that guns were, for the Russians, far more important than butter.

Despite the Soviets' alleged religious tolerance, the entire occupied area was soon subjected to intensive atheistic indoctrination based on a simplified version of Darwin's theory. In the tradition of "oriental despotism" Stalin had been deified, and was often referred to as "Our Sun." A typical approach used in kindergardens by the educational commissars was that in place of the usual Lord's prayer, "Give us this day our daily bread..." the hungry children were told to ask Comrad Stalin for a meal, after which breakfast would be wheeled in. The efficacy of the latter over the former was thus insinuated. Such blasphemy caused some angry nationalists to react by having a group of high school students draw a cross on the blackboard to protest their removal from the classrooms, resulting in the deportation to Siberia of an entire class of sixteen-year olds.

Both mandatory attendance at long party meetings as well as pressure on reserve officers to register with the Soviets caused us to feel increasingly intimidated. In connection with forthcoming "elections" of delegates, various professional groups were given questionnaires to fill out. This was, no doubt, an attempt to give the appearance of democratic plebiscite on the incorporation of the so-called Western Ukraine into the Soviet Ukrainian Republic. As the October 22nd date for the fixed referendum approached, NKVD personnel became quite evident in the streets.

Finally, on that sad date the whole of Eastern Poland was forced to march to the polls. Our caretakers, the Ostrowskis, begged each registered person in our house to be sure to vote; otherwise, they would be held responsible and severely punished for their neglect. On the way to the polls I met Dr. Artur Kopacz, one of the Democratic Party leaders. We were both deeply humiliated at being forced to participate in the Soviet farce, which amounted to renouncing half of Poland's territory, including Lwów and Wilno. There was only one list of candidates headed, of course, by Stalin, the Commander-in-Chief of the occupying Soviet Army Marshal Timosheko, as well as Nikita Khruschev, Aleksander Kosygin, Nikolai Podgorny and other Soviet **apparatchiki** of the Ukraine region. The harsh-looking personnel warned us of the consequences of not voting, and I hoped they would not notice my throwing in a different piece of paper from the official ballot.

As long as the Soviets maintained the appearance of holding "plebiscites" such as this one, and while our government was in exile, Poland was in grave danger of losing its integrity. At this point, I realized that it was time to respond to the call-for-arms of our new Prime Minister in exile, General Władysław Sikorski. He had appealed to create an underground movement to resist both the Nazis and Soviets, and it was obvious that such a resistance was the only way to fight while still holding onto a continuity of a legitimate Polish authority.

Another problem that grew as a result of imposed occupation was the increasing number of Soviet informers and spies, especially among the ranks of frightened refugees. Even some known intellectuals, writers and journalists became outright traitors, as I was to encounter first hand when I visited a Jewish friend, at a gathering of prominent theater people. Without mincing words I criticized the Soviet occupation, only to be dragged into the kitchen by Erwin's father, who warned me that there were several communists in the group, one of whom was strongly suspected to be an agent for the Soviets.

Informers such as these were suspected of infiltrating into each social group. My own family was even implicated in such an endeavor. This was due to a Mrs. Tomanek, who came to our house one evening and asked for me, claiming she was the wife of a Polish infantry major who had been deported to the Soviet Union, and that she had been recruited by the Underground to approach young officers trained in modern weaponry to urge them to respond to General Sikorski's summons. Apparently I was on her list, and she guaranteed to arrange the details for my secret passage though the Carpathians. She looked and dressed amazingly like my mother. I was suspicious and responded that I wanted to stay in Lwów to continue my studies. A few months later, when I was outside Poland, gossip circulated that my poor mother was acting as a Soviet agent and was responsible for the arrests and deportations of several officers. It took some time before the real culprit, the wretched Mrs. Tomanek, was identified and liquidated by the Underground.

19

At about this time, the first couriers arrived from the West via the Carpathian mountains, with the official declaration of the Polish government and armed forces in exile under General Sikorski, and his appeal for the continuation of the struggle for Polish independence and democracy. Within two days this text was secretly published and I distributed the leaflets in the Palace movie house, located in the heart of Lwów. This was my first defiant act against the Soviets, and watching the pamphlets flutter down from the balcony, I felt like a soldier again.

Soon after this incident I was approached by an envoy from the Warsaw Underground (Romuald Tyczyński), having been recommended to him as a potential candidate for youth work. The name of that first clandestine group was the Revolutionary Union for Independence and Freedom (RZNIW), and its leaders were representatives of the Peasant Party, the Polish Socialist Party, the Democratic Party, their respective youth organizations, and the managers of various trade unions. After a few weeks I took charge of the youth sector in my city.[5]

I took my oath of allegiance to the Underground with my close PMSD friend, Jan Lech. In the presence of Mr. Bolesław Zubrzycki and Roman Zagrodzki, together we pledged our loyalty to a truly independent and democratic Republic of Poland in the latter's office at the suburban brick factory. Under the supervision of RZNIW leaders, I began to organize three-man cells with the aim of reaching all school systems from the Lyceum (16- to 18-year olds) to the University, and most of the candidates were eager to join this life and death struggle against Stalinist Russia and Hitler's Germany.

We were all amateurs in matters of conspiration, and had no idea at the time who might have been in charge of the regular military underground. I was fortunate to have contact, through my stepfather, with the then most admired of Polish Generals, Władysław Anders. He was already considered a national hero for leading the cavalry in a valiant resistance against the German invaders, and one of the few who had dared to fight the Soviet Army as well. He had been wounded and captured by the Red Army, and a Russian General had delivered him to my stepfather's hospital on the understanding that his escape would result in the jailing of all medical personnel. General Anders had been originally trained at the Russian military school under the last Czar, and was considered by Moscow as a potential commander of Polish troops under Soviet command. Critical as he was of his Polish superiors' lack of professional preparation for modern warfare, he remained staunchly loyal to the Polish cause and indicated his interest in the new underground movement, as well as possible escape to France.[6]

As the situation in Lwów grew worse, more and more people attempted to cross the Carpathian passes to Rumania and Hungary. About half were caught by Soviet border patrols using police dogs. Several of my friends were captured near Worochta in the Czarnohora range, then released to return to Lwów—presumably to tell the rest of us how difficult the escape was. Nevertheless, young people continued plotting their trip to join Sikorski's army in France, and I was no exception.

I was approached by a young pilot, Andrzej Nahlik, who confided his involvement with the organized evacuation of Polish airmen, sailors, anti-aircraft artillery and, tank officers, through the high Gorgany range to Sub-Carptho Ruthenia, recently retaken by Hungary from Czechoslovakia. This was the opportunity I had been waiting for. He also hinted that the group I was joining would be armed, and was chosen to escort two generals, one of them being General Anders. Unfortunately, as the latter chose another route he was caught and deported to a Russian prison.

I had only a few days to wind up my affairs, during which I transferred my Underground duties to my successor Jan Lech, and informed my superior, Dr. Stanisław Olszewski, of my decision, who agreed that I would indeed be more useful as an anti-aircraft artillery officer in the forthcoming allied campaign against Nazi Germany. Moreover, I came to the conclusion that a large-scale conspiracy against the Soviets could not be successful, and that informers would sooner or later penetrate our ranks to help in elimination of our political leadership.

Unfortunately, I proved to be right, as the later mass arrests showed.

Before the departure, I had two more tasks to complete as leader of the youth sector; the first was to draft slogans for placards which were to be worn during the forced demonstrations by the new authorities in protest against the alleged Finnish invasion of the "innocent" Soviet Union. To the great amusement of the Lwów populace, these signs said such things as "Down with imperialistic Finnish designs on our beloved Russia!" My other job was to contact Professor Kazimierz Bartel, the great scholar and former three-time Prime Minister. I was asked to arrange a meeting between him and three chemical engineers who needed his advice on sophisticated machinery of the Mościce nitrogen factory, dismantled just before German take-over.

These duties completed, it became necessary to secure proper documents to pass through the restricted border region. I acquired them by convincing a Russian lady commissar at the Foreign Trade Institute that our cooperative store was in dire need of "bryndza" (ewe's milk cheese) from the Eastern Carpathian villages.

Finally, my mother packed my bag with warm clothes and had sewn into the locks of my leather briefcase to gold coins, provided by my stepfather. Around my neck I also placed a beautiful golden locket in the shape of a clover, which had passed from generation to generation in my mother's family, and contained small family photographs. I wore this "lucky charm" continually throughout the war. I had to gather last minute information about Lwów underground activities to be passed on to the Polish authorities in exile, and then said goodbye to a couple of close friends. The next morning I rose before dawn, when the street carts were not yet in service, and walked several miles to the central railroad station where I was to meet my contact. As I left, my mother stood on the balcony waving discreetly. I did not know if I would ever see my home or family again.

Once at the station, I saw a number of my colleagues who were also making the trip through the Carpathians. We exchanged only meaningful glances, since we were not to speak to each other in order to escape detection. I located Andrzej Nahlik and kept a close eye on him throughout the first leg of our journey. We moved slowly out of the spacious hall of the station, and gradually watched the Lwów skyline disappear. I was never to see this beautiful sight again. At about noon we arrived in Stanisławów, and I followed Andrzej discreetly to one of the main streets, where we had lunch in a crowded cafeteria full of Soviet officers.

After sunset we went by bus to the south-eastern city of Nadwórna, where we found one of Andrzej's contacts at a spacious, dimly lit restaurant. He informed us where we could spend the night. The small villa had recently been rented to a NKVD officer, and we were to arrive after they had gone to sleep. As we seemed alarmed, our contact also told us this was the safest place because no one would bother to search the house with Russian secret policemen there. We duly arrived at our resting spot before midnight and the middle aged Polish landlady who answered asked us first to remove our shoes before entering so we would not awaken the Russian family, and then served us hot milk before showing us to our bedding on the floor. Before the NKVD captain was up, we had gone.

Again, we set out by bus, this time to Bitków, at the foothills of the Gorgany Ranges, the center of natural gas oil fields, and full of escaping volunteers for the Polish army in France. We reached the outskirts of Bitków at dusk where Andrzej, myself, and a third friend who had made the trip from Lwów with us, Jerzy Buckiewicz, were directed by a representative of the local committee to a house in the hills where Jerzy and I were to be billeted. Andrzej was to be taken to another house nearby. Our hosts, Mr. and Mrs. Rosłan, whose Doctor son had already left to join Sikorski's army, provided shelter for many like ourselves who were passing through the mountains. Since the entire region was under strict control of the pro-Soviet Ukrainian militia who were hunting down escapees, our hosts were taking quite a risk.

Whenever the couple had guests we had to hide. On one occasion an old lady who was failing in memory and indiscreet in conversation came by, and we were told to hide in the closet. I noticed at that point that the doors were short and our feet could be seen. I whispered this to my companion and foolishly told him to jump. However, this made him laugh, and the old lady discovered us shrieked and asked who we were. Mrs. Rosłan explained we were her cousins from Lwów playing "hide and seek". Although we were supposed to wait for General Anders, it was no longer safe to hide at this house. We did not know at that time that he had been caught while trying another route. In any case, not long after this incident, the local militia conducted a thorough search using dogs for the hiding volunteers who had been denounced by someone in the town. Without even saying goodbye we jumped out of the window and crawled under the house. Fortunately, we were not noticed; others were not so lucky.

Later that evening we headed for a slope where other escapees had hidden after the raid. There were thirty-eight of us, among whom was Captain Dobrzański, serving as our commander. The most important man in our group through was our guide, Lieutenant Rosiński, an artillery officer who went by the pseudonym of "Staszek", and who had already served as a guide between Budapest and Lwów, for those wishing to join the Polish army in the West. Also included in our group was Bolesław Zubrzycki, a vice-president of Poland's Democratic Party and his wife, the only woman in our group, as well as the famous glider pilot Bolek Baranowski, who knew this part of the Carpathians quite well.

Others of interest in this group were Tadeusz Gaworski and Kazio Szajowski. Tadeusz was a top sportsman in track and field, as well as in the shot put. He was one of the few who carried a rifle and later became a paratrooper hero of the Underground, under the code name "Captain Lawa"; Kazio was a wrestler and a non-commissioned officer in the Polish army. He was an expert short-wave radio operator and later became an asset in the operations of Polish Naval units in the United Kingdom. The utmost need for caution was made distinct by "Staszek", when some in our group began to smoke. He sternly told them that this could be seen by Soviet border guards patrolling the Bitków region, and if caught, we would endanger all future groups who might traverse the same route.

We began our trek at around 10 p.m., moving south towards the new Hungarian frontier. One of us, the senior non-commissioned officer of the Polish Navy, has been a patient of my stepfather and had his feet so heavily bandaged he could not wear shoes. Because of his involvement with delicate intelligence matters, though, he had been ordered to leave. As a result we had to slow our pace so he could keep up with the rest.

Not all of us had weapons and those who did marched at the front and rear of the group. By morning we were approaching the snowy Sywula peak, almost twenty miles from Bitków. Some of us felt too tired to continue the ascent and wanted to rest in a forester's cottage which our guide had used with another group two weeks earlier. However, since it was not certain if it had been discovered by the enemy, I recommended we rest in the forest for a couple of hours and eat. It proved to be a wise decision, because the group that came by a few days later was caught by the Soviets who had indeed occupied the cottage. Only a few escaped the shoot-out near the cottage.

After a short rest we continued clibming through this cold, snow-covered area until we reached an altitude of 5,000 feet. The deep, rich forests had changed to pine shrubs and the higher we went the deeper were the snow drifts, through which we took turns clearing a path. As the intense cold worsened and the wind hissed treacherously through the pass, we realized that we were only one hundred yards from the Hungarian border. We heard the Soviet patrols and their German shepherds, and saw ski tracks, at which point "Staszek" decided we should make a run for it. Not without great effort, we made it. As we rested not far from the border crossing, we saw a half dozen Soviets pass by just above our heads on the ridge. Fortunately, the winds were blowing towards us so the dogs did not pick up our scent. Although we outnumbered this Soviet patrol, we decided not to attack since it would have disclosed that point of entry and hindered the crossing of other volunteers.

When the danger had passed, we ran down into the valley for about three miles until we reached the timberline, where we stopped to sleep by an open fire. At daybreak we followed the creeks of those rugged mountains in search of the first village we could find. At 8 a.m. we finally reached a Hungarian guard post and were approached by the local gendarmes, who told us to disarm since we were in neutral country. We were then taken to their post and fed a huge breakfast. Afterwards, we formed a regular column and marched to the highway heading south along the river, singing as we went the national anthem with the altered refrain, "Marsz, marsz, Sikorski z ziemi Francji do Polski!" (instead of "March, march Dąbrowski from Italian soil to Poland!).

The journey was exhausting, and by evening myself and two others felt we could not keep pace with the rest of the group. We were left behind for hot milk and a night's rest at the home of a kind Ruthenian peasant. The next day we were taken by horsecart to the Berezov gendarme station, and there divided up among the locals for a longer rest. The kindness and hospitality of these Hungarians I will never forget. They obviously sympathized with our plight and were ready to help, realizing their fate might be soon closely linked with ours, as epitomized in the traditional toast "Poles and Hungarians are like two nephews when it comes to the sword and the bottle."

The next day we were transported in small railroad cars to Chust, the wretched capital of Sub-Carpatho Ruthenia. Its predominantly Jewish inhabitants seemed friendly as we marched through the town boisterously singing military songs. Later that evening, we were moved by train to the next railroad junction at Chop, where we found other Polish refugees, who had crossed the high mountains over another pass. Together we now numbered almost one hundred. The attractive Ewa Runge managed to save her accordion, and led our joyful choir. Later in England she served as Captain Ewa Miszewska, Commander of Polish Women Naval Auxiliaries.

The next morning we were taken by train to Budapest, where

under police bayonets we were marched like criminals through its impressive boulevards to the grim Citadel, to be detained and carefully watched along with hundreds of other Poles.

The conditions were miserable at the fortress, with its abundance of bugs and worms and the unbearable filth which prevailed. Being agitated and discontented, a group of us began planning an escape. Our senior officers advised us though, not to attempt anything because neutral Hungary was in a difficult international situation *vis-a-vis* the Germans, and we should cooperate as long as there was good will on the part of the host government. These same officers, however, also admitted that there were several German agents in the upper echelons of the Hungarian police who were plotting to hand us over to the Nazis. That piece of news made us more determined than ever to outwit our guardians.

A few days later we were relieved to hear that some two hundred of us were to be transported by train to the northern town of Eger, a quaint city with numerous architectural remnants of its long Turkish occupation. At Eger we were marched off to an elementary school building which was to serve as a transitional camp. Finding myself alone with Andrzej Nahlik in a large classroom on the ground floor, and observing that the two policemen had walked around the corner of the building, we quietly opened the window and jumped out. Luckily we both had some dollars, so we checked into a small hotel not far from the center of the city. The proprietors were sympathetic Jews who understood our situation.

We were soon joined by Buckiewicz and Szajowski, and together we managed to establish contact with Polish officers in an old Turkish fortress on the outskirts of Eger. They had been interned after their full units had crossed the Hungarian frontier at the end of the September campaign. They were supposed to be well guarded until the end of the war, and there was a strained atmosphere among those embittered soldiers, forced to remain in idleness for God knew how long. The crux of the matter was that only young officers, trained in modern weapons, were really needed in France, where there

27

were already more "chiefs than Indians". Most of the officers, particularly those over thirty-five years of age were, therefore, supposed to stay interned. This only served to increase the frustration.

Our next step was to return illegally to Budapest and contact the Polish Legation at the fashionable Vaci Utca (Vaci Street), still very active in helping Poles reach France from Hungary. As menekults (Hungarian for refugees), we were not allowed to use the transportation system without prior authorization; I was lucky to have the help of an attractive young woman, whom I had met in a bookstore, and she kindly purchased tickets to Budapest for myself and Andrzej. On December 19, 1939 we waved goodbye to her at the railroad station, and tried to blend into the crowd. Fortuntely no one denounced us to the police at any of the stops along the way.

Once in Budapest we went directly to the pension where Andrzej's aunt and uncle, who had escaped from Lwów, were staying. They filled us in on how to proceed. Andrzej stayed with them while I went to the Hungarian-Polish Relief Society to arrange a place for myself, where I recognized a classmade from officers' school, Władysław Słuczanowski. I joined him in going to a Hungarian student dormitory on the outskirts of Buda where many Poles were residing temporarily, and which was supported by the Polish Legation and the Polish Hungarian Relief Committee.

The next morning brought me in contact with Lieutenant Colonel Emisarski, the military attache at the Polish Legation. He was a handsome, tall officer still serving in Polish uniform, while taking care of the evacuation of those specially selected to go to France. After I reported on our underground experience in Lwów and our dramatic passage through the Carpathian mountains, as a Second Lieutenant in anti-aircraft artillery trained in 40mm Bofors guns, I was put quite high on the list of those chosen to go to France.

At the Hungarian students' union I was fed well and made contact with many fine Polish refugees, eager to serve the cause of freedom. Meanwhile, groups of Hungarian, Polish, and British aristocrats had organized to help in taking care of

28

potential Polish soldiers, not only by finding food and lodging, but also by providing us with social and cultural activities and entertainment. One such event was a gala performance of Polish folk dancing and music provided by the famous Royal Ballet at the Budapest Opera House.

While attending such functions I met the wife of the political councillor of Great Britain to Warsaw, Mrs. Clifford Norton, affectionately known as "Peter", who was deeply involved in assisting Polish volunteers in reaching the armed forces in the West. Later as we became close friends, I asked her why, being acquainted with so many Poles in high standing, she never learned Polish. She responded by telling me: "There are two ways to learn any language, either in the cradle or in bed, and I unfortunately was too old for both."

A traditional Christmas Eve dinner was hospitably offered by the Hungarian Student Union to all Polish students waiting to go to France, and chaired by exiled Bishop Karol Radoński of Włocławek. About three hundred of us attended this moving celebration and after dinner we all sang carols, prayed to soon be back in action fighting to free Poland, and then attended midnight mass at the nearby medieval church.

January 8, 1940 became the date of my departure to France, and I was entrusted with the special responsibility of leading a group of eighty-seven selected volunteers because of my command of French and German. Our personal documents were all faked, particularly in the matter of our ages, since the Hungarian neutrality laws could not accommodate the mass exodus of people eligible for conscription, those between the ages of eighteen and forty-two. Looking youngish, I was, for example, given the papers of a sixteen year old. Early on the morning of our departure, I met Mr. Eustachiewicz, my regular contact at the Legation, who had made our travel arrangements. To decrease our conspicuousness, we were spread out within the long train and were, of course, in civilian clothes. The first stop would be the frontier station near the Yugoslavian border.

At the Document Control Station in Nagykanizsa my identification card was branded with a question mark, but the controller let me go through. Luckily we all passed the inspection and felt great relief as we crossed the border heading for Ljubljana, the capital of Slovenia in Yugoslavia.

As we sped through this countryside, my only regret was not to have been able to visit my dear Croatian friends in Zagreb, although I was able to inform one of them that I might use her address for indirect correspondence with my family in Lwów.

Our next stop, Venice, looked gloomy under gray January skies, not at all the "Pearl of the Adriatic" that I remembered from a previous visit. Hitler had just signed the "Steel Pact" with Mussolini, and though Italy was officially neutral, we no longer knew what the general attitude to us would be. The people seemed friendly, and with my basic Italian I learned that passengers of that international express were by no means pro-German and looked upon us with compassion. As the train moved on, we first took in the spectacular sights of the lake country and then observed the splendid contours of Milan's Duomo Cathedral. Later that evening we stopped in Turin, where we were to change trains. Here I was able to let the men go for a meal in a nearby restaurant. In groups of about twelve, we walked outside for the first time since leaving Budapest. To add to our pleasure, we were served yards of spaghetti with tomato sauce and genuine Chianti. Everyone returned punctually for the night train which would carry us into the long tunnel through the Italian Alps to the French border station.

The train pulled into Modane, which was blacked out for fear of Nazi air raids, and in the bleak, bluish light that remained, we saw our new guide, Lance-Corporal Janusz Jarosz, in uniform, with a crowned eagle on his cap. He was sent by the Second Bureau of the Polish Army Headquarters to verify our arrival and check our papers. Such checks were necessary to prevent infiltration of German spies.

Our group spent the night in the cold, dark railroad station basement which stank of Gaulloises cigarettes. Once safe in France, however, this did not deter us from a short but contented sleep, though the journey was not yet complete. There were still twelve train changes before reaching the northwest province of Brittany, and the far away Coetquidan Army camp, where we would be assigned to units; and so, with a sense of pride, we forged ahead to our destination.

With fresh memories of occupied Poland where the terrors of the Nazis and Soviets were imminent for everyone, and where the ravages of war knew no barriers, it was a shock to see the complaisance and shoddy appearance of French soldiers, enjoying the *"drolle de guerre"* (phony war) atmosphere. Most were well-equipped with red-wine filled canteens and rations of sardines, oranges, *pate-de-foie*, cheeses and other delicacies, while few had weapons to deter the pending Nazi onslaught. Many we talked to felt that they had already "suffered too much for Gdańsk" and the Polish nation, which they did not consider to be a true democratic state. We soon saw that arguing with them was fruitless, as they were more interested in telling stories of the lax discipline of the French Army and luxurious bordellos for "heroic" defenders of the ludicrous Maginot Line. In light of this disappointing realization about French morale, our resolve became greater, and we became a much tighter unit.

In Rennes, we were finally able to stretch out and relax, and were taken to the empty brick barracks of an infantry regiment which had been sent to the German frontier. Around noon the next day we finally reached Coetquidan, and were greeted by the Polish military band playing the 18th century Kościuszko Insurrection March, "Bartoszu, Bartoszu oj nie traćwa nadzieji" (Bartholomew, keep your faith!). Proudly, I reported to the duty officers the arrival of eighty-eight ardent volunteers for General Sikorski's army.

The next two days we were all interviewed for special assignments. I was directed to the anti-aircraft artillery squadron, under the command of one-eyed Lieutenant Colonel Kobielski. We were stationed in the nearby residence of the de Clerville family in Les Forges de Paimpont. I knew most of the officers there, and was especially happy to see my old colleague, Second Lieutenant Henryk Polański, who had distinguished himself in the September campaign by destroying two Nazi tanks with a small caliber 40mm Bofors. I

31

was temporarily assigned to a battery composed almost entirely of Polish-French miners, volunteers under the command of Captain Konstanty Kasprzykowski. The officers were given small unheated pavilions in the forested hills around the lake and took their meals in a charming hotel overlooking the water, while the rank and file were housed in unheated barns and stables. To make the routine more bareable I acted as educational officer, organizing lectures and other cultural activities.

One day, while on a trip to the officers' school at nearby Guer, I was met by the cadet on duty, an opulent middle-aged gentleman whom I recognized as being our last Ambassador in Berlin, the Honorable Józef Lipski. In acknowledgement of the failure of his mission, he joined with General Sikorski as a regular soldier. The majority of volunteers in this school were former diplomats, artists, writers, journalists, who later became the ideological backbone of Sikorski's Army in exile.

Due to a bureaucratic mix-up, I was again transferred, after only a month, to the officers' depot in Ancenis on the Loire, where eighty of us were being intensely trained in the French language, geography and history, as well as the use of French anti-aircraft artillery, to prepare us for service under French command.

During my stay here, and while I was hoping to battle soon with the Soviets in Finland, my roommate, Second Lieutenant Zygmunt Molenda, without my knowledge, proposed to Deputy Foreign Minister Zygmunt Graliński that as an effective orator, I become a public speaker on the latter's forthcoming Latin American trip, the purpose of which was to recruit Polish settlers in Uruguay, Brazil and Argentina. I refused this commendable role, explaining that I had come to France not to increase the civil personnel of our Government in exile, but to fight in the front lines. How ironic it is that I am still alive, while Mr. Graliński was drowned on this journey, along with five thousand British children being evacuated from London, when their ship, the "City of Benares", went down under the attack of a German submarine in the Atlantic.

While waiting for assignment to active service, I found an

excuse, as educational officer, for my first visit to Paris, to arrange cultural activities for our troops in northwestern France. As most Poles, I fell in love with this city, that I had only known from literature and pictures. I met with Lieutenant Colonel Antoni Bogusławski, a poet, and Major Otton Laskowski, a historian, who were in charge of the Education Service for our troops. Of special interest were of course the numerous *"Polonica"* in Paris, most notably the Bibliotheque Polonaise, established on the charming Isle St. Louis on the Seine by two luminaries of the 19th-century so-called Great Immigration, Prince Adam Czartoryski and the prophetic poet, Adam Mickiewicz. This venerable institution was used as the quarters for the newly-created Polish University in exile. As always, obsessed with the continuation of my studies, I went there in hope of arranging at least correspondence courses to work for my master of law finals, and met with the prominent historian, Professor Oskar Halecki. Though sympathetic to my needs, he felt my study efforts would be better utilized in research of Poland's relations with the West. However, any such plan had to be postponed in anticipation of a Spring offensive.

On my return to Ancenis, I stopped for a few days in the historic city of Angers, the temporary seat of the Polish Government in exile. There, to my surprise, outside the railroad station, I met Dr. Olszewski, who had abandoned the Underground operations in Lwów. Since his roommate was absent I was able to stay with him, and he filled me in on the political situation at home. It was not a surprise to learn of the increasing infiltration into the Underground by Soviet agents, making continuation of a clandestine movement in the Eastern territories extremely risky. Olszewski advised me to visit the Ministry of the Interior, where I ran into one of my best pre-war friends, Jan Kozielewski ("Karski") who had just arrived from Warsaw as one of the first secret couriers. He was glad to see me and said he had searched for me in Lwów, hoping to recruite me for similar liaison work between Poland and France.[7] I was tempted, though frightened, at the proposal, and spent the rest of the day with Karski, as we bantered back and forth as to which one of us could outdo the other in this dangerous service. By the next day I was simply unable to refuse the challenge, and agreed that he introduce me to Paweł Siudak, the unassuming director of the Ministry of the Interior's liaison service.[8]

Both Siudak and his Peasant Party colleague from Poznań, Władysław Banaczyk, were happy to get a new volunteer for this exciting operation. They both knew of my pre-war Social Democratic activities and felt my political philosophy was well-suited to the new coalition government of General Sikorski. At the railroad station later that day I was to meet the Minister of the Interior, the sophisticated Professor Stanisław Kot, who was to be arriving from Paris. Upon meeting the Minister, we shook hands and he expressed his approval; he went on to tell me several anecdotes about his tailor, my grandfather Jan Lerski, who was city alderman of Lwów and a veteran of the 1863 "January Insurrection".[10] He then told me to return to my present duties and be patient until they summoned me for assignment as a secret courier. After saying goodbye to Karski, I went back to the dull Ancenis routine to await proper instructions.

Soon our officers' depot was moved to the small town of Pontchateau, and my colleagues and I were able to do some sightseeing in Brittany while awaiting battle orders. We visited, for instance, the prehistoric Dolmens and Menhirs near Carnak, the stone monuments of the Quiberon Peninsula, the great cathedral at Dinard, the medieval fortress town of St. Malo and the exquisite Mont St. Michel. Feeling that our time in waiting should not be wasted, I once again set upon organizing a Soldier's Club to not only keep them entertained and involved with international events, but also to help in appreciation of Polish and French culture. Expressly for these activities my architect colleagues artistically refurbished an abandoned barn on the outskirts of town. On May 3, 1940, Polish National Day, I addressed a crowd of five hundred Poles. In spite of the fact that I became choked with my own tears in describing the tragic situation in our partitioned homeland, the audience was visibly moved.

An unpleasant reminder of the war took place that spring. While traveling back from La Baule (Cote D'Amour) where friends and I celebrated Easter, we were detained at the St. Nazaire railroad station because of a Luftwaffe bombing. Traffic was immobilized and we had to sleep in empty train cars before resuming our trip the next morning. In April, after the Finnish-Soviet Armistice was signed, world attention was drawn to the German invasion of Denmark and Norway. With envy I watched our gallant Highland Brigade, under General Zygmunt Szyszko-Bohusz, leaving the Coetquidan camp as part of an allied expeditionary force.

In connection with my duties as educational officer, a second trip to Paris and the Headquarters of the General Staff was needed. Once again it was an auspicious moment. At Garre Montparnasse it was announced that France, Belgium, Holland, and Luxembourg had just been invaded by Hitler's armies. It was May 10, 1940 and the *"drolle de guerre"* had just come to an abrupt end. People nervously rushed along the boulevards as I walked to Headquarters at the Regina Hotel. After reporting to the officers in charge of educational and cultural programs, I registered at a small hotel just beyond the Madelaine Basilica. The next thing to arrange, in view of the circumstances, was my transfer from the non-combatant officer's depot to the front lines. Through my previous commander, now Major Dobrzański, I was introduced to the senior officer of the anti-aircraft units, Colonel Roman Odzierzyński, who promised to send me with one of the first batteries to the front line.

That night I bolted out of bed as sirens announced a midnight raid, and searchlight scanned the dark night sky for German planes. Their search, however, ended fruitlessly. Unlike Warsaw, Belgrade, Berlin, Rotterdam, and London, Paris was never bombed. There was something unreal and even hedonistic about the carefree atmosphere of the city, when at the same time German armored divisions were cutting across the Low Countries, bypassing the pathetic Maginot Line to attack the heart of France.

General Sikorski displayed an uncritical admiration of the

French, who were full of unrealistic propaganda, like the cocky slogan, *"Nous vainquerons par ce que nous sommes plus forts!"* Moreover, the French politicians were great orators; both Prime Minister Eduard Daladier and his successor, Paul Renaud sounded convincing in their radio broadcasts. Surrounded by such wishful thinking, it was hard not to believe that the French Third Republic was the successor to the Napoleonic tradition and would soon defeat Hitler.

As the Germans steadfastly continued their path into northeastern France, for the first time I had reservations about the military strategy of my hero. Some seventy thousand volunteers had answered Sikorski's call. Why should he allow the French high command to deploy them separately, in small units, and not use them as an entire Polish army corps? The First Grenadiers' Division under General Bronisław Duch, the Second Rifleman's Division under General Bronisław Ketling-Prugar, and the Tenth Armored Brigade under General Stanisław Maczek were all hundreds of miles apart, while the Highland Brigade covered itself with glory, with the first allied victory at Narvik in northern Norway. Was not our good Commander-in-Chief being overzealous to accommodate the French? Nevertheless, like most young officers, I was ready to be sent anywhere rather than sit idly in some cozy little town in Brittany.

Finally my assignment came and the last days in Pontchateau were devoted to forming a viable unit before our departure. I was to be third in command under Captain Jan Działak. Our force was dispatched to Chateaudun in central France to pick up six 25mm guns. After a brief training period we were to join General Prugar's Second Division, assigned to defend the southernmost part of the French German border. The feeling of relief was in the air as we headed into the war zone after so many months of frustrated waiting.

Our unit was an odd mix of people. There were many youths fresh out of elite high schools who had crossed many frontiers to join Sikorski. There were others of dubious character, for instance the four thieves released from Warsaw prison, who required special handling. True to their image, they wore their berets down over their eyes in a swashbuckling way; but most were exemplary soldiers, including several patriotic Jews from Warsaw. Our orderly, Jasiu Popielnicki, was in fact a bit of a scoundrel. He tried to please the four officers and stole chickens and other interesting food which he skillfully prepared. Within the few days this motley group became as one family with one goal, to encounter the enemy.

The morning of June 15th, we reached Chateaudun, France's main artillery center, where we were to pick up guns and other equipment. However, we were immediately informed by one of the few remaining railmen, that Chateaudun had been evacuated and Paris just occupied by the Germans. We were stunned. We had come to France not only to serve in the defense of our homeland, but also cared for France and what she stood for. This was augmented by the age old tradition of French-Polish amity and the feeling that after all: "the neighbors of your enemies are naturally your friends." That the Renaud Government had left the *"ville lumiere"*, loved by all Poles as the capital of their second homeland, was indeed a shock.

We were told that the Chateaudun artillery center was evacuated to Toulouse, supposedly with our guns, and we were ordered to withdraw southwest as well. Minutes later, heavy bombing began; the Germans, unaware of the evacuation, were raining bombs on the railroad station. Lying underneath steel railway cars during the attack intensified the effects of the demoralizing news. The bombing over, we continued our journey, only to come to a sudden halt near Tours. Being the duty officer, I came face-to-face with a 75mm artillery gun and a Senegalese sergeant who was telling us not to cross the bridge over the Loire River. When we asked for his superior, he responded that: "All the French officers have left across the river. I am here only with my gunners and we have orders to shoot anyone who crosses the river." I said to him, "We are your Polish allies, not *"Des Boches"*, you must let us pass to get to our action stations." He let us by but stayed on to defend the bridge. I do not know what became of those brave Senegalese, abandoned by their French officers.

The station at Tours was in a shambles with a train full of wounded soldiers. Hearing Polish from within, we inspected it and saw several men from another anti-aircraft artillery unit. One of them was feverish and told us that the French were deserting on all sides. The Poles had evidently been left behind just like the Senegalese. The sight of those wounded, ill-treated men saddened and angered us as we proceeded on to a major disappointment at Toulouse. Everything was in chaos when we reached our destination, where we learned that the French resistance was collapsing; indeed, at noon on June 17th, the senile head of the French state, Marshal Petain, shamelessly announced the French surrender and upcoming armistice. In disgust, we watched young French airmen drinking in a nearby cafe, toasting each other with *"Vive la paix, la guerre est finie!*.

General Marian Kukiel, the Polish Minister of Defense, advised us through a radio broadcast that we could rejoin our families in France or continue the fight from Great Britain, the last European outpost in the fight against Hitler, under General Sikorski and with de Gaulle's Free French forces. Two hundred and eleven out of two hundred and twenty in my group proudly opted for Great Britain and headed for the nearest port, on the Bay of Biscay.

We reached the town of Bayonne on June 19th and marched some fifteen miles in military formation to the port of St. Jean de Luz, where the two largest Polish passenger ships, the SS *Batory* and the SS *Sobieski*, which had been sent from Britain were waiting for us. My unit boarded the SS *Sobieski* which looked overloaded, carrying over 2,000 passengers. Some twenty thousand Polish troops had left France, which refused to defend herself. The furious Dr. Goebbels, Hitler's Propaganda Minister, called us with contempt "General Sikorski's Tourists" — and we became rather proud of this designation.

Our unit was assigned to man the 75mm anti-aircraft gun and several machine guns to defend against air attacks. The greatest worry would be German U-boats, and we had no escorts whatever to help us in case of attack. In an attempt to

38

elude the submarines patrolling the direct route to England, we headed to the center of the Atlantic. Luckily, the several U-boat alarms given during the journey all proved false. This lurking danger only added to the tenseness of that miserable voyage. Morale among the soldiers was low; the senior officers, of which there were too many, desparate to justify their commissions, were offering bribes to any soldier who would pretend to be under their command; and I was battling a bout of seasickness. With relief we sighted British land on the morning of June 25th.

Near Plymouth, our first sight was the splendid gray contours of the British warships, and second, the blimps. They seemed to be big monsters hovering in the sky, protectors of the important naval base. Cruising slowly, we watched the energetic activities on the pilot boats and finally felt safe again. It seemed that, after all, Britania did "rule the waves."

Once on shore, we bade farewell to the brave sailors of the *SS Sobieski,* who were to return to France to pick up the remaining Poles. Those fine people, whose risk increased with each trip, were certainly front-line warriors, just like regular members of the Polish Navy who fought side by side with the greatest navy in the world—the Royal Navy.

We were treated well by the English, who welcomed us, their new co-defenders (though some were surprised that we were all lilly-white and not coloured!), first by the "lovely cup of tea" at the rail depot and then by waving crowds at all the small stations on our train route to Lancashire, where we were to stay in our first British transition camp. Once again we felt we would be able to contribute to the sacred struggle, even though we were still dazed at how France, one of the greatest democracies in the world capitulated so easily?

At Ashton, which lay between Liverpool and Manchester, we disembarked from our train and marched to the horse racing field, Haydock Park, where the original camp had been set up for Polish troops. The morale of our soldiers was grim and discipline was difficult. They felt that just as in September of 1939, the Polish high command had failed to lead, though they were still loyal to the officers of our unit, as they felt we had done well by them during the evacuation from France. I had to emphasize that with British help we would soon be organized into an effectivve fighting force, which would become part of an invading allied army ultimately capable of defeating the Germans. In those dark days of June 1940 though, they were not easily convinced. The Nazis, with Soviet help, were in control of the European contintent and, at the last moment, even Italy declared war on France and Great Britain. We did not know where our main fighting army units were.

Having learned a little English before the war, I was sent to buy stationery and necessary supplements to our diet from a nearby mining village. The first time I ventured forth, I became involved in a discussion with the railroad clerk at the little station. I told him that we hoped Britain would win, having found such a formidable leader in Winston Churchill. The man was obviously a supporter of the Labour Party, for he sarcastically answered that indeed "Winnie" was a great Tory imperialist, but that as soon as the war was over, they would get rid of him and elect a Labour Party Cabinet to take better care of the working people. I was not enthusiastic with the countryside. This was an industrial section of England, with much smoke along unending rows of identical brick slum roads. In several weeks we were again transferred, this time to Scotland, where we were to meet even friendlier people and see a more attractive landscape.

The Scots, who looked upon us as heroes and were very hospitable indeed lifted our spirits, despite the rainy skies. Our campsite outside Crawford in Lanarkshire on the Upper Clyde River was rough and wet, but it was situated in truly enchanting hills covered with green grass and heather, where only stone walls divided the fields and grazing sheep. In such an environment we were able to settle down and make the best of it.

Our first task, under the command of British General Thorne, was to guard the central Scottish wilderness from possible airborne attack by Germans stationed in occupied Norway. It was hardly exciting to sit for twenty-four hour periods with ten soldiers, armed with machine guns, rifles and hand grenades, in a tent on top of one of those bare hills, while the rest of our forces retrained in the valleys as regular infantry. I used to take books with me on these occasions to study the fascinating history of Great Britain. Though I enjoyed the close contact with my witty soldiers, it was not much of a war!

Early one morning, it finally looked as though the entire Polish army in Scotland was put on alert when scattered shooting was heard in the hills between Crawford and Douglas. But instead of German paratroopers, we found a couple of old kilted Scots hunting rabbits, although soon after, Rudolf Hess, Hitler's top lieutenant, was parachuted into Lord Hamilton's estate not too far from our camp. It was his good luck that he did not fall into our hands first.

The Church of Scotland established a much needed mobile canteen for us. But there were also the cultural needs of the idle troops to be attended to, so I resumed my favorite duties of educational officer. Mrs. Clifford Norton ("Peter"), who had recently returned from Europe with her husband, drummed up tremendous Scottish assistance, and we were provided with equipment and a huge tent which we used as our cultural center. It was partitioned into a reading library and concert or lecture area. We were even written up enthusiastically in the new London publication *Dziennik Polski* (Polish Daily).[10]

On my request several college professors in uniform set up a series of stimulating lectures. Three of the outstanding scholars who gave these talks were Father Joseph Bocheński O.P., a mathematical logician, Captain Tadeusz Sulimirski, Professor of prehistory and archaeology at the Jagiellonian University at Krakow, and Private Zygmunt Sławiński, a civil engineer, who had also been one of the top economic planners of the pre-war COP (Central Industrial Region) to build a stronger Poland.

The latter stressed the need for a West-Slavic federation of Czechs, Slovaks, and Poles as well as Serbo-Lusatians, in an attempt to jointly force the Germans to relinquish Slavic territories. These initial serious discussions of war goals came late in the summer 1940 at a time when the British were

41

barely hanging on, and the Germans seemed about to win the war. We, however, were definitely planning for victory. Our goal was to establish a large regional confederation built of two lesser units: the West Slavic federation, with a possible new capital on the southern slopes of the Tatra mountains in Slovakia—the rural nation which would not be feared by the others as expansionist because of its small size; and the other, a federation between the allied Greeks and the Yugoslavs. In the center, we would have to convince the non-Slavic Rumanians and Hungarians to join the East-Central European Confederation. These were truly fascinating plans, and soon detailed maps were prepared by our bright draftsmen and engineers. Moreover, we decided to approach some of the pro-Polish Czech and Slovak fellow exiles under General Lev Prhala.

We started the *Biuletyn Zachodnio-Słowiański* (West Slavonic Bulletin), the first periodical of this kind promoting the idea that we should let bygones be bygones and join in a union for survival. As busybody educational officer, I suggested that we display in my "świetlica" (soldier's club) a huge map of Europe with markings to indicate the Polish Western frontier on the Odra and Lusatian Nissa rivers where it is today between East Germany and captive Poland. While preparing this map, I was informed that we would soon be having a visit from our Polish Prime Minister, General Sikorski, and our President, Władysław Raczkiewicz, with British dignitaries. I was not quite prepared to declare the purpose of my map to anyone but Commander-in-Chief Sikorski, and instead told General Regulski that I would be using it to show the latest war developments.

A few days later, General Sikorski and President Raczkiewicz were led through the camp. I was introduced as the świetlica's host and led them around the huge tent. When we came to the map, General Regulski explained that I was outlining battlefronts; but General Sikorski scolded him, stating clearly for all to hear that I was actually outlining a future federation of East-Central Europe. He was obviously pleased that we were thinking along those lines, and half-jokingly said that the island of Rugen (Rugia) in the Southern Baltic was once of Slavic background, and therefore should be included. "Yes Sir," I retorted, "you are the Commander-in-Chief," moving the ribbon to including the Baltic island in the territory which was to be the future confederation. Everyone had a good laugh and General Sikorski told one of his aides to take my name down. Two days later a call came from the First Army Corps in the city of Perth that I was to report to General Kukiel. Apparently Prime Minister Sikorski was very much in favor of the Polish-Czechoslovak federation, as well as of the westward expansion of Poland to the territories which had been teutonized, though they were originally West Slavic. He felt that this was exactly the sort of constructive thinking needed for long-range postwar planning. Our Prime Minister had been invited to the White House and wanted to present President Roosevelt with constructive proposals for the future of liberated Europe. I was asked to work with a team of scholars and cartographers to prepare a whole series of maps which would be taken to Washington, D.C.[11] The offer was intellectually tempting, but I declined, explaining that I wanted to remain with my unit and fight with them when the time came. I chose to remain on active duty in hope of physically joining in the battle for freedom. Tadeusz Sulimirski, Zygmunt Sławiński and a third colleague, prominent architect Stanisław Połujan, however, became even more enthusiastic, and worked determinedly on plans for the Federation. As a result, the latter two were soon called to Perth, and Professor Sulimirski became editor-in-chief of the *West Slavonic Bulletin*, in which we published articles concerning the proposed federation and related topics.

We also assisted in the publication of a book entitled **Ziemia Gromadzi Prochy** (The Earth Gathers Ashes) by Józef Kisielewski, who now worked for the Ministry of the Interior in London. It was an important study done just before the war, demonstrating Polish claims to the territories of Eastern Germany which had been Slavic until they became Germanized as the first victims of the *"Drang nach Osten"*. With the help of money from Polish soldiers and officers, we

43

managed to publish the book in 1941.

On August 15, 1940, Polish Soldier's Day, I was asked to address some four thousand soldiers at the Crawford Camp. I opened my address with a *"Nil desperandum"* (Never despair) appeal claiming that the Polish nation is united as in August 1920, when we were able to defeat the Bolshevik Red Army with the "Miracle of Vistula" at the gates of Warsaw. In one of the decisive battles of world history, the Poles had stopped the march of communism into the heart of Europe. I told them that it had happened because we had then, like now, a Government of National Unity, under Wincenty Witos of the Peasant Party as Prime Minister and Ignacy Daszyński of the Polish Socialist Party as his deputy, with the brilliant military leadership of Marshal Piłsudski, and our own present Commander-in-Chief, Sikorski. Now, after the defeat of France, all Polish eyes and hearts were turned to us, the remnants of the Polish Free Army and the nucleus of the future victorious forces which would liberate newly partitioned Poland. This was perhaps the most emotional speech I had ever delivered, and the response was overwhelming. Many were moved to tears, and ever since my reputation as an effective orator both in Polish and English was established.

In Crawford we were finally equipped with modern rifles, machine guns, and hand grenades. Due to our thorough training in Scotland, we were becoming quite an important part of the defensive shield for the island. After Dunkirk, there were only a few British troops in the United Kingdom as a whole, and in Scotland in particular. It would have been easy for Hitler to have invaded the island at this time. His troops had already successfully occupied the Channel islands close to the French coast. After hearing of the systematic *Luftwaffe* attacks on British airports and harbors, a German invasion seemed close at hand.

Early in September we heard that Hitler had decided to blitz London, and soon substantial damage to this city was made. I wanted to go there and see for myself how the British were holding up under the bombing, so as not to have my men deceived by untruthful optimistic newscasts, as they had been in France. It was impossible to get a pass to besieged London, so I deviously got permission to go to Winchester in southern England by saying I had relatives there.

Early that morning I arrived on schedule at Euston Station in London, which was in a shambles having been bombed the night before. The air was full of smoke and the people looked gray. As none of the buses were in service, I walked a couple of miles to a small "bed and breakfast" hotel at Nottingham Place near the Baker Street Station, where I had been told some Polish families were living, and took a good long look at the havoc the intensified German bombing was wreaking on Londoners. Casualties ranged between 300 and 500 a day, and 1,000 to 3,000 injured, while entire neighborhoods were reduced to heaps of rubble. However, life went on in that brave city, its inhabitants somehow managing to remain cheerful in the face of daily terror, and "Business as Usual" signs were proudly displayed in front of bombed out stores.

After I registered at the hotel and unpacked, I went to report to the high-command headquarters at the Rubens Hotel by Buckingham Palace, before visiting some of my friends in the Polish Government. By chance I met Andrzej Nahlik, who was trying to get into the Polish Air Force. As he was pointing out the Zeppelin-type balloons for the protection of London and the huge anti-aircraft artillery guns situated in Hyde Park, an air-raid warning sounded and we found ourselves in the middle of a daytime bombing. This was soon over, and Londoners continued once again with their daily routine.

September 21, 1940 was quite a night in London. Now, at the peak of the Blitz, I realized what such a massive night bombing really meant. After an evening in a cosmopolitan Soho nightclub, I returned to my hotel, and no sooner got into bed, then the shrieking sirens started up. There was a full blackout in effect and searchlights crisscrossed the skies. Whenever a bomber was sighted, the anti-aircraft artillery began its cannonade. The inferno really broke loose when the bombs started falling very near us, and we were told to evacuate the hotel at once, as one unexploded bomb remained in the backyard. We moved quickly to the Bond Street subway station where I saw the pathetic scenes later immortalized by the prominent Royal artist Feliks Topolski; people wrapped in blankets trying to sleep, others hunched over while eating, sitting on the floor.

Early the next morning, I went back to the hotel where I found a crew of specialists disarming the bomb. I was only allowed to run in for my belongings since the bomb had not yet been defused. For the balance of my "vacation", I moved to the place where Andrzej was staying near Earls Court Station, and endured yet another rough night of bombings in that hotel, sitting in the cellar talking with some brave British women who worked for the War Ministry.

While in London, curious about my possible mission to Nazi occupied Poland, I arranged to see Professor Kot. Though friendly, he was noncommittal, being much more interested in finding out about the anti-Sikorski intrigues in Scottish camps. He even called his Ministry's Security Director, Tadeusz Ulman, for an informal cross-examination of my political contacts. I left, disgusted with that team, supposedly dedicated to the war effort of our oppressed country, but actually very much out of step with our preparations for the liberation of Poland.

After another one of those night bombings, by chance I saw Prime Minister Churchill, as that indomitable old "Bulldog" was walking through the debris of a recently hit church in Piccadilly, with a cigar in his mouth. A large crowd applauded him as to convince me that, whatever happened, the Cockneys would follow Churchill's leadership, fighting till the end for every inch of their homeland.

I returned to Crawford on a Sunday, literally a day of rest, and from the railroad station of Moffat in Dumfrieshire I was faced with a fifteen-mile walk, since no buses were running. Happily, after about one hour of walking, I managed to stop a military car and was surprised when an obviously British Captain, Malcolm Scott, addressed me in fluent Polish asking about my parents. His mother was Polish and he had been brought up, like me in Lwów. He now served as one of the liaison officers attached to the Polish Army. At camp there were no changes in routine, but a growing sign of restlessness on the part of many, and a couple of friends even asked me to help them in becoming secret couriers to Poland.

Shortly after my return, the Blitz slackened off and no invasion had been mounted. The British had put up a firm resistance and had bombed Flemish ports, successfully frustrating Nazi preparations. Also, improved defense measures had inflicted heavy losses on the German air-raids with one hundred and eighty five German planes crashing in one day. Many were shot by Polish fighter squadrons.

Once again our troop was ordered to move, this time to much more comfortable housing in Coupar Angus in Perthshire. We were to be the second-line defense of Eastern Scottish ports. My second platoon was billeted in the Masonic Hall, and I was lucky to be placed with a delightful old couple, the Geekies, whose only son Ian had been taken prisoner with the famous 51st Highland Division, and was being held by the Germans in Poland. They treated me like their own son which was very comforting, for at about that same time, I received the terrible news, via Yugoslav friends, of my family's April, 1940 deportation by the NKVD to Siberia. One and one half million other Poles shared their fate; Stalin had proved as cruel to Poles as Hitler.

We were finally being provided with adequate weapons, as well as first-class infantry training by Polish veterans of the Norwegian campaign. A few of the officers, including myself, were also called by the British for practice with heavy caliber anti-aircraft artillery guns installed near the town of Dumferline, not far from Rosyth, the main naval shipyard for British warships and the Royal Navy high command. During our two-week training, we gradually became competent with the newest anti-aircraft artillery guns and even proved our adeptness when we were twice raided by the *Luftwaffe*.

With this preparation we again moved to the northern region of Montrose on Scotland's sunnier east coast, which meant an opportunity to be involved in front-line defenses on the beaches, or so we thought. Our unit was rechristened the Tenth Battery of anti-aircraft artillery, and though still doing infantry work, we were assured assignment to General Maczek's 10th Armored Brigade, once fully equipped. With this in mind, we were now to be under the command of Captain Borys Godunov, a handsome descedent of the pre-Romanov Czar, who had served with distinction under Maczek in France, from which he had only recently escaped.

Hitler was still in command of most of Europe facing us across the North Sea in Norway. We were to construct solid trenches on the Scottish beaches, a task which reminded me of my childhood games in Brzuchowice, for mock battles. What we did not know, was that using the secret Polish Enigma machine, the British were able to decode all of the most confidential Germans communications, and were aware that no invasion of Britain was planned any longer.[12]

Early in spring, 1941, I was presented with offers to use my oratorical skills in America to recruit Polish-American volunteers and to help form another anti-aircraft military unit. Evidently, even if I did go there, I could still be called for underground service, so the Canadian plans met with my approval. While waiting for these special services to come through, I still held my precious positions as platoon commander and educational officer. In this last capacity we succeeded in preparing a dozen of my men for their high school degree, necessary to enter officers' cadet schools. This work was difficult because there were no texts from which to work, and I prepared the notes and lectures myself, for the classes in geography, history, and literature. Little did I know then what important preparation this would be for my later years as a history professor.

Prolonged inaction affected the moral among troops, which was again at quite a low point, and discipline among the men was hard to maintain. For example, non-commissioned officers would occasionally get drunk and pick fights with one another. When rations were cut due to Britain's increasing lack of food supplies and dependency on those from abroad, some of our men took to illegal killing of the salmon catch of local fishermen by throwing hand grenades into the full fish nets. The culprits were disciplined severely, and I attempted to pull my unit back together by having extensive talks with most men individually. I also tried to keep them as constructively busy as possible, and as a result, enjoyed fine relations with most of them.

One day in May, however, German planes bombed the town of Montrose and our garrison was involved in removing the debris. The inhabitants were cleared from the nearby streets, and one of our units was assigned to protect the area until specialists could arrive to disarm the bomb. The famous "four Warsaw thieves", however, were not willing to spend the night at the post because they had dancing dates, so they decided to take care of the bomb themselves. They dug it out and put it on a wheelbarrow. Followed by an admiring crowd, they took it outside the city and buried it. Thank God it did not explode. The "Warsaw Four" got a hero's thanks from the relieved Scots, but we had to punish them for disobeying orders. All they asked was that they be jailed after their dates. No wonder that type of daring man became popular with the Scottish lassies, and even with the older folks.

The spring of 1941 brought a variety of war events, both good and bad. On april 4th, we heard reports of the see-saw situation in North Africa, where the Germans under Marhsal Rommel had just taken Port Bengazi back from the British. One the other hand, on March 27th, the evening news were wonderful. Yugoslavia had decided to overturn its pro-Nazi Regent Paul, in favor of the young King Peter; acting on his behalf the patriotic Regency Council appointed an anti-German Government under General Simovic. This was indeed another important turning point in the struggle of the Slavs against the Germans. I thought at the time that Yugoslavia's unexpected entrance into the war on the Allied side would shorten the war by as much as a year. What it actually did was to critically delay Nazi onslaught on Russia for at least one month. At the same time we heard of the British progress in North Africa under General O'Connor, and that the Italians had just been defeated in the Mediterranean theatre with several of their brand new battleships sunk. The myth of Fascist omnipotence had finally been eclipsed. It also looked as though Germany would soon attack Russia, something we had long thought was inevitable. After they had both eaten away at Poland, they would have had to put a halt to their greediness, or go at each other's throats, and due to the expansionism of both countries, the latter was much more likely.

The second Easter in exile was sad, however, because I not only had to deal with the low morale of our men, but was also full of concern for my family with nostalgic memories of our last skiing vacation in the Tatra mountains. Luckily, I was soon relieved of some of my worries because I finally heard from my friends Wiera Pilawska and Leszek Orski in Lwów, who said they were in touch with my mother and half-brother, who were found in the middle of Soviet Kazakhstan. Soon after these great news I also learned that my stepfather had been sent from prison in Lwów to the Komi region of northeastern European Russia, where he became camp surgeon after saving the life of a Russian guard who fell from a watch turret.

On May 3, 1941, the traditional Polish national holiday, Churchill spoke especially to the Poles in his radio address. He reported that although Greece had fought valiantly, the battle in the Balkans was over. Another small, brave ally had gone down in defeat. I found it hard to understand why the lesser allies were to be sacrificed as a rule.

On May 7th, I took another leave to London to find out when I would be at last called to secret duty.

Mr. Siudak of the Ministry of the Interior could tell me nothing concrete yet about my prospective underground work, and once again I felt very frustrated. My visit to the Czechoslovak Club turned out to be far more rewarding. There I met the famous General Lew Prhala, one of the few Czech commanders willing to fight in the 1938 crisis for his country's independence. Later he had commanded the Czecho-Slovak volunteer legion in Poland and was now in opposition to the president of the Czechoslovak National Council, Dr. Eduard Benes, since we suspected it was through his influence with the Sikorski government that our *West Slavonic Bulletin*, promoting regional confederation, was temporarily banned by

Polish authorities in London. I also had the good fortune to meet the Pridavok brothers, important representatives of the Free Slovaks, who were definitely in favor of a West-Slavic Federation. We discussed the inclusion of other nationalities such as Lithuanians, Ukrainians, Yugoslavs, and Bulgarians, agreeing that such a federation should go beyond joint military and foreign policy to include matters of currency, customs, unions and presidency, while leaving the educational cultural and judicial systems to the autonomous governments.

The next day I went to the editorial offices of *Polska Walcząca* (Fighting Poland), to see its editor, the well known drama critic, Dr. Tymon Terlecki. His paper served as the weekly organ of the Polish armed forces and was published by the Ministry of Defense. Dr. Terlecki suggested that I write a series of articles on the kind of Poland we were fighting for, and another about self-educational work in the army. Before leaving for Scotland, I experienced yet another major bombing of London, this time concentrated in the Parliament area and aptly called the "Westminster Raid". Even though the very heart of that heroic city was again in a shambles, both during and after the raid everyone maintained a sense of pride, expressing the hope that soon Berlin would be honored with a response.

Back at camp, Captain Działak and I were told to report to the main hotel in Perth. We went knowing nothing more than that we were to have this clandestine meeting in room thirty-nine. When we arrived we were greeted by the Peasant Party representative Władysław Banaczyk, who explained the grave situation in Poland, and asked us to help him in recruiting bright, determined candidates for undergroud work. He also confirmed that I was by now at the top for the paratroopers training list, but that they were in need of even more volunteers for special missions. To find such absolutely reliable, level-headed men was a heavy responsibility, but we promised to do our best. My first success was witty lance corporal Aleksander Olędzki, who agreed without hesitation to be parachuted with me into occupied Poland.[13] In the meantime, Captain Godunow promoted me to the function of reconnaissance officer for the battery. I still kept up my favorite duties as educational officer, and was asked to start the war diary of our unit, hopefully a useful source for future war chroniclers.

In the middle of June we were given the assignment of defending the huge naval shipyard of Rosyth, north of the long bridge over the Firth of Forth and in the vicinity of the newly-developed center of naval operations for the entire globe. Strategically, it was thus one of the key areas in the British Isles. We were to continue our infantry duties until the receipt of anti-aircraft artillery equipment, which we would be using to protect that region. Our new camp was at Limekilns on Lord Elgin's estate, on the slope of a hill overlooking the wide river. While in training we were to guard the area against the still possible German airborne invasion.

On June 22nd, Hitler committed his greatest blunder by executing the long-prepared attack on Russia. This was a moment we had been eagerly waiting for, as it opened an entirely new ball game. The conflict of those two totalitarian powers meant that every tank, plane, and soldier destroyed and killed on either side brought us closer to the end of the war. Russia and Germany must have realized by then that, having eliminated Poland from the map of Europe in 1939, the had destroyed the safety buffer between themselves, making a Soviet-Nazi mortal struggle much more likely. As long as the countries of East-Central Europe had been free, they provided for the security of both Russia and Germany, but now it was all gone in one day. There were no news, however, of the fate of one and a half million Polish citizens who had been deported to the depths of the Soviet Union during the last two years. Perhaps, we thought, the Russians would have to suffer much more in order to come to some compromise with the Poles.

Hitler's columns advanced quickly inside Soviet-held territory, moving almost thirty miles a day, and taking a number of major cities. It seemed as though in a few days there would not be one live Russian left on formerly Polish territory. We also realized that Germans would create greater troubles for themselves by overextending their lines of communication. At the end of June, 1941, we learned that Lwów had been easily taken from the Soviets by the Nazis. These news did nothing but increase my desire to land on Polish soil and find out for myself the details of what was actually happening.

On the international scene there was increasing pressure from the British for Poles to almost unconditionally re-establish diplomatic relations with Moscow—a very risky endeavor in view of the fact that the Russians refused to recognize their pre-war frontier with Poland. They were driving some hard bargains in Moscow, while the Poles have hardly been known for their diplomatic skill. Many of us considered General Sikorski a very fine commander and successful organizer, but much too naive in his careless dealings with the Soviets. We did not like the idea that the first man to fly to Moscow to represent the Polish Government was his controversial friend Dr. Joseph Retinger, who had allegedly spent some thirty years in the British intelligence service, and was distrusted by our officers' corps. From the British point of view, it was important that their new Russian ally and the Poles should patch up differences and present a united front, even if this was achieved mainly at the expense of Poland. Meanwhile, we became greatly concerned that some fifteen thousand Polish officers were missing in Russia.[14] Moreover, we were afraid that the Russians would never concede to return the eastern half of the Polish state with Lwów and Wilno to its legitimate control. Such unsolved problems created poisonous suspicions that our leadership was not serving the Polish cause prudently enough, and General Sikroski looked a bit ridiculous touring the units in Scotland to explain everywhere that he had not sold out and does not intend to give up Lwów or Wilno.

The man who did have our confidence at that time was another senior General, Kazimierz Sosnkowski, once the closest lieutenant of Marshal Piłsudski. He led the open opposition to the new Maisky-Sikorski (Soviet-Polish) Agreement and as such resigned from the Cabinet with two other ministers. A new Polish Army was to be created from those volunteers released by the Soviet Union, to be led by the remarkable General Władysław Anders.[15] Because of the lack of officers, it turned out that many of us in Great Britain would be called for assignment with these Polish units in Russia. Naturally, I wanted to be a part of this mission, hoping to join my mother, stepfather and half-brother—all fortunate survivors of Soviet captivity. Unfortunately, the exams for this were given in Russian, and not having learned the Cyrillic alphabet, I was curtly told by Lt. Colonel Marian Jurecki, "Lieutenant, you are out". This was a great disappointment at the moment, but my chance to serve as a secret courier was to come up soon in any case, and I would finally have an opportunity to actively serve my homeland and the allied cause.

CHAPTER II

IN PREPARATION FOR THE MISSION

The long-awaited calling into underground service came as the war was at a boiling point. Hitler was reaching further into the depths of Russia and closing in on Moscow and Leningrad. Kiev, the Ukrainian capital, had fallen, and on December 7, 1941, Pearl Harbor was attacked by the Japanese, which brought the United States directly into the struggle.

Once in London, I reported to the Personnel Division of the Polish General Staff headquarters in the Rubens Hotel near Buckinham Palace, to be directed to Stratton House off Picadilly Street. Here I met with Stanisław Mikołajczyk, the new Minister of the Interior, and Vice President of the Polish Peasant Party as well as the Deputy Prime Minister. Mikołajczyk was a stalky, balding man in his early forties, with an enigmatic personality. Outwardly he appeared to be steely and cold and was neither talkative nor outgoing; when he did speak, his few, emotionless words presented the pensive, self-confident and ambitious man underneath. However, he was not the great statesman that the British press later tried to make him out to be.

I had met Mikołajczyk several times previously, and he approved of my prewar close contacts with the youth leaders of his Party, which became the largest in Poland. Now he formally proposed that I join the courier service as a government emissary between London and Poland, and gave me twenty four hours for a final answer.[16]

Although I had anxiously awaited this moment, these twenty four hours were nonetheless difficult. With my nervous, sensitive nature, I was not endowed with the makings of a war hero and I was acutely aware of these weaknesses. That night, in my nightmares, I lived through the horrors of Gestapo tortures in anticipation of my upcoming service. However, the desire to do something more concrete for my oppressed countrymen, as well as a firm promise given to one of my best prewar friends, Jan Karski, overcame my fears, and the next day I came back to Mikołajczyk with a yes. I was given one week to wind up my army affairs in Cowdenbeath and instructed to begin preparations under the Polish Ministry of the Interior and the British Special Operations Executive (SOE) in London, immediately upon my return from Scotland.

My first assignment was to report to a spacious villa in Wilmslow, near Manchester for a week of intensive parachute training, with some twenty other volunteers from the Polish Army. This residence was surrounded by tall thick hedges so that no outsider could peer in to observe us, and the grounds provided ample space for our physical and technical maneuvers. This unit was in generaly high spirits, with much joking to rid ourselves of the tensions. In this group I was one of three civil couriers, while the remaining were to participate in sabotage and guerrilla warfare. Among them were Captain Bolesław Kontrym ("Żmudzin"), Second Lieutenant Mieczysław Ekhardt ("Bocian"), Second Lieutenant Antoni Jastrzębski ("Ugor"), Second Lieutenant Wacław Kopista ("Kra"), and Cadet officer Adolf Pilch ("Góra"). Some of these men later became well known in Poland as courageous commanders of partisan units and some were killed by Nazis either in battle or in prison.

Our day began at dawn with one hour of "P.T." (intensive physical training), which included running and jumping over obstacles. Afterwards we would go to the Ringway Airport and report to Lieutenant Trice, our Australian parachute instructor. He had broken his leg "while playing soccer," and in our good humor we teased him about this, saying: "We did not know you played soccer in the air, Lieutenant!" Nevertheless, he was able to teach us how to jump safely from an airplane.

The first mild shock came on the first day of training, immediately after being shown the two-engine, spacious

Whittley plane (otherwise known as the "flying coffin"), that was to be used for our jumps. Not having thought about it earlier, I suddenly realized I had never yet been in any plane whatsoever, and here I was preparing myself to jump out of one.

We were then given a flying tour over the airfield, to observe the area between two frozen lakes where our jumps were to take place. Then, back on land, we made a few practice jumps, with our equipment on, but with the plane still stationary. It was with these exercises that we learned how to automatically roll over our shoulders on landing, if necessary, so as to reduce the shock and not to break our legs. The remainder of the afternoon was then spent in observation of others who were making real jumps. This gave us the opportunity to see first hand the do's and don'ts of this tricky operation.

The next day, after an intensive physical training session, we took our first actual jump at 800 feet. As the Whittley approached the field, I made the mistake of saying it would be a similar experience to ski jumping, and when everyone laughed I became quite irritated. It was then that the superstitious Seargeant Instructor informed me that one of my colleagues had written "In loving memory, Lieutenant Lerski" on my parachute cover. Although I landed improperly on my knees, fortunately I managed to jump without mishap. Two of my companions, though, Pilch and Jastrzębski, received retribution for laughing at me, when they broke legs on their jumps.

The next two jumps were from 2500 feet, and one of those times two of us had to jump at once. The most unpleasant experience, though, was a night jump from the gondola of a hot air balloon. When you are jumping from a plane you have the noise of the engine as well as a surge of air pushing you slightly forward, which gives the feeling that you are really not alone in this endeavor. From the gondola, howeverr, the feeling is more desolate, as you jump into deadly silence, and the direction is straight down.

Our last performance was a group jump which each person immediately followed the one before. All went smoothly and the British instructors tried to boost our pride by saying that "Poles are never afraid." We then returned to London after the five training jumps, with each of us going on to receive more specific training in his particular mission.

To become better acquainted with Poland's internal situation, I was placed in the Political Information Office of the Ministry of the Interior, and proceeded to read great amounts of material from Nazi-occupied Poland. This consisted of reports from the underground and clandestine papers of which there were hundreds throughout the country, informing Poles of international and local news, and keeping up their morale. It was definitely an eye opener to me that so many papers were being printed and distrubted within Poland, despite the difficulties involved. In England these reports served to inform the exiled government of the economic situation, police terror, and acts of sabotage on the part of the underground, as well as the other tribulations with which Poles had to deal daily. My assignment with these reports was not only to thoroughly learn the situation in the home country so as to enable myself to move around more easily and effectively on my return, but also to prepare digests for publication and broadcast in the West.

Due to throat infection, it was not until late January that I went to the New Forest station near Bournemouth, operated by the SOE (Special Operations Executive), for further special training. This organization was top secret and run by the British under one of the Cabinet members (first by Professor Hugh Dalton of the Labour Party, later by Lord Selborne, a Tory). There were approximately fifteen Polish candidates for civil underground service at the time. Among them I was pleased to see some of the bright fellows from my battery, whom I had recruited for this purpose. Our British instructors first drilled us in the five fundamental principles that secret agents must abide by while operating in enemy occupied territory. We were told to always have a good cover story, well supported by forged documents, be absolutely discreet, always inconspicuous, know our enemies as well as possible, and be ready for any emergency if the above caveats failed. We were

58

also taught how to follow someone and avoid being followed ourselves.

In being discreet and inconspicuous, we had to be very careful about our manner of talking and dealing with tempting social situations, as well as dress in a fashion that would completely blend in with the environment. Some of the trainees failed in this part and were discharged from the underground service. One, for example, proved to talk too much to inquisitive ladies under the influence of alcohol and had to leave the program abruptly. As if to prove that caution could never be underestimated, one of our British instructors Captain Angelo suddenly disappeared, and we soon learned that he had been found to be a double agent spying for Mussolini, after which he was quickly liquidated.

Familiarity with the enemy was particularly important, for it helped in recognizing dangerous informers, regular police and the Gestapo in any given area. The reports I had read from the clandestine press greatly helped in learning the present situation in Poland and Nazi methods of conducting business.

In our alertness to emergency situations, we were drilled on how to be extremely observant, and how to be sure of ourselves. We were often asked abrupt, unexpected questions for which none of us could be prepared; we had to remain cool and keep our wits about us. Gradually, we all became more confident of ourselves, which made our minds work quicker. Because of this long training, it turned out that we were on the whole more careful and distrusting than those who had not left Poland, since they had been often lulled into a false sense of security.

Other aspects of our instruction dealt with pyrotechnics, particularly with "plastic" explosives, unarmed combat (killing with bare hands), fighting with knives or pistols, and especially instant sharpshooting, where the movement of your body had to be parallel to the object and you had to be able to kill from 200 feet away. This all lasted for three weeks, after which each of us was much better prepared, both mentally and physically, for our future tasks.

The most important specialization, however, was yet to

come, and each person had an assignment that was geared towards accomplishing his upcoming mission. For instance, the fellow who was to be an intelligence agent in the port of Gdańsk (Danzig), was assigned a 6-month job with the Merchant Navy to prepare him for sailor's work in a port city. His background as a city policeman would have been deficient without this supplementary training. I, on the other hand, was put under the auspices of the British Ministry of Information. Ten days were spent in learning opinion sampling skills under the guidance of a Quaker lady, who had investigated the impact of BBC broadcasts concerning private food production on backyard vegetable growing in the southern London suburb of Lewisham. The purpose was to learn to what extent the BBC instruction programs had been effective and how to improve them. The sampling was based on the Gallup Poll methods, whereby a cross section of the population was given well-prepared questionnaires to fill out. Although it did not seem that relevant to me at the time, it proved to be of real use later on in Poland, in organizing a socio-economic and political intelligence network for the civil underground.

A far more exciting task came soon after, when I was sent to the politically radical Rhonda Valley in Southern Wales, to discover within one week the answers to two questions, without being spotted by the ever-present British police for being too inquisitive. I was to investigate the attitude of Welsh miners to Winston Churchill's coalition government, particularly its Labour Party role, and discover the miners' opinions on the amazing shortage of coal in the British Isles. My cover story had me as the son of a Polish miner on leave from the Merchant Navy, who had come to explore and compare the conditions of the Welsh miners to those of Polish Śląsk (Silesia).

After checking into a modest hotel, I went down to the noisy pub, and within two days I befriended a middle-aged miner namesake, George, who invited me to stay at his home. I was able to join him and one of his sons in the mine pit, and went dancing with his daughters. Unexpected information, however, came from George's other son who worked in the aircraft factory near Swansea. He easily shared detailed facts on the nature and locations of his important war production job.

I studiously read the local press and became more or less part of the family. Appearing innocent though gregarious, I completed my report without queries from local authorities and was later told by the British supervisors that I had accomplished my mission well. The main part of my task had been to obtain information on a sensitive issue in a small town, where nosy outsiders were not common. Again, my self-confidence and scouting abilities were greatly enhanced by this worthy experience.

On the whole, I discovered the Welsh were suspicious of the English in general. In specific economic problems they distrusted the Social democratic moderate leadership of the Labour Party, which had entered into the coalition with conservatives and liberals. They definitely did not trust Churchill. As far as the coal shortage was concerened, they blamed the government for poor conditions in the pits and for the fact that they were underpaid.

It was mid-spring, and since the nights became too short for secret flights to Poland, I was sent from London as commanding officer for fifteen civil couriers, to intense physical training at a waiting station in an old farmhouse near historic Tewkesbury Abbey in Gloucestershire. Here I remained for six months, rooming with this unit's British Commander, Capt. Oliver Brown, and his assistant Lt. Perry. While staying with them I was able to improve my English, and brush up on my rusty German, which was essential for my mission. To keep our good shape we had to march, run, row (on the lovely Avon river), cycle, etc. In addition, we were all required to read voluminous material from the London headquarters in order to stay abreast of the current Polish situation. We also received a few British and Polish officials and enjoyed talks with Lieutenant Colonel Peter A. Wilkinson and Major Ronald Hazell of the SOE, set up by the War Cabinet to organize sabotage and resistance in occupied Europe. Mr. Mikołajczyk and his staff from the Polish Ministry of the Interior were frequent guests at that charming hide-out.

The summer of 1942 brought the first American troops to Great Britain, and some of the units were stationed not far from us in Tewkesbury. Our first impressions of them were not too favorable. Appearing to be poorly trained with little military spirit, they were often quite rowdy. For example, one Sunday after a recreational dance, a fight broke out between the black and white GIs, and it took the military police quite a long time to put it under control. From that time on, blacks and whites were given alternate weekends off in order to avoid such disturbances. The British in the area began to complain that: "the GIs are overpaid, overdressed, overdecorated, oversexed, and over here." At this time, it was impossible to visualize them as being the first class front-line fighters they turned out to be two year later.

My next encounter with the Americans was much different. I had taken a brief holiday, and on the way south stopped in the scenic town of Bristol. Walking down from my hotel room I noticed a youngish officer in the hall. Noting his single star, I was convinced he was my second lieutenant peer and began talking to him. We spoke at length about the war situation and even exchanged first names. It was only later that I discovered I had been speaking to a Brigadier General. I went on from there to the picturesque Devonshire coast to forget the war for a few days.

Meanwhile, the growing Soviet pressure on the Anglo-Saxons to open a second front had produced some results, one of them being the unsuccessful August, 1942 raid on Dieppe, where many Canadians, under British command, were killed. This was such an obvious disaster that it seemed as though Churchill was specifically showing Moscow that the Western Allies were not yet ready to help by invading the continent.

At this time, I again began suffering from acute pain in my throat, which resulted in my going to the Paderewski Hospital in Edinburgh for an emergency tonsillectomy. I had been hospitalized for almost one week in the officers' ward with a number of recovering Polish pilots, who exhibited amazingly high spirits, despite their serious injuries. To complete my recuperation, I stayed for a few more days at the old manor house of Lord Elgin's younger brother, Major Bruce, near the town of Elgin in Morayshire, and was also able to visit my best Scottish friends, the Carson family, in Ayrshire.

Back in Tewkesbury came the momentous news of Jan Karski's return from Poland. He had been caught and tortured by the Gestapo and had cut his veins to avoid further torture. Luckily, he was taken to a prison hospital from which he made a miraculous escape with the help of an underground Socialist unit and some of the hospital staff.[17] Janek came loaded with the fullest possible information on the structure and problems of the "Secret State", as well as with specific requests for the West. His most appalling news included a first-hand account of the mass extermination of Jews in the concentration camps' gas crematoria.

Karski returned to the West emaciated after his Gestapo ordeal, but he was a zealous crusader, and became known for his almost charismatic character while speaking to Allied leaders. The Polish Government in exile decided partly on Karski's suggestion that I should be sent to respond to those numerous requests as General Sikorski's personal emissary. My mission would also serve the so-called "Big Four", the largest of Poland's political parties in both wartime London and the Warsaw underground coalition.

Prewar Poland, from 1926 to 1939, was neither a democracy, nor was it a fascist dictatorship. Until his death in 1935, Pilsudski was the authoritarian semi-dictator, despite his Socialist background, and the parliamentary elections were definitely rigged. However, vocal political opposition parties still existed. Created at the end of the 19th century, they grew strong from 1918 until 1926. The "Big Four" were the most important of these organizations, although one should not discount the Jewish and Ukrainian parties.

The Peasant Party probably had the largest membership at the outbreak of World War II because the smallholders were the largest social class at the time. In Poland, the agrarian movement was ably led by Wincenty Witos, who was under Nazi semi-house arrest during the war, while his esteemed deputy in London, Stanisław Mikołajczyk, became the actual

Peasant Party leader. The right-wing Nationalist Party was probably the second largest, and after the 1939 death of its brilliant though controversial founder, Roman Dmowski, was led by the much younger Dr. Tadeusz Bielecki, who came to England in 1940. Third came the Polish Socialist Party (PPS), with many of its able representatives in London. Kazimierz Pużak, its Secretary General, was the real leader, operating from the underground in Poland together with Zygmunt Zaremba. The fourth largest party was actually a conglomeration of groups called the Labor Party. It was chaired by Karol Popiel, and the most important of its components were the prewar Christian Democrats. This group was particularly close to Sikorski, although as a soldier he preferred not to be officially affiliated with any particular party.

Some of these groups were deeply split, and one of my tasks in Poland would be to try to get all the factions to unite and work under one general plan. There were also numerous old and brand new, smaller political outfits which did not enter into the "Big Four", and they were quite unhappy about their secondary status. The most important of these groups was the prewar Sanacja, which was, for the most part, made up of those "Colonels" who were loyal supporters of the old Piłsudski regime. Another such group was the small Democratic Party (Liberal), comprised of philo-Semitic intellectuals, artisans and students. General Sikorski together with his close associates (Kot, Modelski, Popiel), was particularly vindictive towards the leading Pilsudskiites, most of whom were sent to Rothesay Island near Glasgow, where they remained almost interned and thus inactive throughout the war. A depressing story.

Once I was officially sworn into the secret service by the Minister of the Interior, I had to choose the briefest possible pseudonym, because of the vulnerability of radio operations in the underground circumstances. Without much hesitation I decided on "Jur", an abbreviation of Jerzy, my first name, and the name of the attractive Greek-Catholic (Uniate) cathedral in Lwów, as well as the pseudonym of one of the legendary pre-World War II revolutionaries.

The summer of 1942 finally brought exhilarating news regarding my immediate family. They had all survived their deportation to the Soviet Union. My mother, Zofia Sołtysikowa, after being released from her labor assignment in the bull pens of a Kazakhstan farm in Zhana-Semey, where she had been sent with my half-brother and my two aunts, was appointed by Ambassador Kot as his delegate for the Semipalatinsk region. Her main assignment was to help Polish refugees coming out of forced labor, by giving the men money and clothes to join the Polish Army in European Russia. She also helped to organize a hospital, and assisted in registering the refugees to find out where they came from and where they were to go. Luckily, she was able to resign and rejoin her husband before 1942, when Stalin arrested about twenty of these regional representatives under the ridiculous charge of gathering dangerous military intelligence.

My stepfather, Lt. Col. Dr. Adam Sołtysik, who had been deported to the northern tundra of Komi in European Russia, was able to rejoin the Polish Army of General Anders, which had been created after the Maisky-Sikorski Agreement between Poland and Russia. So was my sixteen-year old half-brother Jaś. They were all miraculously reunited in Tockoye in the Fifth Infantry Division camp, under the command of a close family friend, Gen. Michał Karaszewicz-Tokarzewski. Their querries as to my whereabouts were enigmatically answered by Professor Kot, to the effect that I was safe, but must remain incommunicado for at least one year. This was not the best way to dispel their anxieties, but at least I was fortunate to receive their loving letters through the Ministry of the Interior in London, and organize regular food parcels for them.

The final briefing with Jan Karski before my departure was the highlight of my preparation in London. He proved to be a veritable well of information on the intricacies of life in the Underground. Thanks to him I began to live in the spiritual climate of fighting Warsaw, some two months before actually being there.

Karski has presented the free world with the first well-documented horror story of the extermination of Polish Jewry. The influential leaders of American and British Jewry preferred, however, to dismiss that evidence as gruesome anti-German propaganda. Only heartbroken Szmul Zygielbojm, the helpless Bund spokesman, committed suicide in order to convince the world that he, for one, fully believed in the reported tragedy befalling his brethern.[18]

Speaking for the underground leadership, Karski expressed some surprise at the Sikorski Governemnt's bungling of the last Polish-Soviet agreement. At lunch in one of the restaurants near Picadilly, he reproached in my presence the high-ranking diplomat, Dr. Jan Librach, for not securing the recognition of the prewar "Riga frontier", and for blind acceptance of the humiliating word "amnesty" with regard to the forcibly deported Polish citizens. Why accept devious Soviet semantics? Dr. Librach used ail of his skills to convince us that Gen. Sikorski had to sign the agreement in order to get General Anders' army and as many Polish citizens as possible out of the Soviet Union. From Karski's reactions I became aware of the unbending attitude of Poland's genuine underground leaders regarding any sort of compromise with Russia on territorial or political issues. They remembered only too well that "stab in the back of 1939" and the mass deportations to Siberia.

Karski and I spent the traditional Christmas Eve dinner with Ambassador Edward Raczyński, who was also Acting Foreign Minister, and his charming wife at the basement Rectory of the Polish mission on Devonia Road in North London, as guests of the jovial Monsignor Władysław Staniszewski.

The core of my assignment was to be defined by General Sikorski after he returned from his third visit to the United States. In the meantime, I was talking to the ministers in his Cabinet, senior department directors and most importantly, to the exiled leaders of the four major political parties. I was also encouraged to attend sessions of the National Council to familiarize myself with the issues and personalities involved. I attended, therefore, the inaugural meeting of the Second

National Council, held in February, 1942 at the Polish Embassy residence in Portland Place. It was here that I heard President Władyslaw Raczkiewicz's memorable call to all exiled Poles, for unceasing efforts to work to multiply Polish assets as "ambassadors of Poland's cause" in the Free World.

As President of the Republic-in-Exile, Raczkiewicz, a distinguished looking gentleman, was primarily, though not totally, a figurehead. According to the 24th Article in the 1935 Polish Constitution, he had special wartime powers such as calling the National Council into session, and was also obliged to appoint his successor. He was at no time, though, able to act unilaterally on behalf of the Polish State because of the October 15, 1939 Paris agreement, which stated that in any of his decision making powers he had to consult the Prime Minister and through him the coalition leaders of the four major parties.

Vigorous in spite his age, the new Chairman of the National Council, Dr. Stanisław Grabski, a former economics professor of mine from Lwów, had just been released from a Soviet prison and was asked to take that position after the 1941 death of the previous chairman, Ignacy Jan Paderewski. The Maestro requested that his body be buried only in free Poland, so for the time being, President Roosevelt had it placed in Arlington, Virginia, with the Marines, where it still lies. Grabski was at this time understandably a fervent anti-Communist, and organized a seminar of some fifteen prospective democratic leaders. He invited me to these weekly meetings in Stratton House, which I enjoyed quite a bit. The most articulate among the participants were Dr. Witold Hulewicz and Mr. Antoni Wójcicki of the famous Jagiellonian University of Kraków. Both historians of education were seriously involved in discussing the type and character of future Poles, as well as in reform plans of past wrongs. They were very much imbued with liberal Western ideas.

For security reasons I was forbidden to reveal the true nature of my stay in London to anyone, even my closest friends. This rule I abided by strictly, even when at a party in a plush nightclub, my English friends, Sir Clifford and Lady

Norton, seemed to be trying to get me to be more talkative than necessary. They must have had some inkling as to the true nature of my plans, but the details they were not to get from me. I only revealed to them some of my "fascinating" work with the Polish government in London.

Most of the time I was still in uniform, while gradually buying unassuming civilian clothes suitable for Warsaw at Selfrige's on Oxford Street. Particularly important was the purchase of a strong pair of boots which I would need for my journey. I acquired these from a renowned shoemaker, not far from Hyde Park Corner, who had been recommended to me by an SOE liaison officer. When I picked up the boots, the merchant smiled in an understanding way and informed me that he had just made a similar sale to a young Norwegian gentleman.

Born and brought up in the city of Lwów, and witness to the ongoing bitter dispute over territory between Poles and Ukrainians, I was deeply convinced that these two nations had much more in common when faced with Russian and German threats, than their national leaders had been ready to admit. In 1918, the fratricidal struggle over this area brought on a large number of victims on both sides, and over the years, the Poles did not fulfill their promise of an Ukrainian autonomy and a separate university in their national language. At this point in time, the news from Eastern Poland was increasingly bad, as tensions between Poles and Ukrainians grew under the Nazis, with mass terror against the Polish minority spreading in Volhynia. One of my self-appointed tasks was to convince Gen. Sikorski's Cabinet that a rapproachement was necessary before the situation deteriorated further.

While awaiting Sikorski's return I spent many hours with the exiled leaders to learn all I could of their viewpoints, hopes and ambitions. I was particularly impressed by the President of the right-wing National Party, Dr. Tadeusz Bielecki and his brilliant Socialist protagonist, Adam Ciołkosz. Since my high school years I had considered Nationalists ("Endeks" — popular acronym for National Democrats), who in the 1930s ominously dropped the "Democratic" half of their original party name, as political adversaries because of their economic conservatism and anti-Semitic platform. Prime Minister Sikorski preferred to deal with the older and more liberal leaders of this large movement, which represented Poland's rising middle class, namely Mr. Marian Seyda of Poznań, and Professor Wacław Komarnicki of Wilno. However, these two experienced politicians did not command the loyalty of the mainstream of this historically important political party, created by the late Roman Dmowski. Sikorski definitely acted in a highhanded manner by selecting them for the Coalition Cabinet over the more representative leaders. Since, according to my oath, I was to be the secret envoy representing the four parties of national unity, I put aside my strong aversion to their ideology and decided to interview those "Endek" leaders in Britain who held the confidence of the overwhelming majority of young "Endeks", both in Poland and in exile, as well as those who supported and were approved by Mikołajczyk and Sikorski.

Dr. Bielecki, who had once been Dmowski's closest assistant, became Chairman of the party shortly before the war. My meeting with this man was arranged by a couple of personal friends who were in touch with him. Dr. Bielecki received me in his Hampstead apartment and was obviously grateful for this first chance to communicate through me with his counterparts in Poland. He asked that I convey his pessimistic analysis of the Moscow and Anglo-Saxon policies towards Poland. Unfortunely, his sobering scenario proved prophetic, as he correctly foresaw the Soviets' plans for dominating East-Central Europe with Anglo-Saxon acquiscence. Despite our ideological differences, he was warm and certainly well prepared for a thorough assessment of the international situation, particularly the Big Powers' cynical attitude towards their smaller allies. He had no illusions as to what was really happening behind the scenes, claiming that Prime Minister Sikorski and his immediate entourage were careless in accommodating their British and American mentors. In particular, Bielecki was strongly opposed to the Maisky-Sikorski agreement. Along with others of his persuasion, he already saw that Stalin was pushing hard and that the West was ready to placate him at the expense of Poland.

The Social-Democratic Marxist Adam Ciołkosz, Bielecki's opponent and classmate from the Jagiellonian University of Krakow, was an accomplished dialectician, with an impeccable anti-totalitarian record. He had the best contacts with leaders of the British Labour Party, exiled leaders of the Second International, and was a special trustee of the underground Polish Socialist party (PPS), working under the name "WRN" (Freedom, Equality and Indepenence). Ciołkosz critically analyzed General Sikorski's naivete in his short-sighted compromise with Russia, and openly opposed the Premier's "soft" foreign policy in the National Council debates. His total distrust of Communist Russia was the main reason for opposing the dishonest Anglo-Saxon attitude toward Poland's territorial integrity and freedom. Despite their fundamental differences, these two men were in complete agreement in their gloomy assessment of the Soviet Union's goals with respect to East-Central Europe.

It was not easy to gain the confidence of those ambitious exiled partitions, but like Karski, I became a sort of young "father confessor" to Poland's wartime leadership in London, and later in Warsaw. While I occasionally had different ideas on the issues at hand, as envoy my personal views could not be a part of my reports to the Polish underground. I had to put myself more or less on "automatic pilot" and take in everything I saw and heard and repeat it verbatim, uncolored by my own biases.

Another important figure in exiled leadership was, of course, Deputy Premier Mikołajczyk. He was what you might call a self-made man; once a prosperous farmer, successful in political life and unlike many other exiled leaders, he made a praiseworthy attempt to learn English. He was calm, persevering and certainly knowledgable of the complex political situation in occupied Poland.

Other Cabinet members were less impressive, preoccupied as they were with fictional party politics and petty political and

70

personal animosities. For instance, Karol Popiel, who was Minister of Public Administration (a rather redundant creation in an emigre ministry), and main supporter of Gen. Sikorski, bragged about the strength of his tiny Christian Democrat Labor Party and pretended that it was an equal partner with the three much larger movements. In actuality, his movement's strength was more potential than real and his claim for equality with the larger Peasant, Socialist and Nationalist parties, was necessary to obtain equal funding. He was a skillful political operator and wanted to secure the underground leadership for his prewar friends. As a result, most of his instructions dealt with personalities and showed little insight into the international situation or the socio-economic needs of the Polish nation. Similarly, Popiel's associates in London, General Izydor Modelski, Monsignor Zygmunt Kaczyński, security boss in the Ministry of the Interior Tadeusz Ulman, and the quarrelsome French-Polish editor of the *Narodowiec* daily, Michał Kwiatkowski, shared that hangover of frustrated prewar opposition to the post-Piłsudski Sanacja regime. Individually, they were all good people, but politically, fighting their petty battles, they seemed out of step with the real struggle of the younger Poles.

Typical of the generation brought up in a totally independent Poland, I considered wartime party quarrels to be one of the most annoying hindrances to our success, both at home and abroad. The truly great leaders of World War I (Daszyński, Dmowski, Korfanty, Paderewski, Piłsudski, and Witos), had been succeeded by their respective secretaries, generally men of lesser caliber, who were unable to forget their own phobias and grievances. With this in mind, I realized that one of the main tasks of my mission was to heal some of those old, true or imaginary wounds and, for the sake of future Polish generations, to work for a common cause in our life and death struggle for freedom, independence and social democracy. To accomplish this, I had to have empathy for human strengths and weaknesses alike, and rather to listen than to talk, for any other way would fail to gain the confidence of all concerned.

The most crucial was to be my mission for Gen. Sikorski

himself, whose following was much stronger in Poland and among Allied leaders than among Polish troops in Scotland. I had admired this man since early childhood, almost as much as I did his chief adversary, Marshal Piłsudski, who jailed in the Brześć Litewski fortress some of those politicians who had failed to support his *coup d'etat* in 1946. Others went into political exile. I was only nine years old when I saw General Sikorski, then commander of the Sixth Army Corps of the Lwów region, reviewing the troops on his white horse on May the Third, a National Holiday. He was a good looking man, an effectivve public speaker, popular with the people as a brave officer, and also respected because he was a well-educated man with a Civil Engineering degree, not only a professional soldier. My family was particularly fond of him. With these childhood memories and a profound respect for the man himself, I had welcomed the news of his leadership after the fall of 1939 and now looked forward with anticipation to becoming his personal envoy to fighting Warsaw.

Sikorski finally returned from his last trip to the United States, and at 11:30 a.m. on Monday, February 8, 1943, I met with him in the Kensington Palace Gardens office. He looked straight into my eyes and asked a rather strange question, "Do you think that your memory is as good as that of my classmate, your father, Miecio?" I answered that I hoped that it was. I knew that Sikorski had, as an upperclassman at the Lwów School of Technology, been kept busy with political and paramilitary activities, while my father, eager to score well, was primarily occupied with his studies, enabling him to help Sikorski with some difficult examinations. "Lieutenant, you are being sent to Poland as my personal emissary and we must have absolute mutual confidence. I have picked you partially because of my friendship with your family and our previous contacts in Scotland, but mainly on the basis of what I know of you through the Ministry of the Interior, your prewar political stand for social democracy and especially Jan Karski's strong recommendation."[19] This friendly approach would have been more elevating if I had not at that very moment become aware of the General's personal vanity. I suddenly noticed that he was no longer looking at me, but was gazing into the mirror at his numerous war ribbons. He evidently liked the "Mirror Hall" of the secessionist Rothschild mansion which he had himself chosen as his London office.

Sikorski correctly realized that the most obvious question I would face from underground leaders was the Prime Minister's assessment of the war calendar, with special emphasis on the timing of final victory by the allies. It sounded unbelievable, but with his typical self-assurance, the Commanderr-in-Chief informed me that within three months the North African Campaign would be over, to be followed by the Allied invasion of Sicily. The General went on:

It is then that we will have our chance to terminate the war, as early as the summer or fall of 1943, providing the Mussolini regime falls, as a result of the heavy bombardment of Italy. Our Polish intelligence cell has been approached in Ankara, Turkey, by secret envoys of Hungary and Rumania, with the dramatic proposal of front switching, in case of an Allied invasion through northern Yugoslavia's Ljubljana gap to capture Vienna, Prague, and Budapest, ahead of the Red Army. I submitted these proposals first to Prime Minister Churchill and later to President Roosevelt, with the former's strong support of the southward ["soft underbelly"] invasion.[20] The American President, however, was reluctant to follow such a bold idea, mainly due to the logistical obstacles in such rough terrain, although he assured me that in case of Mussolini's collapse in 1943 he might overrule the Joint Chiefs' of Staff preference for a more orthodox invasion from England with the use of Western Europe's well developed railroad and highway network. There is no doubt, at any rate, that such a major onslaught would break the Nazis not later than the summer of 1944. Please convey these strategic concepts to General Rakoń ("Grot" — Stefan Rowecki), Commander of the Home Army (Armia Krajowa), the Delegate of Civil Government and the KRP (underground representation of the four coalition parties). This is the way I, as Commander-in-Chief see the major war developments which will affect Poland's liberation from the Nazis, either by the end of this year, or at worst by mid 1944, depending if the Allied

invasion occurs from the south or more likely from the west.
[Unfortunately he proved to be wrong on both accounts!] *Being
in touch daily with the A.K. high command through short wave
radio, we will send further instructions for a general national
uprising, giving them ample time for the final action.*
I realized that this was the main message for me to carry.
The General continued:

*Your next duty Lieutenant will be to assure General 'Rakoń'
of my absolute confidence in his thorough preparatory work as
well as my full support for his crucial efforts to unify all armed
underground organizations of varied political coloring under his
command within the Home Army. You will have to use all your
powers of persuasion, stressing in your discussions with the
political leaders of the entire underground spectrum the obvious
need for military unity in the struggle with the common enemy.
There is no place for partisan separatism by any clandestine
armed unit. I am thus reaffirming, through you as my special
messenger, the unequivocal orders for structural unification of
all fighting Poles under one central command. Similarly, I
demand from the politically overambitious General Staff of the
Home Army to transfer all non-military agendas as soon as
possible to the network of Civil Underground authorities under
the Delegate and his respective Departments, so as to avoid
duplication and lessen the chances of jealousy or genuine fear of
militarism in the liberated country. In response to Karski's
mission, I have decided together with other coalition leaders in
exile to invite the true representatives of the PPS-WRN to the
KRP (Krajowa Rada Polityczna — Home Political Council)
underground representation of the wartime coalition of the four
big parties, in lieu of the so-called Polish Socialists (P.S.), with
their avowed aspirations for risky cooperation with Communist
agents of Moscow, recently organized as the Polish Workers'
Party (PPR). It won't be easy, but you have my full backing to
pressure all the coalition leaders at home in the matter of a
patriotically reliable presentation of the Socialist movement."*
I was very pleased with these clear-cut instructions.
*I am sure people will be curious in Warsaw about how I
evaluate my own Cabinet colleagues. As you know, prior to my*

departure for the United States, I promoted the hard-working Minister of the Interior Mikołajczyk to the position of Deputy Premier and Acting Premier in my absence. I did so because this self-made, ambitious Peasant leader not only loyally supports my policies, but also because of his notable progress in stature as a democratic statesman. I worry, however, that such a quick rise to prominence is already turning his head. With his lack of seld-criticism, he may unnecessarily antagonize other politicians of the coalition. In spite of these shortcomings, I find him most helpful among my ministers and therefore rely on his common sense.

In other words, Mikołajczyk was definitely the Number Two man to watch in future, although he was only forty years old and lacked international experience. Sikorski had not much good to say about other Cabinet members, and seemed annoyed with some of them, particularly with his enthusiastic supporter Professor Stanisław Stroński who served as Minister of Information and Documentation.

When you report to General, 'Rakoń', assure him that we are doing our best to increase, as he requires, the supply of weapons and ammunition from the air. For this purpose, I have just secured in Washington the delivery of a squadron of Americna Liberators to replace the smaller and slower British Halifaxes. The First Polish Airborne Brigade is being trained in Scotland to parachute in support of the forthcoming uprising at home. We would very much appreciate all critical comments for further improvement of our supply operations including better preparations of secret paratroopers.

Naturally, I was curious as to my assignment after the completion of reporting duties. "Yes, we instruct the Delegate to take advantage of your English training in gathering non-military data for our underground authorities and through them for us in London." I interjected here that in time of general uprising I would prefer to be used in the front lines as a fighting officer, but was advised to request this from the Home Army Commander-in-Chief. The Prime Minister indicated, however that I might eventually be sent back to the West, like my friend Karski, as the Secret State's envoy.

Gen. Sikorski was especially interested in a parallel build-up of various governmental departments under the Delegate as counterparts of the existing ministries in London. He suggested, therefore, that the remainder of my time in England be spent in acquiring as much information about Government operations as possible, under direction and supervision of my superiors from the Ministry of the Interior. Specifically, I was told to implement his order of the creation of a new Department of Foreign Affairs, to be headed by his personal friend Roman Knoll, who had created in the underground an elitist group called the Patriotic Association, which fully supported Sikorski's policies. Along with this nomination, I was to inform that experienced diplomat, selected to be the future Foreign Minister, that he should immediately begin schooling young cadres for foreign service in the democratic spirit, thereby replacing the snobbish prewar team of Colonel Józef Beck, whose unrealistic foreign policy was rightly disliked by Sikorski and his colleagues. Beck acted as though Poland was one of the big powers, but distrusted France, was anti-Czech, anti-Lithuanian, and did not do much in attracting national minorities to support his policies. In the face of expansionist Germany and the Soviet Union, he had to have some allies, but was not doing enough for a closer cooperation with the smaller neighboring countries.

Our meeting was almost at an end, and Sikorski returned once again to the question of our mutual trust. He kindly asked if I had any doubts or unanswered questions, and since I did have a few, I asked for another appointment so that I could think them over carefully. My request was granted, and it was agreed that we meet two days later, on February 10th at 12:30 p.m.[21]

In preparation for this final meeting, I took advantage of Karski's readiness to discuss the problems transmitted by him from Poland's Underground leaders. My questions finally composed, I reported back to the General at the agreed time. He became angered with only one of them, that which dealt with a number of controversial members of his entourage, derogatively called by many the "Black Cabinet." Although I was aware that this particular subject might be met with great consternation by Sikorski, after having been urged to dispel all my doubts, I felt I must alert him to the fact that a number of his close associates were distrusted by many officers in the Polish Armed Forces, and probably by the Polish underground leaders as well. "What do you mean by the 'Black Cabinet'? Are you another of those Endek anti-Semites?" he asked me sharply. "No, sir, definitely not. Many of your staff who are, justly or unjustly, considered to be controversial are not of Jewish origin." I was thinking for instance of Count Adam Romer, Director of the Prime Minister's Office, Monsignor Zygmunt Kaczyński, the Christian Democrat member of the National Council, and General Izydor Modelski who purged the officers' corps from the true or alleged enemies of Gen. Sikorski, none of whom were Jewish. Others, however, like Dr. Stefan Litauer, head of the Polish Wire Service (PAT), Stefan Aubac, who as I found later was a very decent, patriotic journalist with useful international contacts, and particularly Dr. Józef Retinger, the *eminence grise* in the "kitchen cabinet," or Professor Ferdynand Zweig were indeed of Jewish descent. Retinger was especially distrusted because of his excessive influence on the Prime Minister, though he was not a member of the Government. Sikorski maintained a chummy personal relationship with this shadowy figure, who served as a sort of confidential *"cicerone"* in England. The Premier put responsibility for hiring Aubac and Litauer on Professor Stroński, and although I did not take issue with him, it did not make much sense to me, since after all Sikorski was the ultimate boss, while Stroński, himself once a leading "Endek" despite his partly Jewish origin, was simply a member of the War Cabinet. The Commander-in-Chief then grew even more articulate in defense of Dr. Retinger when I explained that the latter was generally suspected of being either a British, or possibly even Soviet cover agent who in the interwar period was denied an American visa for his complicity with the leftist President of Mexico. "First of all," stated Sikorski "Recio was baptized, and his godfather was Count Zamoyski of Kuźnice himself. Moreover, unlike most of our braggart diplomats, he does have valuable British contacts. This was recently proven when I asked him to arrange an important conference with Sir Stafford Cripps, the Marxist Labourite member of the War Cabinet, who had just returned from his ambassadorial post in Moscow. Retinger did it within 48 hours. I need him because he serves me well and you should not listen to malicious hearsay," the Prime Minister explained with unusual rancor.

Aside from this touchy issue Sikorski ended our meeting in a friendly manner, telling his Secretary Kułakowski to show me three documents to memorize: The Altantic Charter, President Roosevelt's Four Freedoms, and Roosevelt's personal letter to the Polish Premier to which he attached great importance. It implied the American blessing in two significant matters, which was bound to evoke enthusiasm in Poland; the first being the President's support for Polish territorial claims against the German aggressor with regard to East Prussia with its main city port of Konigsberg, Western Pomerania up to Kołobrzeg, and the Opole region in Silesia. The second point dealt with Roosevelt's general approval of Polish plans for a close Federation with Czechoslovakia, and possibly a larger Confederation of the entire East-Central European region.

Mr. Aubac of the alleged "Black Cabinet" had the bad luck of being my boss's next visitor, and as I sat at the amiable Adam Kułakowski's desk studying the three documents, I heard angry outbursts from the Prime Minister's office, after which they both emerged. The General stopped and stared at me for a moment, for in his fury he had forgotten I was still there under his instructions. Sikorski was a man who liked to be admired and wanted those people around him to be liked as well. He was also hot tempered, and since I had just finished talking to him about Aubac, he jumped on the poor man. Sikorski quickly recovered, and patted me on the back in a somewhat patronizing way. This was to be my last encounter with the then actual leader of fighting Poles.

My last briefing conference was at the Prime Minister's office with the Cabinet ministers serving as the Committee for Home Affairs (KSK). Those present were Chairman

Mikołajczyk, Secretary Siudak, Minister of Industry and Chairman of the Socialist Party's Foreign Committee Kwapiński, Minister of Justice and "Endek" Komarnicki, Christian Democratic Minister of Public Administration Popiel, and Minister of Defense General Kukiel. This meeting was mainly to reinforce and confirm by the "Big Four" Coalition all that General Sikorski had already told me.

In preparing psychologically for the most important mission of my life, I went on a thorough confession to Monsignor Staniszewski, the Rector of the Polish church on Devonia Road in North London, and had a wonderful evening with the witty Father, as well as the other inhabitants of the rectory.

In final preparation, my mail to the Polish Underground leaders was microfilmed and placed in special belts. The official message of my mission was then radioed to Poland on February 11, 1943:

"Jur" takes belt #31/13 and the mail film and photographic plates to be delivered to the government's Delegate. He is the envoy of the Government and the representatives of the coalition parties. He has special recommendations from General Sikorski to be handed to his Deputy, the Delegate and Commander-in-Chief of the Home Army (A.K.), the PKP (Political Coalition Committee), as well as to the Director's Departments of the Interior, Propaganda and Press, of the Delegate's Bureau to the Bureau of Social Welfare and the Patriotic Society and eventually to all those whom the official contact authorizes; from Minister Mikołajczyk to the Delegate, to the political committee and the Triangle (the cryptonym for the Polish Peasant Party); from other members of the Government's Committee on Home Affairs (KSK), precise recommendations to their opposite numbers in the PKP; the representative of the "Circle" (Polish Socialist Party) directed his remarks to both groups of the party. Upon completion of his mission, his employment in the Delegate's Office is left to the decision of the Government's Delegate.

I signed this Document on the same day at the London office of the Ministry of the Interior at Stratton Street, and on February 18th a cable was sent to the Delegate's office in

Warsaw, announcing my mission and the fact that "Jur" takes with him belt #30/13, with $90,000.00 U.S., 145 pounds sterling, and $390 in gold." Also, the same cable announced that, like courier "Lis" (Tadeusz Samotus) I would be bringing two radio stations, Rebecca 495 and 431, with quartzes, and anti-typhus vaccine, and some books.22

I must have beat all the records for weight as a paratrooper, due to my stoutness combined with the heavy mail, money belts, and special radio equipment. The latter had recently been invented by brilliant Polish engineers, namely, Edward Wygard, Stanisław Grycko and Stanisław Lalewicz at the Mill Hill secret research headquarters, in northwestern London. I understood nothing of the workings of this ingenious equipment, only the fact that it was too heavy. As for the money, I was told by an American military attache, Brig. Gen. Robert A. McClure, that a certain amount of the American contribution was earmarked for Jewish organizations in the Warsaw ghetto, and I was duly honored to be entrusted with such a delicate mission. With all of this equipment, I was drven to the S.O.E. Station #20 at the Audley End mansion in Essex, where some fifty well-trained men waited impatiently for the final call.

Some of these regular army officers were political fanatics who looked upon me with suspicion, as they did upon all civil couriers selected by the unpopular Professor Kot. Moreover, they were in favor of replacing General Sikorski with General Sosnkowski, a distinguished Piłsudskiite, who was uncompromising in his wish to halt Soviet aggressions, and refused to give in to British and American pressures on any territorial concessions to the Russian Ally. These fine men were evidently not aware that I also had an important military mission to the Commander-in-Chief of the Home Army, and thought instead that I was a troublesome "kociak" (kitten, from the word Kot - cat) agent on some sinister party errand. One of those ultra patriots, a ferocious looking shooting instructor, even expressed a desire to make me a living target for my involvement with Socialist and Peasant leaders whom he considered to be dangerous scoundrels.23 The majority of prospective paratroopers, however, were truly supportive of each other during this final period of anticipation for the flying operation during the next full moon. And for that matter so was that model gentleman, the commanding officer of the Waiting Station at Audley End Major Józef Hartman ("Papa"), who showed his warm parental support for all of us, while the delightful British F.A.N.Y. (First Aid Nursing Yeomanry) ladies did everything in their power to make us confortable, serving as drivers, cooks, secretaries, and cheerful friends.

As part of operation "Spokeshave" (SOE-Polish crew to Poland No. 22), called into action on February 16, 1943, I was included in a team, with radio expert "Bor" (Czesław Pieniak), and two non-commissioned airmen, "Oko" (Piotr Nowak) and "Pionek" (Kazimierz Antoni Człapka). After a light supper we dressed for our trip. Our civilian clothes had to be thoroughly checked to make sure that there was no indication left of their English origin, the standard joke being the London bus ticket in the pocket. I was annoyed that my spectacles, which broke during training, had not been sent back from repair. They were needed for my shortsightedness and astigmatism in my right eye, but my assignment was too urgent to postpone the flight, so I decided to deal with my handicap at a latter time.

Major Harold B. Perkins of the Special Operation Executive was in his usual exuberant mood waving his cane around as though it was a conductor's baton. "Tell the Polish people," he said, "that here in England live their best friends, who will never desert them in need. We will simply add to the mounting German losses those of the Russians killed daily at the Eastern front." I began to wonder about the true feelings of the Anglo-Saxons and their war policies. But this was only wishful thinking, a pep talk in broken Polish which did not reflect official British attitude.

Helen, one of the F.A.N.Y. chauffeurs, drove us in a shuttered hearse-like car to the highly secret Tempsford Airport in Suffolk (its name was not disclosed to us). Although this vehicle was as dark and stuffy as a coffin inside, we were in high spirits after waiting long months for our clandestine assignments to materialize at last. Once by our Halifax plane, we were met by the jovial representative of the Polish General Staff, Lt. Col. Michał Protasewicz, and the distinguished representative of the famous Polish Air Force, Col. Wacław Makowski. Soon we were in the experienced hands of the crew from Polish Special 138 Squadron, Captain Mieczysław Kuźmicki, the Janik brothers, one of whom was a radio operator and the other a tail gunner, and two equally well seasoned airmen. They took us firmly under their wings as if we were kids. Though we tried to relax it was not that simple, as we checked with apprehension our supply of deadly cyanide and dexedrine, just in case of emergency after landing. Suddenly I realized that my lucky charm, the golden clover given by my mother, was missing.

CHAPTER III

EMISSARY "JUR"

Once airborne the exhaust gases along with the general excitement of that moment brought on one of my migraine headaches, so I laid down on the floor of the plane, while my companions nervously moved about. We were approaching occupied Denmark, and shafts of searchlights guided heavy anti-aircraft gunfire. One of the starboard engines had given out and it became obvious that we had to fly back to England. However, as soon as that had been determined, the other engine on the same side came to a halt and the pilot bellowed to the telegraphist to send an S.O.S. to England that we were going down over the North Sea — not a happy prospect. The top door of the plane cabin was opened. Shivering, we were getting ready to escape through that hole with a rubber dinghy. Apparently, this was our only chance of survival if we endured the impact of the crash from a ten thousand-foot level, the chance being less than fifty-fifty. Remembering that Gen. Sikorski was eager to obtain American Liberators, which were better planes for such far operations, I found myself swearing loudly: "To hell with the Halifaxes!" Kazik, one of my companions responded in his phlegmatic way, "Some other time Jurek, some other time, please."

Meanwhile we were quickly losing altitude and speed. The air hissed menacingly through the open door. Capt. Kuźmicki told us to pile ourselves together on the cabin floor, protecting our heads by reclining on each other's bodies. Only the radio operator remained seated by the pilot, sending the S.O.S. so that our location could be determined. Kuźmicki stayed calmly at the controls, and after ordering Janik to "scram," he suddenly yelled: "We are ditching at any moment! Gentlemen, say your prayers, and lets hope they won't be your last!"

The pilot then made one final attempt to start the paralyzed engines and to everyone's relief, with a bark and a roar, one of them responded. Incoherent in his joy, Kuźmicki yelled out: "The son of a bitch," and then again, "Good lad!" We were all overjoyed with the brand new prospect of living a few more years after such a close call. As the excitement died down, I realized that I had been airsick for some time.

There were no more insults to the old Halifax, as it brought us back to East Anglia's shores. Our S.O.S. had been received and the sky was lit by hospitable searchlights. Finally, after reaching the original airport of departure we were met by quite a reception committee. Major Perkins, the airfield British Commander, and the concerned officers of the Sixth Bureau of the Polish General Staff stayed up throughout our aborted operation. They congratulated the brave crew on their razor's edge escape. The F.A.N.Y. ladies were on hand as well, of course. Helen, the willowy driver pretended not to notice the altered state of my once white flying outfit which she earlier graciously admired. Emotionally exhausted we were driven by her back to our luxurious residence at "Number Twenty." Here Lieutenant Betty came running out to greet us and handed me my sorely missed clover-shaped golden pendant with tiny family photographs, which she had found in my room. The beautiful Pamela asked about her fiance, Alex Odrowąż, who had been on another plane. It was much later that she was to learn of his tragic death that very night over the Pilica river. His shrouds had become tangled and the chute never opened.

We remained at Audley End, having three more days of leisure, when the persistent Captain Kuźmicki insisted on having us once again as his cargo to occupied Poland. In the meantime, I was lucky to regain my spectacles. As the snow had melted in our target area, we now flew in brownish-khaki overalls. Our team was greeted as old pals by the crew, and to me personally the polite hope was expressed that they would not need to scrub down the cabin after this second trip.

Luckily, it was a very different flight. All four engines hummed smoothly until we came over the Vistula River and then over the completely darkened Warsaw. The pilot announced that, most likely, an air raid was sounded down there because of our appearance in the skies. Soon we found ourselves in the bright moonlight over the Pilica River in central Poland, searching for the promised lights of the Home Army's secret receiving station.

Our Halifax descended fast, and to everyone's tremendous exhilaration we saw with our own eyes a regular cross composed of red lights in one direction, and white ones in the other down the middle of a spacious meadow among the trees. This symbol indicated not only the exact position of our desired landing space, but the direction of the wind as well. The cross was made up of men lying down, holding small electric torches in their mouths, and the red color by covering the light with red blotting paper. It was hard to contain our joyous excitement. All doubts that clandestine reception stations, secret liaison arrangements, etc., were but a propaganda product of the fertile imaginations of the Rubens Hotel Staff officers evaporated at once. Our brothers were there just below expecting us with no less excitement. The Kuźmicki crew came up one by one and hugged us with affection. The next moment we were sitting around the windy hole, waiting for the sacramental "Go!" command and the green light.

First went ten heavy containers with tommy guns and ammunition, then "Bór" was dropped. The plane made the third round, and it was my turn into silent emptiness. Sharp opening of a white umbrella. Just below was a thin pine forest with a large clearing. We were dropped from the low altitude of 350 feet to prevent drifting over the woods. I barely missed a pine tree, but had a good, soft landing without any need to roll over. Kuźmicki came around to drop "Oko" and "Pionek", then gave a "good luck" signal with his lights and disappeared. He was killed in action over Poland a few months after delivering us safely.[24]

Seconds later, as the hum of the plane died away, I found

myself firmly grasping the rough hand of a peasant soldier of the Home Army from the nearby Radzice Duże village in the Kielce District. What a thrilling experience! We exchanged brief passwords with this authentic member of Europe's largest and best organized Underground Movement.

Soon we were approached by a young officer from the Polish Air Force, whom I later identified as Jan Mikołajczyk, unrelated to the London politician. He was a brave man from Wilno, and we later became good friends. As our parachutes, overalls, containers, money belts, and weapons were being eagerly taken by the local unit, we were told that they had been waiting several nights for us, until weather conditions permitted the completion of the operation. Everyone was moving as quickly as they could, for all of this work had to be done fast so as not to arouse the suspicion of the Germans in the vicinity, and force us to fight for our lives. There were approximately sixty people involved, and the whole operation from our arrival took less than one hour. We were later told that our silk parachutes were used to make underwear by the local women.

As we entered the village of Radzice Duże, the dogs began to bark loudly and we feared they might alert nearby German patrols. However, we arrived without incident, and once inside the school building everything quieted down. Our hostess was the local schoolteacher, Irena, who served us a fine meal of scrambled eggs and sausage. We also swallowed dexedrine to fortify us for our journey to Warsaw, as we sat and listened to new instructions. Before leaving England we had been given a few addresses and names of people to contact on our arrival, but at this point we were given additional contacts in Warsaw, becasue one could never be sure how long one address might still be safe.

Just before dawn, we were taken by horsecart to the railroad junction at Opoczno. Two others were filled with well-armed Home Army soldiers in civilian clothes, a small unit to protect us. At the station we saw German gendarmes for the first time and hoped there would be no confrontation. Our hopes granted, we passed freely. The faces of our guides and protectors were unforgettable, full of concern for our mission.

Pani Irena purchased tickets to Warsaw for the four of us and boarded the train with us. It was full of women smugglers who had purchased forbidden food items to be sold on the black market. They were nervous, but skillful in hiding lard, eggs, butter, etc. Without this service the capital city would probably starve under the German blockade. Those shrewd old ladies were trying to use us for hiding some of the contraband, but we were not cooperative, aware of our more important function.

The train stopped at Radom, a junction station well-known for its particularly severe Nazi control. The yelling gendarmes were a real menace to everyone. As a result, we awaited our arrival with trepidation, even though we had good documents and knew our cover stories perfectly. I was supposed to be one Stanisław Adamczuk, a minor clerk in Warsaw's city government. The real Adamczuk was dead, and his documents had been brought to London by Capt. Józef Zabielski, the first paratrooper/courier to return to the West, who had played an important role in our training by teaching us how to use our documents, and as how to function in the occupied city.[25]

Our trip to Warsaw was carefully watched by Irena, and she quietly approved of our outward calm as we successfully passed the Radom checkpoint. She got off with us at the Warsaw West Station, since the Central Station was known for a greater concentration of German police. In the approaching darkness we moved quickly through the fields of the Ochota District towards the capital city's beckoning lights. Warsaw appeared to be bustling with life, as if to spite its enemies. It was unbelievably exciting to be there, and we had to quickly blend into this Warsaw mood.

Irena first took me to the address on Asnyka Street that Jan Mikołajczyk had given me at the reception station. The occupant was Dr. Janina Krassowska, a psychiatrist from the Tworki Asylum, and an intimate friend of Mikołajczyk's doctor sister. The former was not at home when we arrived, so we were taken to her mother's apartment in the next block. There I parted for good with my three companions and was led into

Mrs. Krassowska's flat by her maid, who was quite aware of what to do. I was obviously not the first young man to hide at that address. She served a warm meal and informed me that Witold, Mrs. Krassowska's son, had just been released from jail after a ruthless January roundup. He was evidently in hiding while working in the office of the clandestine Attorney General.

Moments before the 8 p.m. curfew the old landlady appeared and welcomed me as if I were part of the family. She had lost her husband and one son at the beginning of the war, and was now totally dedicated to serving the nation. She was one among tens of thousands of Warsaw women who daily risked their lives and their families' lives by participating in the Underground struggle, and I soon learned that without these heroic women the Secret State could never have attained its level of success. They provided the infrastructure of the Underground. Liaison service and hideouts were a main part of their functions; others carried weapons and were involved in the dangerous distribution of the clandestine press. Their particular services were extremely perilous, and a large number of them were killed throughout the war. Their effectiveness, however, lay in their unpretentious style of activities; they behaved in a very unassuming way and were, therefore, hard to pin down by the Germans.

Before retiring that evening, I was given the last clandestine bulletins and magazines. Although I was too tired to read through them all at that moment, I could not help being struck by the alarming news that the Delegate of the Polish Government, Dr. Julian Piekałkiewicz had been arrested on the day of my arrival. This was most unfortunate for me, for one of my main missions was to report Prime Minister Sikorski's and Mr. Mikołajczyk's instructions to this learned man. Now all my contact addresses would have to be "burned" because no one know how the Delegate had been betrayed or his personal capacity to endure Gestapo torture in silence. I quickly decided to deal with this issue the next day, for at this point I was too fatigued to think clearly, the dexedrine being no more effective.

The next morning, February 21st, I was awakened by the rhythmic marching and nostalgic singing of German infantry. I looked out from a corner of the window and saw those pathetic men in their *feldgrau* uniforms. Yes, they were well armed, but nothing reveals the actual mood of soldiers like their singing, and it had been only weeks since their major defeat at Stalingrad, the watershed of World War II. I was pulled back from the window very quickly by my worried hostess, however, for she was concerned that someone indiscreet should notice me.

I did not leave the apartment for a few days since I was not yet on the official list of those living in this house, and therefore, had to be very careful not to be seen by anyone. After a couple of days Mrs. Krassowska's son, excited by the news of my presence in his home, appeared along with his doctor sister, who was a bit jealous that she had missed the opportunity to host a paratrooper from England. I had to refuse her invitation, though, to participate in some clandestine meeting of the erratic "Zryw" group that was to be held there, being under strict instructions not to get involved with this sort of activity until I had delivered all my oral presentations to the proper authorities. The "Zryw" was a controversial left-wing organization, and was part of the so-called Christian Labor Party, their leaders being radical atheistic members of the intelligentsia, which even included some outward Communists. Politically they were dangerously irresponsible.

My problem now, however, was how to get in touch with those clandestine leaders I was instructed to talk with, so I decided to use the alternate contact of the Polish Peasant Party, given to me by a prewar friend. Aware of my mission when I had visited him at Cambridge, he told me that his fiancee was living in a big apartment block in the Solec District near the Vistula River, and that she was closely related to the woman activist "Black Marry" (Maria Szczawińska) of the Underground Peasant Party, whose members played a key role in the Delegate's office.

I indeed found the young woman at the address I had memorized, and she promised to arrange the meeting as soon as possible. Meanwhile, to familiarize myself better with the wartime atmosphere, I began walking along the busy streets of Warsaw. It was still cold and windy, but I enjoyed some delicious hot meals at the Warsaw bistros. Well-trained by the British, I looked with suspicion on the belligerent young men who courted danger with their semi-military dress and loud discussions. At one restaurant, listening to my favorite singer, Lucyna Romanowska, I noticed two paratroopers, "Filip" (Jerzy Mara-Meyer) and Stanisław Stach, who had been selected by me in 1941 in Scotland. One was dressed in the brown NSDAP uniform of the Nazi party and the other displayed a swastika button. Although I was aware of their fearless work with the "Peasant Battalions" in carrying out reprisals for the deportation of Polish children from the Zamość area, I was not prepared for this foolishly overdone cover. These two men, recently in charge of the so-called *Chłostra* Battalions, became executioners of the Underground's courts. On one occasion, for example, they were sent to shoot a worker named Kozak who was found to be an informer to the Gestapo. Dressed as Nazis, Jerzy and Staszek located their suspect in the Warsaw suburb of Włochy and told him they wanted to take him to the Gestapo's boss at Szucha Street. Kozak was eager to go, and on the way proudly admitted that he had just betrayed an Underground radio station, whose two operators had been caught. Instead of Szucha (Gestapo headquarters), Kozak was taken to a dark place outside of town and shot in the name of the Polish Republic. This was one of the many successes these two men had. They also eliminated a dentist who had betrayed a couple of Jews living in Warsaw under false documents. Obviously such operations went to their young heads, and they became much too loose and braggardly in their behavior. Without mincing words I scolded them for immaturity and lack of self-discipline. Later that spring they were both killed in an unnecessarily bold expedition against some *Volksdeutchen* (Poles of German origin turned Nazi), undertaken on their own initiative on Miodowa Street in the heart of the city.

About a week after my arrival, I was informed by "Black

Maria" that I would be meeting with "Grey Maria" (Maria Modlibowska), Deputy Director of the Delegate's Office in charge of all outside contacts. I was instructed to wait for her at 6 p.m. on the busy corner of Poznańska and Nowogrodzka Streets at the electric train station. It was a pleasant surprise to see that my contact, a tiny, well-dressed woman was an old acquaintance, who had been a famous pilot before the war and the first woman courier from Paris to Warsaw in 1940. I was actually to meet with her and her boss, the new Director of the Delegate's Office, "Grabowiecki" (Stefan Pawłowski) at the top flat on Sixth of August Street. The appointment was set late in the day to elude the overly curious caretaker. This left us little time to exchange information before the Nazi-imposed curfew.

I rushed to the meeting place, and was surprised to find the two other couriers, "Cap" and "Lis", well installed in that apartment. As they led me inside, I was assailed by heavy smoke and a rush of cold air. They had just burned some compromising papers so that we could barely see each other. My friends noisily introduced me to the elegant Mr. "Grabowiecki", who was to arrange my appointment with the new Delegate (Jan Stanisław Jankowski, working under the pseudonym "Doctor"). But another tall figure appeared unexpectedly through the smoke screen insisting that I must have brought some special material from Deputy Premier Mikołajczyk for himself, "Nowak". This gentleman's military bearing impressed me at once. He was also known as "Zieliński" (Stefan Korboński), the newly appointed Head of the so-called Civil Struggle, and was thus in charge, among other crucial activities, of the well researched executions against traitors. At the same time, this Peasant Party activist was responsible for non-military radio communications with London.[26] We made arrangements for a separate meeting on Sunday morning at 10 o'clock outside the National Museum.

The ladies who took care of the "birdies" (i.e., us paratroopers) were affectionately nicknamed "aunties", and here I was introduced to "Auntie Wladka", Mrs. Władysława Lelech, the widow of a Lublin judge who had been shot by the

Germans. She took me a long way to the northern workers' district of Wola, where I would be lodging with another recent widow, Mrs. Maria Śnieżko, whose husband and only son were likewise killed by the Nazis. Her two-room apartment at 8 Działdowska Street was clean and cozy. However, my new landlady was not informed, for her own safety, about my real role, but was told that I was a young innocent scholar from Lwów University who had just escaped Ukrainian harassment to continue studies in the capital. I assumed the name Jerzy Gordziewicz (my mother's maiden name), the first name remaining real to avoid memory lapses as we were advised in England. The new identity papers for that easy-to-remember fictitious person had been fabricated without much delay by one of my courier colleagues, "Konik" (Jan Cegłowski), whose older sister was employed in the city agency, and could fake such documents using actual photos. I was also provided with a solid Labor *Ausweis* which testified that I was employed by a genuine railroad construction company. Its courageous boss, Mr. Mazalon, had a number of underground activists "working" for him. I was supposed to be one of his field accountants inspecting actual work sites. In this ingenious way I was duly registered as a *bona fide* resident of Warsaw working for the German war effort.

As an added precaution that would free me from carryng around or even displaying any incriminating papers, in my bedroom a trusted carpenter constructed an excellent hiding place for secret archives under the floorboards of my room. Mrs. Śnieżko was seldom home during the day, and was usually at the nearby house of her old mother, so there was no worry about her discovering this spacious hiding place which was to hard to open for any unintroduced person. The patriotic determination of the Wola workers, whom I met and observed in clandestine action, was truly impressive. Most of them proudly belonged to the PPS-controlled trade unions before the war. The few visitors that Mrs. Śnieżko received in her apartment showed a good grasp of the international situation. Before long I found that they ferreted out the news from B.B.C. radio bulletins in the Polish language or from the underground press.

Early in March I was told by Auntie Władka to again meet with "Grabowiecki". At last I could unload my memory to the Delegate, the actual boss of the Secret State. Upon meeting the "Doctor," I was pleased to find an extremely calm, well-organized man in his late fifties. We both had the feeling that we had met before, and then remembered that we had skied together in the Tatra mountains in 1939. "So you are from Lwów," he said. I then took this moment to tell of my wish to meet with the leader of the Uniate Church in Lwów, Archbishop Andrzej Szeptycki, in an attempt to reduce tension between Poles and Ukrainians. "Permission not granted," he replied. "We tried this ourselves recently, and one of the negotiators, Mieczysław Rettinger, was denounced by one of the Ukrainian monsignors and arrested by the Gestapo. Secondly, knowing who you really are, I am aware that too many people in Lwów would easily recognize you as the prewar youth leader, and then we would all be in trouble. Therefore, I demand that you not even visit your native city.

After this initial exchange and the Delegate's confirmation that the entire shipment of London mail and money had been received, I gave an oral report of Gen. Sikorski's evaluation of the war situation. Jankowski, who had previously served with distinction as Social Welfare Director of the Underground, was particularly happy with Gen. Sikorski's clear demand that all military units from the entire political spectrum should, without delay, submit to the orders of the Home Army Commander and his General Staff, while all non-military activists should be organized by the Delegate in departments which would parallel the London Ministries in exile. The "Doctor" assured me that these were his own views and it was only on such conditions that he accepted the heavy responsibility of Civil Head of the Underground State. He instructed me to discuss the pertinent details with the proper departmental directors and was pleased that my mission to the General in charge of the A.K. would include civil as well as military matters.

Jankowski was aware of the powerful influence of the Peasant Party leadership, and although one of them,

"Grabowiecki," a member of that party, was present and taking notes, the "Doctor" stressed that he did not belong any more to any political party, and like Gen. Sikorski, whom he respected greatly, saw his role as a unifier and organizer. Regarding my special instructions to create a new Department of Foreign Affairs under Mr. Knoll, the "Doctor" informed me that the latter was forced to go into hiding with his wife outside Warsaw because of a special Gestapo search. I was assured that Knoll would be contacted, and that I would be able to deliver his nomination in person.

Jankowski finally asked about the character of my special training, and afterward assigned me to the Department of Information under "Dolęga" (Stanisław Kauzik), signaling the end of the interview. This department was to gather all the information needed for the Delegate, to transmit it to London and publish guidances for the clandestine press in addition to the official monthly *Rzeczpospolita Polska*.

My meeting with Korboński was scheduled for 10 a.m. the first Sunday in March. As he approached me at Jerozolimskie Allee, I was somewhat taken aback by his conspicious sporty dress. He looked like an army officer in disguise. The streets outside the National Museum were empty so he took me for a brisk walk along the Vistula. Suddenly a four-man patrol with machine guns appeared about one hundred yards away and Korboński asked me if I was armed. I had nothing of that sort as I had not planned on getting into a stupid fight with ordinary German policemen just two weeks after my return to Polish soil. Although he offered me one of his pistols, I refused to become involved in such an unnecessary confrontation. Nevertheless, I did admire his nerve. Luckily, these stiff gendarmes passed us by without notice. It is hard to understand how this heroic man and his equally brave wife survived those terrible six years, always being in the center of the storm. Their narrow escapes even became legendary. For example, one time when Pani Zosia was carrying a radio station from one broadcasting hideout to another across a busy thoroughfare, a gallant SS officer offered to help her carry the heavy parcel. She willingly obliged. Luckily no questions were asked and she escaped the situation without mishap.

Fortunately, my delicate mission to the Socialists proved easier than I had anticipated. My first contact with the mainstream of the WRN was established through Korboński, who introduced me to "Marcin" (Zygmunt Zaremba), a very impressive organizer of the worker's resistance in Warsaw. He had grown a long beard in order not to be recognized, since, before the war he started, he had been quite well known as a member of Parliament and as a public orator. We were introduced at the gate of an old apartment building, and he gave me an address where we should meet later on. I also met the aging leader of the Polish Socialists, "Paweł" (Wincenty Markowski) through my prewar colleague from Lwów, Kazimierz Dorosz. As it turned out, Markowski was another Lwów acquaintance. He was going against the majority of that grand old party of Poland and its genuine leaders. Arciszewski, Puzak and Zaremba had much more right to represent the working class than the left-wing Marxist intellectuals, who had toyed with the idea of a popular front with the pro-Moscow Communists.

Well-provided with instructions from the London Foreign Committee of the Socialist Party and the sound arguments by prominent exiled leaders, I was able to convince Markowski and his common-sense wife Jadwiga that the time had come for their full submission to the Supreme Commander of the Home Army and unification with the mainstream of the WRN.

At my scheduled meeting with "Marcin" I found that he already knew of the Foreign Committee's request that the recognition of the Polscy Socjaliści (PS) splinter group be denied, and that they be possibly merged back into the party mainstream. "Marcin" heartily approved of this proposal and insisted that I meet with "Bazyli", (Kazimierz Pużak), the venerated Secretary General of the PPS. The meeting was then arranged for a Sunday at noon at the historic Powązki Cemetery near the grave of the Socialist pioneer, Bolesław Limanowski.

I had already met "Bazyli" once, just before the war at a rally in Lwów, when we both addressed a large gathering before the city council elections. At the time, he was energetic, robust, and red-faced but already graying; now, when we met at the cemetery he looked smaller, a little hunched, and wore a long gray mustache, which changed his appearance dramatically. However, he still had the same strong, concentrated expression, as always. He was known for his organizational skills, intense personality, and for speaking only briefly but with purpose. He was certainly one of the most important, almost legendary figures of the Underground during this time. My request to "Bazyli" from London was that he should go there with me to become the constitutional successor to the President of the Polish Republic, thereby denying Poland's enemies the chance to call us aristocratic reactionaries. He was adamant, however, that his place was not in exile, but here with the Polish workers in his role as Secretary of the Polish Socialist Party, and dismissed the request by saying that the aging "Stanisław" (Tomasz Arciszewski), was going to be sent to London for that purpose instead of him. Our meeting came to an end when Mrs. Komarnicka, Secretary and liaison for the WRN leaders, discreetly signaled us from a nearby grave that we should part in different directions.

Through my prewar contacts with the left-of-center youth leadership, I was fortunate to establish excellent working conditions with the fearless Leszek Raabe and his Socialist Fighting Organization called the *Socjalistyczna Organizacja Bojowa.* He both organized and commanded this group, which was the most active in attacks on selected Nazis and liquidation of proven traitors. I also became involved with the daily underground publication *Demokrata,* of which Raabe was a founder. The paper's editors were Grzegorz Załęski, Rafał Praga, and Kazimierz Dorosz. My role was to write some of the editorials on international affairs. Our contact point was a pastry shop on May the Third Avenue, run by a pretty young woman who was a refugee from Poznan. When necessary, I was able to leave materials with her to be taken to the editorial room in "Grzegorz's" nearby apartment.

At the Żoliborz hideout in a northern suburb of Warsaw,

through Leszek I also met the fascinating group of young socialist intellectuals, *Płomienie* (Flames), led by Karol Lipiński and my prewar ski and tennis pal Jan Strzelecki. They also produced a Socialist youth magazine, under the same name, theoretical in nature and attempting to change the Marxist dogma to blend with future needs. The members of this sophisticated group were well-read, open-minded, and inspiring.

Dr. Józef Fell, a Jewish Lwów acquaintance and one of the prewar leaders of the Association of Independent Socialist Youth (ZNMS), and now editor of another Socialist paper entitled *Wolność* (Freedom), helped me in establishing contact with the underground Jewish Bund representative Dr. Leon Feiner, known as "Berezowski." Dr. Feiner, typically Aryan-looking with a long gray mustache, could easily mix with Poles outside the Ghetto without being suspected of his Jewish role. His Marxist (but non-Communist) party before the war already had its strongest support among Jewish working people in Poland, and as such it closely cooperated with the PPS. Now, once again, it played a leading role in the Jewish conspiracy in the Warsaw Ghetto and others. Feiner was the one who represented Bundists of the Ghetto in the Polish underground world. I was in full agreement with his appeals for more effective aid from the West. Feiner was aware of my mission to the Jews and the transfer to them of a substantial sum of United States currency, brought by me, and although he was personally grateful for bringing this help, he did not consider it enough for their desperate situation. Taking into account the tremendous lack of medical assistance, food, clothing and weapons, it was only a drop in an ocean, especially considering that Jews in America were rich enough to help more substantially.

The representation of the right-wing National Party, *Stronnictwo Narodowe*, continued to be a problem. Although they did surrender their well-trained military units, the National Military Organization (NOW), to the Home Army, the semi-fascist National Radical Camp (ONR), their main splinter group which was now using the cryptonym NSZ (National

Armed Forces), remained defiant. Later this was to cause a great deal of trouble for Polish leaders both at home and abroad because they remained actively anti-Semitic. At the last stage of the war they displayed an independent strategy apart from the Home Army, which even led to some local understandings with German commanders, mainly because of their predominantly anti-Communist stance. Regretfully, I was never allowed to argue or even meet with any of the NSZ leaders, because it was believed that the hostility between them and the A.K. (Home Army) was so strong that nothing, even my persuasion on behalf of Gen. Sikorski, could ever reconcile them.

The National Party's genuine leaders were, from the beginning, fully involved in the formation and conduct of the "Secret State", though their actual London representatives were kept outside of the establishment because of their criticism of Gen. Sikorski's compromising policy with the Soviets. I was the first political envoy to have talked with Dr. Tadeusz Bielecki, President of the National Party in London, Professor Władysław Folkierski, President of the Party's Supreme Council, Marian E. Rojek, editor of the thought provoking Party organ *Myśl Polska* (Polish Thought), and Dr. Edward Sojka, their watchman in the crucial Ministry of the Interior. The underground leadership in Warsaw deplored Sikorski's highhanded selection of the unrepresentative Wilno Professor Wacław Komarnicki, and veteran Poznań journalist Marian Seyda, to serve in his cabinet. Therefore, they appreciated the opportunity of listening to the sceptical analysis of the international situation conveyed by me from their true leaders in London.

I found the National Party's Underground Chairman, Dr. Stefan Sacha, to be quite impressive in his clear understanding of both the national and international struggle. He was realistic in his discussion of the underground's potential, and not eager to push for a premature uprising. When the interview was almost over, he asked me whether I knew one Jan Kornas from Lwów. "Of course, I know him only too well," I replied. "He was chairman of the violent *Młodzież Wszechpolska* (the official youth movement of the National Party), which was responsible for a number of assaults on Jews and those of us who tried to defend the Jews. It was Kornas who led some twenty-five medical students in a physical assault on me on May 28, 1938. I barely survived, suffering five head wounds in addition to having my front teeth knocked out."[27] "I know well," said Dr. Sacha, "about the unfortunate event, but Kornas regrets it now and he is very useful to our cause. Training the NOW cadet officers, he would like very much to apologize to you in person and ask you, as the official envoy from London, to preside over the clandestine oath ceremony in the officers' school which he runs."

Although I accepted this bizarre proposal, it was not without reservation. Needless to say, my previous experience with the man had not been pleasant. For protection I asked a paratrooper sharpshooter, Stanisław Stach, to bring his pistol and follow me to Marszałkowska Street, the main commercial thoroughfare in Warsaw. He was to leave me alone with Kornas only after I signaled by scratching my ear that all was well. Kornas looked the same, and began our discussion by asking my forgiveness now that we were facing the same mortal enemy; following our conversation in the apartment at Hoża Street, a week later I did witness the oath of allegiance to the Home Army and Government in exile by some twenty young men under Kornas. I learned later that he was killed as a fearless participant in the 1944 Warsaw Uprising. *Tempora mutantur et nos mutamur in illis...* Regardless of my personal reservations about the "Endeks" ideology, I had to admit their Underground leaders were able men. Unlike some of their counterparts in London, they seemed to have gone through substantial ideological transformations regarding the need for democratic reforms and their once negative attitude to the Jews.

Perhaps the most complicated problems were those surrounding the smallest member of the coalition, the Christian Labor Party (Stronnictwo Pracy). This outwardly pro-Sikorski formation was actually an uneasy fusion of the prewar Christian Democrats and a few ambitious small groups eager for an equal share of the London funds available for the four major parties. Their exiled leader, Karol Popiel, had told me how upset he was about the penetration of his movement, which was ideologically based on the *Rerum Novarum* and *Quadragesimo Anno* encyclicals, by totalitarian elements of the ZRYW movement. Popiel and the exiled leaders were concerned that the true Christian Democrats were losing influence to the dynamic younger representatives of the "Zryw" and "Unia" groups. The latter organization was made up primarily of young intellectuals once serving the prewar "Sanacja" regime, who had gone through a democratic evolution in their views. Primarily, "Unia" strove for amelioration of contradictions in society as well as a federation of East-Central European nations. The "Zryw" group was particularly eager to get my support, but even as they wined and dined me, they were not convincing enough to assure me that they had any mass influence or substantial accomplishments in their favor. Though they did have some effective military units known as Cadres (Kadra), they were newcomers to the political struggle, with a popular front attitude for closer cooperation with the numerically weak Polish Communists and their Soviet masters.

I also attended several meetings held by the left of center Democratic Party, Stronnictwo Demokratyczne, to which Supreme Council I was elected *in absentia* as its youngest member just before the war.[28] As a liberal-progressive party deeply involved in resisting anti-Semitism, this group had played a constructive role in providing the Home Army with dedicated intellectuals, particularly for its BIP (Information and Propaganda Office) Sixth Department. At this time though, the decimated movement had already lost most of its original leaders who had been assassinated by the Gestapo. The Party's new mainstay were courageous young girls recruited mainly from the liaison staff of the Home Army Headquarters. Unfortunately, I had to report to them that although I was fully sympathetic with their commitment to the democratic cause and to their active opposition to any anti-Semitism in Poland, despite my affiliation with them before the

100

war, now as a public servant to all the political groups I could not be associated with a party which was unfortunately outside the official coalition in Warsaw and London.

Within two months of reaching Poland, I was able to talk to representatives of almost every group in the underground, including such small ones as the two Syndicalist organizations. One was the ZSP (Association of Polish Syndicalists), led by the busybody Stefan Szwedowski, which was steering towards the pro-Communist left. The other was the Syndicalist Union led by an able architect, Erazm Kulesza, which was anti-Marxist. Some of these encounters had been unnecessarily risky for myself, because not all of the organizations were appropriately discreet. For example, most of these ambitious smaller outfits decided to face the establishment of the Big Four coalition by federating into the S.O.S. group (Społeczna Organizacja Samoobrony or the Social Organization of Self-Defense). I was invited to their meeting by the popular Polish writer, Zofia Kossak-Szczucka, founder of the philo-Semitic organization of the Catholic intelligentsia FOP (Front of Poland's Revival), who were mainly involved in assisting the hiding of Jews. When I went to this gathering on the corner of Nowogrodzka and Bracka Streets, in a large Victorian flat owned by Count and Countess Lasocki, I thought it would include only a few representatives. To my surprise, however, there were about forty, rather loud people. I quickly turned and left, saying that I was trained not to expose myself to such a large number of evidently amateur conspirators. Although at the time I must have been considered as rude, I was sure that I was right. The heroic Mme. Zofia Kossak-Szczucka was soon after jailed in Pawiak prison to be put in Auschwitz, probably resulting from one such obvious indiscretion. The two organizations which held the best record for secrecy turned out to be the Home Army itself and the Polish Socialist Party (WRN).

My mission with various Underground groups was now completed, although I still had to personally deliver Sikorski's nomination to Ambassador Knoll. On a cold day in early spring, a youthful liaison man, Andrzej Leśniewski, and I took a suburban train to the Wesoła Station where we were met by another prewar Foreign Office official, Dr. Tadeusz Chromecki, who showed us through the pine forest to a desolate spot where a middle-aged man, dressed as an old fashioned country gentleman going for a hunting trip, waited with his charming wife, ready with her picnic basket. Once settled in that rustic situation I raised my cup to congratulate Ambassador Knoll on his nomination as director of the Foreign Affairs Department, and presumably Poland's Foreign Minister after the war. The session with Knoll was quite enjoyable as he was widely known for his wit. We also talked of serious things, as he was out of touch with the most current Warsaw and London news, having been in hiding for several months. We discussed at length the Western Allies' shifty attitude towards Poland. Near the end of our time together, I finished with Sikorski's request that Knoll train a young staff (different from the snobbish prewar MSZ "bubki"), in preparation for their duties abroad after Poland's liberation. Knoll, in turn asked that I attend some of these training sessions, which I did with pleasure a couple of times within the year.[29]

By the end of March my mission was completed except for the most important task, which turned out to be my meeting with Gen. "Grot". Some jealous intelligence officers of BIP, the information arm of the Underground military establishment, had attempted to keep me away from the General. They probably feared that my message from the Premier concerning the necessary division between the Civil and Military sectors threatened their excessive political influence, which was objected to by the four coalition parties in both London and the Underground. Concerned friends from the Peasant Party had informed London that I was being prevented from fulfilling my mission by some internal intrigue, and as a result Gen. Sikorski sent, along with my promotion to First Lieutenant, an order to A.K. headquarters that I had to be received by Gen. "Grot" personally. All this time, in the seam of my overcoat I had been carrying photocopies of notes from my two meetings with Gen. Sikorski, which referred to this particular mission. As a rule I preferred not to carry any such evidence, but in the case of crucial liaison between Gen. Sikorski and his counterpart in Poland, I wanted to be able to refresh my memory so as not to leave out any points.

Karski and other people had told me elevating stories about the dynamic "Grot" regarding his conscientiousness and abilities as an underground boss. Before the war he had published on the fight of the cities, which accounted for his theoretical competency; and during the war he put his theories to work and grew in the people's imagination to become almost a mythical hero, the foremost statesmanlike figure in the entire wartime underground.

The morning of my most important date, I rehearsed a concise report of the instructions contained in my notes, and then went to meet "Krystyna", whom I knew as a Social Democratic youth activist. She was one of the most effective, though inconspicuous liaison women of the BIP. We met at an appointed time on the streetcar stand, and although we did not exchange words, she smiled approvingly at my punctuality. I followed her onto the streetcar heading back toward Narutowicz Square in West Warsaw. We got off at Niemcewicza Street and went into the nearby flowershop, where "Krystyna" disappeared after leaving me in the hands of Mrs. "Berg" (Major Janina Karasiówna), the great personage in the Home Army Headquarters in charge of all communications, both within and without Poland. She gave me the latest information from the Eastern front, all the while testing my conspirational abilities. We quickly set off for our *rendezvous* with "Grot", and I was amused when she told me not to look at the street names, nor memorize the route; evidently she considered me a novice at conspiracy. Then she said, "We have instructions from the London Chief of Staff that the Commander of the Home Army should receive you in person." Sensing her resentment that I had contacted London when I encountered difficulties in meeting with "Grot", I quickly attempted an explanation: "I am sorry that I had to use such methods, but I had been clearly instructed by Gen. Sikorski himself to discuss certain matters solely with the A.K.

Commander and the Government's Delegate. Failing to reach the former through Karski's contact, I was told to pass on all information through his nosy subordinates. I complied with this request in all cases which were not reserved for direct transmittal to Gen. "Grot". Then I notified London of my inability to implement the Commander-in-Chief's orders, being barred by the prying Major 'Malicki' from direct contact with the General." Mrs. "Berg's" response was more sympathetic, and through the years we became close friends, until her mysterious death in South India.

It became clear that we had reached our destination when I spotted a couple of young men strolling about at their leisure. Olek, a paratrooper who had been one of my subordinates in Scotland, was among them. He was now in the special Security Service assigned to protect Gen. "Grot". We soon arrived at a modern apartment house at Spiska Street, the very place where the heroic "Grot" was arrested a couple of months later, on June 30, 1943, after being recognized and followed by a Polish cavalry cadet of German descent.

We rang the bell twice and were informed by an elderly lady that the "Professor" was not ready yet. I did not have to wait long, however, before I heard energetic steps in the corridor. A strikingly handsome, medium-sized man in his prime with graying black hair entered the room, looking strong-willed and determined. As his penetrating gaze bore down on me, I reported: "General, Sir, Lieutenant Jur reporting as emissary of the Commander-in-Chief." The General nodded and said, "You are a tough one, but you were correct not to trust these special reports to Malicki. Go ahead:"

First of all, Gen. Sikorski and his Cabinet would like to assure you, Sir, that they regard your work with the highest approval and esteem. I was to give you the Prime Minister's assessment of the war situation and London's views with reference to the organizational structure of the Underground. According to the Commander-in-Chief, the war will end in 1944, as a result of the planned Anglo-Saxon invasion from the West. There is still some slight chance that it may end this very year, providing that fascist Italy capitulates this summer. Gen. Sikorski conceived the plan for the invasion of Europe through the northern Balkans and submitted it to the Allies. Because our military attache in Turkey was approached separately by Hungarian and Rumunian intelligence couriers with an offer to switch the front, it would mean abandoning the Germans in favor of the Western Allies in case of the latter's invasion of South Europe's "soft underbelly". This would permit the East-Central capitals to be liberated before the Red Army defeats the Nazis on the Eastern front. If successfully implemented, the Anglo-Saxons would be in Poland before the Soviets. Unfortunately, due to American reluctance to undertake the risk, mainly because of logistics, the soft underbelly invasion scheme had to be postponed, even though Prime Minister Churchill was apparently in favor of it. Gen. Sikorski declared to me on February 13, 1943, that the African campaign will surely be over in three months, followed by the invasion of Pantellaria and Sicily. If, as a result of the massive bombing of Italy from these new bases Mussolini surrenders, then the Allied operation in East-Central Europe through northern Yugoslavia would still be feasible later this year.

The A.K. commander listened attentively, while Mrs. "Berg" carefully noted almost ever word of my report.

Gen. Sikorski briefed me shortly after his return from discussions with President Roosevelt and his top advisors. Polish-Soviet relations were dealt with and, evidently, Roosevelt showed a sympathetic grasp of Poland's precarious position. He promised that Poland would certainly emerge from the war undiminished in comparison with her prewar territory. Sikorski presented the Polish ideas regarding Western lands, particularly the crucial need for the liquidation of Germany's East Prussia enclave. This seemed to meet with Roosevelt's understanding and the promise of support. Similarly, Gen Sikorski believes that we will gain substantial border corrections in Western Pomerania, which would substantially shorten our border with Germany by moving it up to Kołobrzeg.

Roosevelt also solemnly promised to support a reborn Poland, and Gen. Sikorski asked me to memorize the contents of the President's personal letter, which summed up their discussions.

In this document Roosevelt reassures the Polish government that it is his deep conviction that Poland will re-emerge as a free, independent and undiminished state. Apparently Roosevelt fully approved the plan for an East-Central European confederation, and authorized Sikorski to speak to other leaders of those nations, with the guarantee that both the President and his administration support this constructive idea as the best postwar solution for the area.

To preserve personal integrity, I interjected my own concern for the Eastern lands, and asked Gen. Sikorski why, among so many words and promises, there is no specific mention of the prewar Riga frontier stipulated in 1921 which would secure the future of Lwów and Wilno? He answered that in Roosevelt's opinion, for considerations of Stalin's prestige, some concession in the East might be necessary to appease the heavily bleeding Russia. As for the fate of Lwów and Wilno, Sikorski had no doubts about their remaining in Poland, and would brook no further discussion.

The Commander-in-Chief also told me to assure you, Sir, that he has made the necessary arrangements in the United States to get new Liberator bombers to be used for transporting paratroopers and additional supplies for the Polish squadron which cooperates with the resistance movement. These will replace the Halifaxes which had a smaller flying range. Sikorski was promised that from June, 1943 we would have six Liberators at our disposal.

Gen. "Grot", interrupted several times with precise questions, indicating his excellent orientation on the international situation and cool political judgement. "The Prime Minister and government in London ask you, Sir, to again participate in the periodic meetings of the Home Political Council." He responded quickly:

From the next meeting on I will participate again, but I could not attend as long as the Polish Socialists' faction was included. I am glad that this has finally changed as a result of the now united stand of London politicians indicated in instructions brought by you, "Jur". I am particularly happy that patriotic elements of the Polish Socialists have decided to return to the mainstream of the legal underground *WRN* socialist organization. *I am also informed by the new Delegate, with whom we are working in complete harmony, that at the last meeting of the Home Political Council held in the suburb of Praga, the matter was definitively solved. Unfortunately, some of the "Polish Socialists' clearly gravitate toward Communism, their main source of inspiration. I am convinced that some of them are collaborating with Soviet intelligence and there are agents provocateurs among them judging by the recent Gestapo assault on the Henryk Wachowicz group in Łódź and the Nazis' arrest of the paratrooper/courier who preceded you, Karol Buka. Under these circumstances, I could not, as the Commander-in-Chief of the Home Army, tolerate such a deplorable state of affairs. That is why I informed the Delegate and London that until the Socialist situation was clarified, I would refuse to participate in meetings of the Home Political Council.*

"General Sir," I said, returning to my report, "the Prime Minister confirms through me his basic order directed to all military units operating in Poland to immediately surrender to you as Commander-in-Chief in the homeland. This policy was approved by the entire Cabinet. The moment is approaching when this unity will be imperative in facing the withdrawing of the enemy by general uprising. Such an action must be under one leader and acted upon according to one plan. On the other hand, Gen. Sikorski and his government ask you to transfer as soon as feasible all the bureaus and agencies of a primarily civil nature to the Delegate's office." "Grot" quickly stopped me saying, "I realize that you are touching on the problem of the so-called 'Teczka' (File), referring to the local administrations and the Bureau of Press and Information." "Yes, Sir," I resumed, "the political parties in London are concerned that these various cells of both civil and political nature, while still under the control of the military Underground, may gain too much power, as in the case of the prewar militaristic *Sanacja* anti-democratic regime." Drawing himself up, the General responded:

I hope that as far as I myself am concerned, there are no doubts about my democratic principles and practice. When I

107

started with Gen. Michał Karaszewicz-Tokarzewski and the SZP (Service to Poland's Victory) Underground army, we worked closely with the leaders of mass political movements. As early as the end of 1939 we anticipated the growth of a civil apparatus in the Underground. For obvious reasons, however, the military resistance was organized earlier and more efficiently. I do understand the Commander-in-Chief's concern and have already issued an executive order to eliminate "Teczka" and to transfer that administrative institution in its entirety to the Delegat's office. We only wish to retain in the military structure the administration of regained territories in the West, because we anticipate that they will necessarily remain for some time under strict military control. But even in this matter, we want to coordinate our efforts with the civil authority. As to alleged Sanacja influence, I do not take kindly to the various insinuations on the part of London politicians. Long before the war I was one of those commanders who knew their constitutional limits, and would never allow any political use of the armed forces.

I do need the BIP, however, and it is irreplaceable in certain respects. After all, the army must have its own information and propaganda apparatus. We must provide our guerrilla units with material against the Nazis, and the same holds for the local cells all over the country. We have our own underground printing shops, radio teams and propaganda operation "N" in the German language, all organized by the BIP. London must understand that the Home Army cannot be deprived of this effective arm, developed at the beginning of the occupation four years ago.

I hastened to reassure "Grot" by saying, "General, the instructions I received were mainly dealing with 'Teczka' and Minister Popiel's long-range plans for rebuilding public administration. With regard to BIP, these instructions were neither definitive nor precise. The General then concluded by saying, "You will see, we are in the process of clearly delineating these issues, and thanks to the good will and high qualifications of the new Delegate and his level-headed objectivity, I am sure that soon these controversies will be resolved."

Our conference was then interrupted by Mrs. "Berg" to warn us of the approaching curfew. The meeting, which had already lasted almost three hours, had gone quickly, and I now hastily formulated my one personal request. "I know from my job description that prior to my eventual return to London I will be assigned to the Department of Information in the Delegate's office, to make use of my special British training in gathering non-military information. As a soldier, however, I would like to also have a purely military assignment in the case of an uprising, so as not to be then idle in some bureaucratic job." The General looked me over as if he were sizing me up for service in his army. Knowing of my anti-aircraft artillery background, he promised, in the event of mobilization, to give me a position in the unit whose task would be to attack several German AA gunposts at the former Mokotow airport. "First you must take those guns from the Nazis and learn how to use them, to provide umbrella protection for liberated Warsaw." He then asked Mrs. "Berg" to arrange for my on-call status with the army, and finally shook my hand. I left the apartment first, it was getting dark, but Olek came up to me mischievously with a bag of apples and offered me one; underneath were several hand grenades.

I walked to the streetcar stop at Grójecka and was soon joined in the small crowd by Gen. "Grot". He looked smart in his gray winter sportscoat and smiled to himself; perhaps not only to himself. I never saw that manly leader again. After his arrest, he never broke under torture, and was killed in a Berlin jail, as one of the reprisals for the Warsaw Uprising of 1944.[30] For the first time since my return to Poland I felt total relief, because even if I were captured by the Gestapo now, I had at least completed my major duties and could finally relax.

One of my remaining minor assignments had to do with support for the Uprising. Major "Kotwicz" (Maciej Kalenkiewicz), also a paratrooper from Great Britain, had already been working for the Underground for an entire year, and I had news for him from London regarding his original plans of Western support for the General Polish Uprising. It was "Murka" (Maria Kann), the writer of children's stories involved with "Kotwicz" in the task of training young Poles for the Air Force, who arranged for me to meet him at her mother's apartment at noon on March 26th. It was next door to the Gestapo Pawiak Prison pharmacy on Dǉuga Street. Exchanging news and ideas, we suddenly heard shooting in the street. Unfolding before our eyes was the daring liberation of sabotage leaders by the Senior Boy Scouts (Szare Szeregi or Gray Rows). The jail truck ("Buda") was quickly opened and some twenty young men escaped in all directions, amidst the cannonade of machine guns. We knew instantly that we had to make a run for it. It was only a matter of minutes before the area would be encircled by Nazi forces. I asked "Kotwicz" as senior officer to jump first from the window, and then poor Murka, who was watching us with horror, almost pushed me out the door. Never in my life had I run so fast as in that desperate effort to escape Nazi entrapment. Before I knew it, I found myself in Wola, a good couple of miles away from Dǉuga Street.[31]

Reports of the increasingly tragic Jewish situation came through several Poles, who had volunteered to stay in touch with the leaders of Jewish organizations both inside the Ghetto and out. After killing almost one-half million hapless people who were deported from the Warsaw Ghetto to various extermination camps, only about forty thousand fit young men and women remained to perform various "productive" tasks for the German war effort. I saw them often, silently marching in pathetic work battalions under strict supervision of the well-armed German police and their watchdogs. You could sense the tense determination on the part of this "labor force", fully aware of what was to be their future. Apparently most of them decided to fight for their human dignity, rather than give up passively to the final "solution". They received some, but not sufficient amounts of weapons and ammunition from the meager amounts supplied by Home Army contacts and the local secret production.

Although it was rare to find prewar Jewish acquaintances still alive after a year of ghetto exterminations, I was happy to meet a number of my Lwów friends in Warsaw. All of them had changed their names and were posing as non-Jewish Poles. One of these encounters took place at the church of Saint James, where I was attending my first mass after my return to Poland. To my surprise, praying next to me was Dr. Tadeusz Owiński, our family dental surgeon, and a member of our KTN skiing club in Lwów. In church we pretended not to know each other, but a few days later, having need of a good dentist, I inquired as to his whereabouts, and went to see him. In his waiting room I met our prewar skiing champion, Zbigniew Jakubowski, but of course sensing some clandestine involvement, we pretended not to know each other. Dr. Owiński began work on my infection, as in continuation of prewar dental work, only asking the whereabouts of my family.

These meetings on the street with Lwów Jews, whom I had known well before the war were never too safe. One such incident happened while I was walking home just minutes after a meeting with the Delegate, at Mokotowska Street. Here I ran into my prewar neighbors, Dr. Bizio and Helena Rappaport. While we were still a good distance apart, he shouted, "Jerzyku, my name is now Rapacki." Naturally, they had changed their identity for protection. The Rappaports were delightful people, but I had to warn them that such open enthusiastic acknowledgements could endanger us all.

Even more dramatic was the streetcar encounter between myself and the Jewish-born mother of one of my companions, Andrzej Nahlik, the Polish pilot, whose wedding with an attractive English WAAF girl I had attended only a few months earlier in London. Knowing that we had left Lwów together, and seeing me in the crowded street car, poor Mrs. Nahlik exclaimed with great concern, "Where is my Andrzej?" Evidently she had no knowledge of my current status, and I had to pretend that I knew neither her nor her son. "Aren't you Jerzyk Lerski?" she asked. "Madam, indeed I must look like him, because it is not the first time I have been mistaken for that man." Of course, she recognized my voice and became even more convinced that her only son must have been killed as an airman. It took quite some time to pass a message to her through some trustworthy contacts, assuring her that Andrzej was safe.

Another Jewish contact I made while in Warsaw did not come from such a chance meeting as those mentioned. I tried on my own to locate one of my best prewar friends, Erwin Axer, a rising star of the theater and finally got in touch with him through Krystyna Wieńszczak, an able playwright. Erwin had acquired so-called Aryan papers, and was living at the apartment of a Christian lady whom he married after the war, and who was the sister of well-known actor Jan Kreczmar. Our meeting was quite an emotional experience because we had known each other as classmates since we were ten years old, and together even won the tennis doubles championship. He informed me of other Jewish friends, the poet Jan Kott and his wife Lidka (nee Steinhaus), who were in hiding in this same Żoliborz district. I inquired about Erwin's family, and found that his father, a prominent Lwów lawyer, had been killed by the Nazis. His mother Pani Fryda was in hiding with Christian friends in Warsaw, and his brother Ryś was with the Jewish Fighting Organization (ŻOB), in the Janowska Street camp for the internment of Lwów Jews. He refused all our attempts to secure his release by bribery, because he felt it his duty to stay with the combatants until the very end.

On another lucky day, I went to a large coffee house at Nowy Świat Street to listen to a recommended pianist, Zieliński. To my joy, it turned out to be my other Jewish classmate, Jan Gorbaty, who had later attended the Lwów Conservatory. At the intermission, he approached my table unostentatiously and told me that our mutual friend, the Lwów tenor Leszek Finze, had saved his life by bringing him to Warsaw and finding him this job. Finze was a Pole of German origin who, in May of 1938, had dropped his membership in the jingoistic *Młodzież Wszechpolska* as a protest on the brutal assult on me by a gang of narrow-minded students who resented my philo-Semitic stand. He had to face a more serious problem later, when his parents opted to become the so called *Reichsdeutschen* under the Nazis. As such, they were designated as having been born Germans, and forced to cooperate with the German

112

authorities. When they made this move, Leszek turned against his own parents and moved to Warsaw to work as a vocalist. With him he managed to bring several Jewish colleagues, including Gorbaty, and helped them in finding work and safe lodgings. Through a prominent philologist, Czesław Fiszer, who was living outside the Ghetto with Aryan papers and working with his older brother on a construction crew. I learned that one of our scoundrel classmates, Izio Dornberg, was blackmailing his Jewish co-religionists, telling them that he would reveal their attempts to pass as Aryan Poles in Warsaw if they did not pay him a set sum of money.

Horror scenes happened to Jews not only behind the Ghetto walls, but sometimes in front of our eyes in the middle of the day. While returning by street-car near the Ghetto wall, from a secret meeting in the Żoliborz district, we suddenly came to a quick halt. During the war the first part of the street cars were reserved *"Nur für Deutsche,"* (for Germans only); on this occasion a pale Jewish boy had just run from the Ghetto straight into this first section. The Germans, after stopping the car, turned the boy over matter-of-factly to the policemen among them. The child was shot on the spot in front of everyone present. There was a general devastating feeling of impotence among those of us Poles in the back of the car, for the Germans were all armed and we were not. There was absolutely nothing we could do to stop this murderous act, and it was terrible beyond description.

By Easter week, 1943, young Jews remaining in the Warsaw Ghetto were preparing as best they could for their final battle. On Monday of that week, I had an appointment in court at Krasiński Square, near the Ghetto. The meeting was to have been with Judge Piotrowski ("Baryka"), who was in charge of the Ukrainian question in the Department of the Interior of the Delegate's office. This meeting never took place, though, for as I approached the edge of the square, I saw an SS unit firing into the Ghetto. A preliminary battle of the Ghetto had just begun, and as a symbol of the centuries of coexistence between the Poles and Jews, the Polish White and Red and the Jewish White and Blue flags, were proudly displayed side by side on the rooftop near Muranowski Square. I had heard that one or two small Home Army units were trying to help the Jews in their fight. These were selected groups, experienced in street fighting, who gave technical assistance in attempts to break through the walls, as well as assisting people to escape through the sewers after the fighting had stopped. Brave as these attempts were, however, the help was far from sufficient. The next day, a writer friend of mine, Krystyna Wieńszczak, and I walked through the Old Town towards the Vistula River, going as close as we could to the besieged Ghetto. We felt entirely useless as we listened to the continuous shooting, and watched, half paralyzed, the fire and smoke hang over the district, as if to outline the desperate and lonely struggle of those heroes inside.

For security purposes, it was mandatory for over-exposed underground workers to withdraw from circulation from time to time, and since I badly needed a rest, a long-planned getaway from Warsaw for Easter was arranged. I was exhausted from the stress that had accompanied my mission. Moreover, I had also become known to much to too many people in Warsaw at that time, so laying low for a while was almost routine for me. Mrs. Zboromirski, a friend of my first landlady, recommended that I visit the Children's Hospital near Kielce, where her son, Jerzy, was hiding. The *Gestapo* was after him, suspecting his involvement in underground activities, so he left the city and was posing under a faked name as a gardener at this distant hospital. Marysia, the sister of Jan Mikołajczyk, the man who had received me on my return to Poland, happened to be the doctor in charge of this Catholic hospital. So, I decided Kielce would be my destination for this brief respite, and boarded a train for there on Good Friday. I was very anxious to see some of the guerrillas in action and note their methods of operation. As the train passed through the forests outside of Kielce, I could not help but wonder where they were operating. Some of the most daring of their number, "Ponury" (Jan Piwnik) and "Nurt" (Eugeniusz Kaszyński), were my paratrooper comrades.

The guerrilla units were involved in sabotaging railroad

transport with plastic bombs; but they were also active in such endeavors as liberating political prisoners, punishing notorious Gestapo officers, receiving paratroopers, and mainly training cadres for the final uprising. By the end of the war, some one quarter million people, mostly young, had been sworn in to these "forest" units of the world's largest underground army. In daylight, the little towns and railroad junctions seemed to be under the Germans, but the night belonged to us and they knew it. As a result, frequent reprisals were carried against these villages, which only made the resistance spirit that much stronger.

I was warmly welcomed at the hospital. It provided a convenient underground "mailbox" under the protection of the courageous Sisters of Mercy and two women doctors. In no other place outside Warsaw had I felt such a strong feeling of simmering resistance and survival of the Polish patriotic spirit as I did in this Kielce area. We went to the traditional early Sunday Mass of the Resurrection at the old Cathedral of Kielce. The city had changed in character, as had most of the small Polish towns, because the Jews had been forcefully removed. In their place came Polish people deported from western Poland, and gone were the ancient Synagogues and little Jewish shops.

My true identity was not revealed at the hospital, even though its residents were mostly patriotic Poles. One could never take too many precautions. With my hosts I visited the beautiful countryside, which brought forth memories of my favorite novels by Stefan Żeromski about the struggle against Tsarist Russia. He described to perfection the rolling old mountains, pine trees and deep forest jungles of this area: ideal country for guerrilla activity. Nothing, however, seemed to make me forget these burning skies over the Warsaw Ghetto, seen just before my departure to this romantic region.

After a week I returned to Warsaw, which was still under an umbrella of heavy smoke coming from the fighting Ghetto. The clandestine press, particularly that of the Home Army, gave compassionate accounts of the Jewish struggle, comparing them to the biblical David, fighting the modern Goliath.

Actually it proved more like a new Masada, and the first one since the ancient Jewish armed resistance.

A year before the Ghetto Uprising, Catholic intellectuals concerned about their Jewish co-citizens, organized in major Polish cities a special Council to help Jews ("Żegota"-Rada Pomocy Zydom). This was done in close cooperation with the military and civilian sectors of the Secret State. As Gen. Sikorski's envoy, I discussed those difficult matters with various dedicated leaders of "Żegota," namely Ferdynand Arczyński, Władysław Bartoszewski, Witold Bieńkowski, Maria Kann, Zofia Kossak-Szczucka, Maria Anna Lasocka, and Henryk Woliński. We were all sadly aware that much more should have been done by us to save Jewish lives, but adversities of the cruel Nazi occupation combined with a shortage of funds proved to be insurmountable. The fact, however, that at least one hundred thousand Polish Jews destined for extinction did survive the Holocaust on Polish soil, should be attributed to the selfless work of "Żegota" and thousands of fearless individuals of all social classes, most of whom were subsequently recognized as "The Righteous Gentiles" by the Yad Vashem Institute in Jerusalem, where by now there are more tamarisk trees planted by them then by philosemites of all other nations combined. The truth of the matter is that as much as some of us would have wished to, at that time, we Poles alone could not decisively help with any major operation to relieve the Jewish fighters. Both the western and eastern allies were too far from Warsaw and not ready at all to act on the Jews' behalf. One night later in May, when this second Warsaw battle of World War II was over, Soviet bombers did attack the city, lighting it up with flares. Much damage was done to Warsaw buildings, but nothing was achieved for the few Jews still hiding in the Ghetto cellars and sewers.[32]

Throughout this horrible time, we continued our underground activities and never thought of ourselves as instant heroes, candidates for military awards, decorations or easy promotions. To preserve mental sanity we tried to live as normally as possible. For young people that meant harmless

116

flirtations and occasional dating during holidays. Being of amorous disposition, I had quite a problem of choosing the "number one" sweetheart from among those remarkable young women of the Warsaw underground. Remembering the English proverb "safety in numbers," I decided to be in love with most of them, and thus greatly enjoyed Sunday outings along the Vistula River. At the same time, I made up my mind to marry one of those A.K. heroines immediately after the victory.[33] The most important element of those wartime affections between young men and women deeply involved in dangerous underground operations and clandestine higher studies was mutual respect, which helped many of the friendships to survive and develop until this moment.

One of my companions, the brilliant "Magdalena" (Zofia Straszewska), insisted that I help her A.K. boss, "Olicki" (Dr. Aleksander Gieysztor), in briefing for a London mission of special envoy "Zych" (Jan Nowak — Zdzisław Jeziorański). After clearing such delicate cross-cell matters with my immediate supervisor, I met the secret courier at the "Elektrownia" contact local of the Home Army's 6th Bureau (BIP) in one of the inconspicuous apartments at One Marszałkowska Street. Having already heard praises from "Zieliński" (Korboński) about "Zych's" daring round trip to neutral Sweden on behalf of the sophisticated "N" propaganda section of the A.K. among German troops, I decided to perform a similar *mutatis mutandis* function as Karski did in the case of my mission to Warsaw. Hence the origin of a unique "Trojka" team of wartime secret envoys working ever since in perfect harmony with each other. I found my successor very attentive and completely dedicated to national unity both at home and in exile for the duration of the war. Moreover, this conference started a lasting bond of true friendship based on mutual good will and full trust, essential in the performance of our respective duties.[34]

Life in Warsaw was changing fast in a kaleidoscopic manner. Walking from another secret meeting across the spectacular Poniatowski Bridge, I was recognized by the Pawłowskis, our family friends from Lwów, and their lovely daughter Hanka invited me to her birthday party. Along with a number of other young people, we had a good time singing, dancing and enjoying a cold buffet. For a few moments we could pretend that there was no war. However, the sweet illusion could not last long. Since the streetcars were out of order, I jogged in order to get home before curfew. Being shortsighted, I ran into a German police patrol. Absentmindedly, I apologized in English, "I am so sorry", instead of the expected, "*Verzeihen Sie bitte*"; thank God they took me for a harmless fool and let me go. Another time, trying to beat curfew, I ran in the dark under the walls of the "Small Ghetto", an abandoned portion of the entire Warsaw Ghetto which had been sectioned off. The next thing I knew, I was facing a four-man German patrol. "*Hande Hoch!* they shouted and began searching my pockets for weapons. One of them bristled, asking "*Was is das?*" "*Da schauen sie bitte*", I calmly replied knowing that the item he had discovered was only my bulky spectacle case.

On May 15, 1943, something happened which made my mission into Poland personally most rewarding. On that day I became sentimental while remembering our prewar celebration honoring my mother's name day. I decided to pay a visit to my first cousin, also named Zofia (Supińska), and as a gift for her I purchased a black alabaster statue of a bulldog with a cigar, which in occupied Europe symbolized Winston Churchill and his tenacity. As I climbed the stairs to Zośka's flat on Słupecka Four, an elderly smiling man opened the door, and before I had time to say anything, he introduced himself: "I am your father, Jerzyku". We had not seen each other since I was three years old, due to some unintelligent divorce arrangement. He looked seventy, and somewhat hunched over, but his eyes were sparkling with joy. Mieczysław Lerski was an unassuming old man, though he had once been quite famous as a pioneer skier and mountaineer[35]. Professionally, he was a civil engineer before the war, in charge of construction of roads and bridges in the southeastern Stanisławów region. While it was impossible during this first unrehearsed encounter to cover the twenty years which we lived apart, gradually we were able to develop a warm,

118

intimate relationship. He was a quite witty, balding man of medium size, with a serious heart problem. This unexpected friendship, I am sure, did a great deal of good to both of us.

I had to move in a hurry from my apartment in Wola because my landlady claimed that during an unexpected house search by the German police, several of my gold coins, hidden in the kitchen chimney, had been stolen. She was more frightened than usual, and I decided to move at once. The very same person who had found my first lodgings, "Auntie Władka", took me to her relative's house at 12 Francuska Street in Saska Kępa, an attractive residential district across the Vistula River. Mrs. Irena Pietruszewska was one of those fearless ladies who allowed her house to be overused by paratroopers. When I first visited the place, I pointed out the security dangers involved in such overcrowding. Nevertheless, it was hard during that summer of 1943 to find hiding places for everybody. Living there were two other civilian couriers, having a good time in that noisy place. The man of the house was in London, but his square officer's hat still hung proudly in the hall entranceway.

While settling confortably into new living quarters, I was also assuming my duties at the amorphous Department of Information. It was thrilling to be a part of the growing infrastructure of the Secret State in anticipation of the postwar Reconstruction. The overly inquisitive director of the Department "Dołęga" (Stanisław Kauzik), was a neatly dressed man with gray hair and blue eyes. A typical political manipulator, he knew many people and pretended to know everything. Though personally courageous, he was rather careless and absent minded. He held his official appointment at the attractive old apartment on Skorupki Street, occupied by the Warsaw librarian Dr. Stanisława Sawicka. She tried admirably to keep order in the manifold agendas of her boss, but was later arrested anyway.

I was also assigned to the newly created SIP (Information and Propaganda Section) under "Konrad" (Kiryl Sosnowski), a truly dedicated gentleman from Poznań where he served as director of the St. Wojciech Catholic Publishing House before the war. He organized a clandestine nationalist group called the Fatherland *(Ojczyzna)*, which operated mainly in Western Polish areas incorporated into the German *Reich*. Though definitely right-wing in his prewar political views, "Konrad" was a wonderful chief, who entrusted me with the information side of his section, and later with the editing of an official news agency monthly release, *Kraj* (The Homeland). I undertook to develop a competent network of informants throughout the country to gather important political, cultural and socio-economic news in their respective regions, by way of concise weekly, and longer monthly analytical reports. It was essential to train these well-selected people in filling out questionnaires regarding those specific problems throughout various areas of the country. The summaries of these weekly reports were to be coded for radio transmission to London, while longer and more synthetic monthly summaries were sent through Budapest and Lisbon via neutral diplomatic pouch. In building my network, I was mainly looking for social scientists, politically aware of the importance of everyday changes. For special reporting on Warsaw's daily events, I used yet another ready team, the Girl Scouts *(Szare Szeregi)*, recruiting bright kids from eleven to fourteen years of age, who collected information from their respective city districts to be delivered every evening to a place designated by their leaders. I then picked up and edited these reports for "Nowak" (Korboński), to be transmitted via short wave radio that very night. That quick telegraphy set I had been parachuted with was used in this particular operation known as the *Świt* (Dawn) secret radio station. These broadcasts were ostensibly coming from inside Poland, but were actually from the exiled London Ministry of the Interior station at Bletchley Park in East Anglia. In order to make it look like the fresh news were broadcast from within Poland it had to be sent to England within a twenty-four hour period. In some cases, broadcasting of warnings to singled-out Nazis especially cruel in thier methods was quite effective in frightening them.

To find the right people to work for our information center I had to travel to Kraków, the actual capital of the Nazi General

Government, under Dr. Hans Frank, as well as to Lublin. "Konrad's" *Ojczyzna* (Fatherland) also had effective communication with Western Poland, incorporated with the Third Reich including the industrial Śląsk (Silesia), thus providing us with ample material for evaluation.

One of my most rewarding experiences had to do with the so-called cultural intelligence. Our Kraków agent was Dr. Hanka Kutrzeba, a sociologist and daughter of the renowned historian, Dr. Stanisław Kutrzeba, ex-Rector (President) of the 600-year old Jagiellonian University. One day I walked with her along the Vistula, she told me that she had to take me to her father's apartment to show me some "treasures." One of the curators of the medieval Jagiellonian library had a German name, Kuntz, so he was not watched too closely by the Nazis. They never suspected that in spite of his German descent he was really a Polish patriot. While on the job, he carefully listed professors coming from famous universities like Gottingen and Heidelberg, and whenever any of them delved into the archives, he noted which of the illuminated manuscripts disappeared. In this way, he created a valuable roster of missing material. Miss Kutrzeba passed on this list to me in the bathroom of their house, as she was very concerned that her father should not be involved in such a dangerous transaction. After receiving this precious report. I hid it in the false botton of my suitcase, and hoped that it would reach Warsaw without mishap.[36]

As I was now ready to go back to Warsaw, I asked my cousin Murka Gargulińska to make a reservation in a sleeping car for me. As the train was to go through the annexed territories near Piotrków and Tomaszów, I knew I had to be particularly careful with my secret documents. I went to the station early in order to beat the 6 p.m. curfew, which had been temporarily imposed in Kraków as punishment to the populace for frequent transgressions of Nazi rules. Since the train's departure time was still a few hours away, it was standing well outside the platforms. I was able to board it and quickly found my compatment, undressed and confortably went to bed in the top bunk. When the train finally moved into the station, a sudden noise awoke me, as two German army officers came into the compartment with two disreputable Polish women. They were angry to find me there. "What is the matter?" I asked. "This is the women's compartment and you are not supposed to be here." Of course, Murka had forgotten to specify that the ticket should be for a man. The conductor soon arrived to settle the disturbance and he told me that I would have to leave immediately. "Allright," I said, "but find me another bed." His reponse was, "There is only one bunk available, and it is a compartment occupied by two *Gestapo* officers." "I'll take it," I said. He replied that he was not supposed to allow anyone else to travel with them because, "you may leave them stiff at the end of the ride." At this point I began to bluff and said, "How can you be sure that I am not one of them?" He finally gave up, shrugging his shoulders and led me to the compartment, where I told the two officers my sad story. They laughed and said, "Had we been in your position, those two army men would soon have left us alone with those whores." "Maybe so," I replied, "but this Pole had no such luck." Having amused them, I was allowed to travel in their company for the entire journey.

Coming through the annexed German territory, we were stopped, as was expected, for a general inspection of papers by the *Grenzpolizei* (border police). Luckily for me, my unwitting Gestapo guardians refused to let them disturb us and I had an easy passage with my precious material, which would eventually be used well after the war to recover those stolen manuscripts.

On another trip connected with my work, I went to the Lublin district. In traveling there, I had to have a good cover story, because entering and leaving that area in 1943 was under strict control. It was arranged that I should be a guard for the *Karpatengesellschaft* transport company, whose loaded trucks traveled from Warsaw to my native city of Lwów. My additional duty was to deliver a small transmitter to Lublin, where I would leave the truck. Once at my destination, I was to establish an information cell, and my contact was to be Zofia Karpińska. She was a well-trained sociologist from Poznań

University, working for the "*Społem*" Cooperatives' headquarters in Lublin. This was the main consumer's cooperative chain in Poland, and Zofia's job there would help her keep in contact with people in that entire agricultural area. enabling her to get information we needed for our regular reports. She readily agreed to work for "Konrad" and me. In addition to the general social and economic data that Zofia would gather, she would also be observing the changes in the nearby Majdanek Concentration camp, and inform us on the Communist guerrilla movement in the region. Therefore, she also had to set up a regional network of people that would report to her. This is how our project grew to even larger proportions. Prepared for swearing in by me, she handed over a valuable report on Majdanek to be taken to Warsaw.

On returning to my quarters at Mrs. Wacława Hercelińska's house, I ran into my petite prewar secretary from the SD Youth. Her name was Staszka Rosiecka ("Penny"), and I had known her to be a dedicated girl of leftist orientation. "You are supposed to be in London," she exclaimed. "In London?" I replied. "You must have been misinformed. I have a good job in Warsaw. Come and see me when you are in the capital," I said, giving her a false address. Her manner seemed too flagrant, and I wanted out of the encounter. However, she insisted that, as an old friend, I must visit her at her mother's house that evening. "I can't do it," I replied. "I am going back to Warsaw right away, but," I capitulated, "we can have lunch together." She took me to a rather grim looking restaurant in the basement of a house, where after ordering my favorite meal of boiled beef with cucumbers, mashed potatoes and horseradish sauce, I noticed a sinister group of German speaking civilians at the next table. She had just warned me that they were the local *Gestapo*, when suddenly one of them approached the table and addressed my companion. He had brought a number of photographs for her to identify. She looked confused and asked, "Not now." Well, I thought, this is it. I am going to be arrested in a moment. I bowed my head over the plate in an attempt to at least partially hide my face. When he returned to his table, I asked her bluntly if she was working for them and she replied, "In a way, yes. I work for the Labor Exchange Office *(Arbeitsamt)*, transporting people from the Majdanek concentration camp to forced labor in Germany. This helps me keep in touch with some of our prewar friends as well as underground leaders incarcerated there to identify those being sent to German camps and keep track of their whereabouts." Her story seemed strangely amiss to me, and I wanted to say goodbye. That same afternoon, I reported "Penny" to the local A.K. intelligence officer, and told him she appeared to be a typical *Gestapo* informer. I later learned that she was, in fact, under oath and working for Lt. Łopatniuk from Lwów, all this time risking her life as a target for either side.

No longer with the truck, I was now faced with the problem of getting back to Warsaw. Since the Lublin area was tightly restricted in order to contain guerrilla units during the "Pacification Process," no one was allowed in or out of the city without a pass. There had been a great deal of reprisals against the Germans because of their deportation of Polish children in Zamość region. As a result more and more SS units had been called in to control the restless part of that country. In order to get my return pass, I had to go to the German Police headquarters. While I was at the front desk, confident of my Berlin accent, I addressed the woman officer and suddenly realized that I had been interjecting English idioms into my German speech. She looked at me suspiciously and told me to come back the next day, at which point I insisted I had to return to work at the *Karpatengesellschaft* Warsaw office immediately. Nevertheless, she kept my documents and refused to give me a pass that day. Smelling a rat, I decided to leave as soon as possible without a pass, rather than go back to Police headquarters. Early the next morning, I walked north from my lodgings and came across a formidable Polish police patrol at the end of a wide deserted street which led northward to Warsaw. Meanwhile, on the other side of the street, were four German policemen. Loaded with sensitive material, I knew I would be tortured if my double deck briefcase was dismounted. Without hesitation I walked straight across to the

Germans. When they asked me why I was coming suddenly to their side I explained that I wished to deal with the best police in the world, rather than those Polish scoundrels. They laughed with satisfaction and let me pass without further questions.

Marveling at the success of my stratagem, I tightened my grip on the satchel, tried not to reveal my relief, and went quickly uphill on my way. A mile or two later I hitched a ride with a middle-aged German truckdriver from Stuttgart, who proved to be surprisingly decent. Deeply concerned about the situation on the Eastern front, he was convinced that the Germans were losing and obviously appreciated the chance to talk to a Pole about the war problems. Finally, after a couple of hours, we reached the Mińsk Mazowiecki near Warsaw, and he let me out, and from there I took the train to my temporary home in Saska Kępa.

Gradually, as my network expanded, we were able to regularly collect material from all over the country. It was usually delivered by reliable railroad personnel. As traditional elite of the Polish working class, they were known to be trustworthy in these types of operations ever since the Socialist Party started its struggle for national independence at the end of last century. In summer of 1943 I began to edit the *Kraj* (Homeland) news agency of our Department. My deputy and main features' writer was an able penman Włodzimierz Wnuk, who had been miraculously released from the dreadful Gusen concentration camp because of a TB infection in the bone marrow of his leg. The release was arranged by his influential uncle Wacław Krzeptowski, who, although helpful to Włodek, was really a despicable character in his treacherous role as leader of the phony *Goralenvolk*. This was a small group of opportunistic highlanders who pretended to be of prehistoric German origin. Their patriotic countrymen warned Krzeptowski that he will be hanged sooner or later: "Wacuś bedzies wisioł!" (Wacław you will be hanged!") Though grateful to his uncle,Włodek did not support his collaborationist policies and left Zakopane for Warsaw, where he joined his Poznań classmates in the clandestine *Ojczyzna* (Fatherland)

Catholic movement. Because of his health condition I usually walked to his hideout at Pańska Street to pick up his well-written material for *Kraj*.[37]

Step by step I was getting acquainted with other departments of the well-structured Secret State, and was particularly impressed with the widespread Education Department headed by "Sadowski" (Czesław Wycech). He had been known before the war as the leftist, anti-clerical president of the Teacher's Union. An efficient organizer, and a no-nonsense activist, he managed to construct the three-tiered regular system of grammar, high school and university levels, also using German tolerated professional schools such as nursing, mechanics etc. An amazing achievement. Wycech and his competent assistants mobilized tens of thousands of courageous teachers to instruct hundreds of thousands of students throughout Poland and kept their hopes high for the future.

This gave me a chance to complete my own studies at the underground Warsaw University. The classes were held in groups not larger than ten at the given Professor's or reliable student's private apartments. They lasted a couple of intensive hours, during which we had the privilege of listening to outstanding legal scholars, who were also taking great risks, as several such study groups were arrested by the dreaded Gestapo squads. It was the final (fourth) year of law studies covering mainly civil law subjects. Among my new classmates were two of my old colleagues with changed identities for reasons similar to mine. I was highly impressed with the younger students who exemplified to me the flowering of that generation with their total commitment to clandestine military duties and serious academic work, in conjunction with their regular jobs for a living. These, I found, were the three character building ingredients which ultimately produced that unique A.K. generation of dedicated, responsible patriots which any country could envy. Many of these brave men and women were to be prematurely killed in the abortive 63-day long Warsaw Uprising of 1944, while the links between those who survived have often proven no less strong than family ties. Such was to be the lasting bond between those who studied and risked their young lives together for a common cause in such demanding circumstances. For example, one of my fellow students, Zbigniew Rapacki of Warsaw, became in exile the godfather of my first son Thomas, after I became in Paris the godfather of his first son Jan.

In April, 1943, powerful shock waves resounded with the horrible news brought forth by the devious Nazi Propaganda Minister Dr. Goebbels concerning the discovery of mass graves of missing Polish officers in the Katyń Forest near Smolensk in Russia. Our first reaction was that nothing coming from such a source could be trusted, but soon the bare facts began to speak for themselves. We heard by radio that Gen. Sikorski's Government in London had turned to the International Red Cross in Geneva for an impartial investigation. On my humble part I selected a reliable friend who volunteered to go with the official Polish Red Cross delegation from Warsaw to the site of the massacre for a thorough, on-the-spot examination. Janek Mikołajczyk's detailed report left no doubt whatever that these Polish officers had been killed at least a year before the German invasion of the Soviet Union. The growth of small trees and bushes which had been planted to hide the graves clearly indicated the time when this greatest tragedy in Polish-Russian relations occurred. Similarly, the dates on thousands of family letters found with the bodies showed that no word had reached these 4,143 officers after the spring of 1940 (another 10.000 from the Ostaszków and Starobielsk camps remain unaccounted for). I knew a Katyń widow, Mrs. Jadwiga Hertz, whose numerous postcards and letters written after that time had not been found together with the previous ones which Janek duly brought back. So at least in this horrendous crime the villains were definitely not the Germans, but Stalin with his N.K.V.D. police aparatus; a fact which Moscow prefers to disavow to this day.[38] From that moment on, the crisis between the Poles and Soviets assumed major proportions. Responding with anger to Polish attempts of investigations by the International Red Cross, the Soviets abruptly severed diplomatic relations with the Polish Government in exile, showing similar hostility to our Underground. Once again we were to face mortal enemies on two fronts. To survive between such millstones, Poles had to remain tough as diamonds for centuries.

Just after that ominous breach in Polish-Soviet relations, we tragically lost two top leaders of our struggle. First came the arrest of Gen. Stefan "Grot" Rowecki, whose prestige could not be equaled by any other military man in the underground. And the second upset came with the mysterious plane accident just outside of Gibraltar, on July 3, 1943, in which Gen. Sikorski was killed with his vivacious daughter, Zofia Leśniowska, and his able staff. The Goebbels' propaganda machine stated that the British meant to rid themselves of an increasingly inconvenient Allied leader, at a moment when Churchill needed better relations with Stalin. Of course, there are many other possibilities, such as Nazi or Soviet sabotage. In any case, Gen. Sikorski's unexpected death was felt by me as a great loss because regardless of his shortcomings, he was very charming in dealing with me as his trusted personal envoy.[39]

Covert radio transmissions quickly carried the word that Władysław Raczkiewicz, the President of the Polish Republic in London, had appointed Deputy Premier Stanisław Mikołajczyk as the new Prime Minister, and Gen. Sosnkowski as the new Commander-in-Chief. I was well aware that these two men did not get along at all, and expected serious friction between them. That sad summer of 1943 also brought more disasters for the underground leadership. The Gestapo captured the National Party leader, Dr. Sacha, as well as two successive heads of the Intelligence Division of the A.K. They also arrested the hard-working deputy head of our "SIP" Division, Zbigniew Sadkowski. Though tortured in Gestapo Headquarters, he did not betray any of our hideouts. As a result of those arrests, the Underground feverishly set to work in uncovering treacherous informers, finding new meeting places, and devising new codes, in order to elude the Nazis.

Gen. Sosnkowski appointed without delay the inconspicuous Gen. "Bór" (Tadeusz Komorowski), to replace Gen. "Grot" as officer in charge of the Home Army. I remembered Count

Komorowski from before the war. He had been in charge of the Ninth Cavalry Regiment in Trembowla and later of the school for cavalry officers in Grudziądz. Though a fine gentleman and excellent horseman, he lacked the charisma of his predecessor, needed for such a crucial assignment. The other experienced leader who could have been chosen for this position was Gen. Tadeusz Pełczyński ("Grzegorz"). Though highly respected as Chief-of-Staff, he was remembered as the prewar Pilsudskiite boss of the military intelligence (Second Bureau). As such, he was less acceptable to the coalition parties than was the apolitical Gen. Komorowski. Gradually, it became obvious that the real center of decision-making in the underground was shifting to the civilian sector, with its efficient Government's Delegate Jan Stanisław Jankowski, and strong willed Kazimierz Pużak, the Secretary General of the PPS, who had become a dominant personality in a wider political arena.

Before long, the *Gestapo's* arm opened out to me. Luckily, the A.K. counter-intelligence had planted a few Polish secretaries in *Gestapo* headquarters. One of them appeared at 12 Francuska Street to warn me and my roommate Włodek Wnuk that we must immediately abandon present living quarters to avoid imminent arrest. It seems that one of the woman neighbors had denounced this house and its occupants. I quickly gathered up my belongings and left within the hour.

My main work had been done out of the top floor of a large apartment building on Sixth of August Street. The landlady, Ewa Daczkowska, knew I was using her premises for underground work, but did not know that it was there, under the floorboards, that I kept my official archives. This was known only to myself and my loyal subordinate, "Basia" (Magda Rudowska), who came there periodically on her liaison errands. I again had to face the problem of finding another place to live, and not wanting to stay with different friends every night, I decided to return to the Wola suburb, once again trusting Mrs. Śnieżko. She agreed to rent to me, as she remembered that I had always paid well before. After such a close call with the *Gestapo*, I decided to reveal my new address only to "Basia", whom I trusted absolutely. One day she came to me with a personal request, to enlist the services of her older sister, Zofia; as I had been empowered by my superiors to administer the special oath of the "Secret State", and since we really needed this type of dedicated young person in our service at the Department of Information, I accepted the request. One sunny morning a few days later, I inducted the beautiful redheaded Zofia into the underground liaison service, atop the roof of an apartment building which overlooked the city. She too turned out to be a very capable person and performed admirably alongside her sister during the Uprising, in the course of which both of them were wounded.

Many of those liaison women paid with their lives in the heroic work of maintaining the underground's communication network. Although the list goes on and on, I remember in particular two dedicated ladies from the small Democratic Party, who worked for the Bureau of Information and Press (BIP). They were caught on the street carrying handbags full of clandestine newspapers and other incriminating materials. These wonderful young fighters, "Helena" (Hanka Csaki) and "Krystyna" (Zofia Warzyńska), were subsequently tortured at the Pawiak prison, but they never betrayed any contacts, names or addresses. Such was the heavy price paid almost daily for the growth of the "Secret State".

Almost every aspect of normal existence was stubbornly maintained during the occupation, so that no area of culture would be allowed to die out. In our musical endeavors, for example, according to Nazi regulations we were not supposed to play the patriotic composition of Frederic Chopin. But on the contrary, I often heard the "Etude Revolutionaire" or "Polonaise As Dur" as I walked through the suburbs. In the literary field, our writers continued to create, albeit only for "their drawers", preserving their manuscripts for publication during better times. Literary evenings were also organized, whereby a group of intellectuals would gather together for play or prose readings from current writers. One such meeting to which I was taken by Krystyna Wieńszczak particularly stands out in my memory. Karol Małcużyński, the brother of the famous pianist, and his wife, were hosting a prose reading of Stefan Otwinowski's works in their attractive flat at Mazowiecka street. Among those present were the prominent poet Czesław Miłosz (future Nobel Prize winner), and the fascinating preacher Father Jan Zieja, when suddenly our illegal soiree was silenced by the sound of shooting in the street. The German police were evidently after two young men who had thrown a bomb into a nearby restaurant frequented by the Gestapo. It seemed for a moment that a large part of Warsaw's literary elite would be caught and eliminated. Luckily the police did not search the neighborhood houses.

Particularly difficult was the life of actors. Walking down Francuska Street, I was stopped by Janusz Strachocki, one of the great theater directors and an old skiing friend. He insisted on taking me home, where he told me the following story: "I was approached by a once famous actress, who is now in disrepute for cooperating with the German propaganda office. She proposed that I should work with her in one of thoses hallow productions which are intended as diversions from resistance efforts. When I refused, she pointed out that I had two sons to feed and educate which I should consider in such a decision. I quickly retorted by saying," he continued, "for my sons, I must preserve my good name." Strachocki chose to remain faithful to the classic roles of Polish drama, which he had so memorably performed on the Lwów stage before the war. The BIP department of the Home Army even enlisted some prominent theater people like Stefan Jarema and Krystyna Wieńszczak to work on puppet shows, which were later shown during the sixty-three day Warsaw Uprising.

The variety of cultural involvement enlisted by the underground may be hard to believe, but it was absolutely necessary to give vent to the creative needs of those who were otherwise silenced. Captivated by such artistic activities, I truly admired the young enthusiasts involved in them, but worried that they could not last long.

Of my upcoming return to London I was to learn in a rather unusual way. Later in November, while waiting for a street-car,

I saw "Jan" (Witold Bieńkowski) from the Delegate's office. He smiled at me knowingly and whispered, "Congratulations. They have decided to send you back to London." Somewhat taken aback, I replied, "Isn't it strange that you know this before I do? Moreover, I am not particularly interested in returning." For a number of reasons I was not eager to leave Warsaw, even though the mood there was extremely tense, due to the increased roundups and mass executions. In addition, I was thoroughly immersed in my work, having formed a network capable of gathering an even greater amount of useful information. Being most comfortable with my underground companions I was anxiously anticipating joining them in the fight, when the call finally rang out 'for the Uprising. I was eager to complete my law studies. In spite of my actual desires, England was to be my destination again. "Jan" continued in a half whisper saying, "'The Doctor' and 'Bór' have decided to send you at the Prime Minister's special request, because the last two couriers 'Sęp' (Stanisław Łuczkiewicz) and 'Andrzej' (Benedykt Moszczyński) are missing. They were probably caught somewhere on the way by the Germans, and emissary 'Stanisławski' (Stanisław Ołtarzewski) was mysteriously stopped by some factional intrigue in Budapest."

Indeed soon after this streetcar encounter with "Jan", official orders were given through "Konrad", who informed me that by the end of November, 1943, I would transfer my duties as head of the Information Service to my successor "Wiktor" (Alojzy Męclewski), and begin preparing for the new mission as emissary of the Delegate, various departments, the four coalition parties and the Armia Krajowa to the West.

CHAPTER IV
TELL THE WEST!

The completed mission from London to Poland had offered me a panoramic view of the "Secret State" which I hoped could survive until the end of the war as the substructure for the Polish Government on our freed Polish soil. In December, though, I filled out this enlarged view with a plethora of detailed information in preparation for my return to our Government in exile.

As I once again undertook intensive meetings with the respective political leaders, I saw more clearly than ever that the four years of struggle against impossible odds had taken its toll. With the loss of many top leaders, the level of statesmanship had somewhat declined, although those remaining were all as sincere in their duties as they were brave and kind. While providing me with pertinent information, these men wined and dined me, in hopes of impressing me with their individual achievements.

My own Democratic Party, not a member of the ruling coalition, had suffered the greatest losses since the beginning of Nazi occupation. It had paid a heavy price for its total commitment to the cause of freedom. In 1943, this small party of progressive intelligentsia was dominated by an architect of Jewish origin, Jerzy Makowiecki ("Malicki"), who was also a high-ranking officer in the Home Army's BIP unit. Bitter over not being admitted to the "Big Four", he wished me to perform the miracle of convincing the exiled London establishment of the Democrats' importance to be included in the ruling coalition. This of course, would be nearly impossible, for at that time the Democratic Party was in a state of disarray and factional struggle caused by Communist intrigue.

Only slightly better was the story of the Christian Labor Party. There had been an influx of new political cliques within its ranks, but the prewar leaders with their Catholic ideology intact seemed to retain the upper hand. Aside from their emphasis on the future federation of East-Central Europe, there was little new in their *desiderata.*

The right-wing National-Democratic leadership had been badly affected by Nazi terrorism. By the beginning of 1944, "The Square", as it was known to the introduced, was led by the aging Stanisław Jasiukowicz assisted by his younger lieutenants Władysław Jaworski, Zbigniew Stypułkowski, Father Jan Stępień and Wiktor Trościanko, all able people of good will. Their military units, including some of the heretofore reluctant semi-fascist National Armed Forces (NSZ), had loyally joined with the Home Army. Having witnessed the Holocaust, most of those "Endek" leaders had, as I saw it, sincerely revised their anti-Semitic views, with some even sacrificing their own lives to help the Jews. Such was the case of Stanisław Piasecki, editor of the prewar literary magazine *Poprostu* (Straightforward). The "Endeks" were particularly concerned with German postwar reparation payments to ruined Poland, and strongly advocated that we should regain our historic lands, once inhabited by Western Slavs, by substantially moving the Polish border at Germany's expense. In general they definitely seemed to move for a genuine democratic representation of the middle class and what was left of landed gentry. Their special request to me was that I testify to their full support of Dr. Tadeusz Bielecki, their Party's Chairman in London, who had been kept outside the Coalition governments of Prime Ministers Sikorski and Mikołajczyk respectively.

Numerically strongest during the war was the Peasant Party, known by its cryptonym of the "Triangle." Its charismatic leader was ex-Premier Wincenty Witos, who headed the 1920 Government of National Unity during the Polish-Soviet War, won almost miraculously by the Poles. Afraid of his immense popularity, the Germans now kept him under constant

134

surveillance on his farm in Wierzchosławice. He was thus unable to participate in any underground activities. Their Number Two man, highly respected for his intellect and integrity as former Speaker of the Parliament Maciej Rataj, had been shot by the Nazis together with a Socialist editor Mieczysław Niedziałkowski early in the war in the Palmiry Forest near Warsaw. Next in command was the current Prime Minister in exile Stanisław Mikołajczyk. Like its partners from the Christian Labor Party, the Peasant Party leadership was very suspicious of some A.K. General Staff officers for once being closely linked with the late Marshal Piłsudski and his undemocratic successors. It was mainly for these reasons that the Party was the last Coalition member to subordinate its battalions ("Chłostra") to the central Home Army Command. They claimed that the new Commander-in-Chief General Sosnkowski, should without delay relinquish his constitutional position as Successor to the Presdient of the Polish Republic. Holding two such key jobs seemed to them too much for any one man, and the ghost of the semi-totalitarian "Sanacja" regime of prewar years was heavy on their minds. Influenced by the powerful Peasant Party, the other three coalition components also unequivocally demanded that I convince Gen. Sosnkowski to resign his civil position. This was to be my uneasy mission to President Raczkiewicz and the Government in exile.

When it came to the discussion of Soviet territorial demands at our expense, the "Triangle" leaders, Stanisław Osiecki, Kazimierz Bagiński, Wincenty Bryja, Adam Bień, and Józef Grudziński, were as adamant as others at that session. Their senior, Osiecki, admonished me on the crucial importance for preserving Poland's integrity: "Tell them in England that we the leaders of Polish peasantry cannot understand why our beloved country, which was the first to resist Hitler's aggression, should be forced to give even an inch of its soil to the rapacious Soviet Union, which helped Nazi Germany immensely during the first two years of this terrible war."

Ideologically I felt the closest affinity with the venerable Polish Socialist Party (WRN-PPS), and was looking forward to my farewell conference with its main leaders. Their distinguished looking Chairman, Tomasz Arciszewski ("Stanisław"), presided, but main roles were played by the astute "Bazyli" (Kazimierz Pużak), and the sophisticated politician "Marcin" (Zygmunt Zaremba). There were two more representatives of Party's trade unions and their military units whose names were not revealed to me at the time. Pużak again announced that Arciszewski will soon be sent by some "safe route" to London to replace Sosnkowski as the choice of the Secret State for constitutional succession to the Presidency and spokesman of the Polish working class, which should help us with the British Labour Party and the Second Socialist International in general. Pużak also claimed with conviction that the P.P.S. had more experience in dealing with Russian Communists than any other Party in the world; therefore, I should warn the London Polish establishment that any wishful thinking in that respect may prove to be fatal for our cause.

Zaremba impressed me with his penetrating analysis of the deteriorating international situation between the Allies. He undertook to prepre a thorough analysis of Stalin's designs on Europe in general, and on Poland in particular. They asked me to help "Marcin's" assistant Maria Dziewulska in translating the lengthy document into English before it was microfilmed.[40] As such, it was then to be covered by the inocuous label of a German *Antigrippin* medicine, which I would take with me across occupied Europe to be delivered through the intermediary of the P.P.S. Foreign Affairs Committee to Deputy Premier Clement Attlee of the British Labour Party. Evidently Polish Socialists believed in the brotherhood of the non-Communist European working-class, considering it their duty to share with the Western comrades their great anxiety about Soviet expansionism and totalitarianism. I solemnly promised to do my very best in that aspect of my new mission. Finally, I was asked to assist old "Stanisław" (Arciszewski), whom they all seemed to admire for his glorious revolutionary past and unbending attitude in defense of Social Democracy, when he hopefully reaches London later that year.

136

There were only two men in the Polish underground administration who recommended territorial concession to Russia. One was Roman Knoll, the newly nominated Director of Foreign Affairs. I once again met with Ambassador Knoll at his suburban hideout. His recommendation was that the Polish Government in London, as a gesture of goodwill, propose an exchange of population across some newly established border, leaving Wilno in the north and Lwów in the south together with the Borysław-Drohobycz oil-fields within the Polish State; with all Poles to the east of this new frontier to be relocated westward and all Lithuanians, Byelorussians and Ukrainians to be sent across to the eastern side. I was also told to meet with that able young historian of Jewish origin, Dr. Ludwik Widerszal, a BIP expert on the international situation, who was later assassinated together with the great historian, Professor Marceli Handelsman, and the Democratic Party leader Jerzy Makowiecki, by madly anti-Semitic fringe elements of the military Underground. Somewhat naively, the unassuming Dr. Widerszal asked me to recommend to his friend Adam Tarnowski of the Foreign Ministry in London that we should rely on the British sense of fairplay and not destroy this valuable alliance by our opposition to their pressure on territorial concessions to the Soviet Union. He believed that in order "to remain in the game," some compromise on our part was advisable, but felt the Anglo-Saxons should be trusted with regard to safeguarding essential democracy for postwar Poland. In other words he believed that we should put more emphasis on national independence than on the untouchability of our prewar Eastern borders.

While I was conducting these conferences throughout December 1943, I learned from "Marek" (Ferdynand Arczyński), who belonged to the pro-Soviet splinter of the Democratic Party, that along with the two young Socialists Leszek Raabe and Jan Rosieński, I was to be turned over by the Communists to the Nazis and be eliminated. I immediately passed on the warning to Leszek and went about all the necessary precautions for myself, by changing glasses, hairstyle, clothes and whereabouts. Leszek, unfortunately, did not take the warning seriously enough, for on Christmas Eve I learned that he had disappeared. As he had been not only the heroic commander of the Socialist Fighting Squads (SOB), but at the same time also the Deputy Chief of the entire Civil Struggle (KWC), on my way home I had to alarm his superior, Korboński, of Leszek's arrest to avoid a possible chain reaction.[41]

Christmas Eve of 1943 was an auspicious day for me. Not only could I thank God that I had not been caught by the Gestapo like so many of my friends this past year, but I was able to celebrate this memorable evening with my own father for the first time since my childhood. Zośka, my first cousin, managed to serve the traditional twelve-dish meatless meal. To make this never-to-be-repeated experience last longer, I spent the night with the family at Słupecka Street, before going to Church.

Almost equally exciting was my last New Year's Eve in Warsaw. It started in the afternoon with a semi-business date to find out from an attractive young lady any news about Leszek Raabe. She was our contact point in her little pastry shop. Unfortunately, as told by Leszek's wife, he disappeared like a "stone in water." Nevertheless, we tried to enjoy a popular music concert at a large coffee house in Nowy Świat. The place was packed with young people who likewise did their best to forget about the hard realities of everyday life. Such was the face of wartime Warsaw... I escorted my charming companion to her home, and hurried over by depressing man-rikshaw to the Straszewskis' family villa in faraway Mokotów, where a crowd of close friends gathered to meet the New Year. Since we were all deeply involved with underground activities, our conversation was far from festive merrymaking, as we discussed in earnest the future of our generation. My optimistic predictions during that emotional occasion, stimulated with French champagne, turned out to be desperately wrong. Foolishly playing on Adam Mickiewicz's famous cabalistic prophecy of the significance of "44," I talked about 1944 as the year of deliverance, with Germany being defeated by the Allies and our Poland becoming once more a free nation. Instead, 1944 was to bring the disastrous Warsaw Uprising with the death of the gentle Andrzej Straszewski, who co-hosted that memorable party together with his two sisters Zośka and Margot. Our lively discussions lasted until sunrise, which marked the end of curfew.

The six of us then went for a brisk walk to the Natolin Pavilion overlooking the Vistula Valley, before attending early Mass at the historical Church of Three Crosses in the middle of town to spiritually bring in the New Year. The Church was badly damaged nine months later in the Uprising. That night I made up my mind in selecting at last one of those wonderful A.K. ladies as my sweetheart, but due to circumstances it was to remain a purely platonic relationship, despite its lasting intensity across oceans and continents.

Definitely the most important of the pre-departure briefings was a long conference with the head of the Secret State, the Government's Delegate Jan Stanisław Jankowski, who was soon to be officially appointed as Deputy Prime Minister by the President of the Republic. This calm and well-organized lean man began with a serious admonishment that I am to serve as Poland's Secret Envoy to the free Western world. In addition, he made it clear that besides taking a large amount of mail on microfilm from all eight departments, one of my major tasks was to press the London government for precise instructions for underground authorities regarding their attitude toward the Red Army which was about to enter Polish territories in a major pursuit of the withdrawing German armies. In particular, the "Doctor" requested that they forward without delay a realistic assessment of the recent Teheran Conference of the Big Three, instead of their rosy and overly optimistic propaganda broadcasts. The underground leaders sensed that something was going very wrong between the Soviets and our Anglo-Saxon Allies and they felt they had a right to know the whole truth.

On their part, they decided to send the following instructions to the regional Delegates, who had been the first to meet the Soviet Commanders: "The Deputy Delegate for each prewar province of Eastern Poland shall step forward to greet the respective commanders of the Red Army, bearing the national flag and proper identification, and declare them welcome on Polish territory as 'the Allies of our Allies'. He will assure them of the full cooperation of the local underground administration and Home Army units in the area in the sacred struggle with the common German enemy, expecting the same good will from the Soviet side." The fact that it was to be the Deputy and not the regional Delegate I was to tell only the Prime Minister in London himself.

My next assignment was to tell the West about the increasing terror of German brutal reprisals since mid-October. We needed to secure immediate intervention of our Allies in the form of special bombing raids aimed at stopping Nazi street roundups and mass public shootings of young Polish civilians. For the record, the Delegate complained that the London Ministery of Information, now under Professor Kot, had been remiss in appraising the underground leadership of the real international situation, and had not given them any ideas about Poland's future foreign policy. Moreover, Dr. Stefan Litauer, the head of PAT (Polish Telegraph Agency), i.e. official propaganda, was singled out as being a dangerous Soviet agent in the Government's apparatus. Mr. Jankowski insisted that the latter be removed from his vital post at once. He also blamed the Ministry of Interior under another exiled member of the Peasant Party Władysław Banaczyk, for deteriorating communication with the Secret State and for concentrating on partisan contacts with his power hungry Party. As an example, "Doctor" used the highhanded actions of the Ministry's representative in Budapest, "Fietowicz" (Józef Fietz) who was responsible for blocking the Delegate's envoys' passage to England.

The "Doctor" emphasized his smooth cooperation with the new Commander of the Home Army, General "Bór", and the Chairman of the rump Parliament "Bazyli" of the Polish Socialist Party, working in agreement on major political and structural issues. He very much hoped that similar unity prevails in exile, at least until the hostilities end. Winding up his well conceived instructions, the Delegate asked me to meet

140

with the representative of the Advisory Council of Clergy, which desired to pass its important suggestions to the Vatican through official Polish channels. Finally he emphasized with whole sincerity: "Remember, Jur, when you talk to our people in London or to anyone else in the free world, forget about your youthfulness and low military rank, and do not bow too low to anyone. You are going there with quite a mandate as our spokesman." What a wonderful man, I thought, to head the Secret State in times of trial. But before the end of the war, together with fifteen other leaders of that State, he was kidnaped by Soviet authorities for a show trial in Moscow and never returned to his native country.[42]

Contact with the clandestine Priests' Council was soon established through the Director of the Delegate's Office "Grabowiecki." I met with Father Elter of the Society of Jesus at his office by the Church. After a while, we were interrupted by loud knocking at the front door downstairs. Father Elter, without losing his composure, asked if I were a practicing Roman Catholic and I nodded my affirmation. "Let's go to the Confessional in the chapel quickly," he said, "and if it's the *Gestapo*, I will explain that you came for the Sacrament." Indeed it was the *Gestapo*, but they were not intending to arrest me. They were simply looking for convenient lodgings, to be requisitioned for some of their units withdrawn from the East.

As we resumed our discussion Father Elter, who had prewar experience in Rome, spoke of the need for immediate replacement of the present German bishops with new Polish ones in the regained lands. In the case of the anti-Polish Bishop Karl Maria Splet of Gdańsk (Danzig) for instance, Bishop Tadeusz Zakrzewski was suggested. Father Elter also frankly expressed criticism of the three potential candidates for Cardinal Hlond's position of the incumbent Primate. First of all, it was suggested that the latter, having spent the war years outside Poland, should rather stay in Rome to strengthen the Polish role in the predominantly Italian Curia. The three "contestants" were: Zygmunt Choromański, the overambitious Secretary of the Bishops' Conference in Warsaw; Stanisław Adamski of Katowice, who became very controversial as a

141

result of his giving permission to young Poles in Silesia to serve in the German Army; and finally, Archbishop Józef Gawlina, considered to be more of militaristic character as chief chaplain of the Polish Army in exile. The Council proposed in the first place the learned Father Czesław Falkowski, prewar Chairman of the Theology Department at Wilno University, or secondly, another Professor of the same School, Father Antoni Pawłowski, neither of whom were yet ordained as bishops. Apparently they were both fully immersed in Warsaw underground structures, which made them well aware of actual problems of the suffering population in the country. Father Elter did not mention the future Primate of Poland's Christian Millennium, Stefan Wyszyński, or the future Pope Karol Wojtyła, who was at that time still studying for priesthood in Kraków.

Father Elter placed the strongest emphasis on orderly Church organization under the new Polish administration of the former German dioceses for East Prussia, Gdańsk, Western Pomerania, and Lower Silesia. He was convinced that the Church would have to play a crucial role in the forthcoming reconstruction period. This required a well-organized network approved by the Holy See and saintly prelates with administrative talents. Before I left the Jesuit premises, we prayed together for the success of my mission. I departed feeling encouraged that there was so much foresight and wisdom in the Church of Poland's preparations for the new era, perhaps the most critical in her long history.

My last Warsaw conferences happened to deal with fascinating youth problems. Although I had never joined the Boy Scouts movement in my school days considering it somewhat infantile, I changed my opinion after observing their splendid performance in the underground. Without forgetting about educational and character building goals, they became particularly effective in minor sabotage operations vividly described by Aleksander Kamiński ("Hubert") in his superb story about two real heroes, "Wojtek" and "Czarny", under the title *Stones on the Rampart (Kamienie Na Szaniec)*, the most significant book published in the underground.[43] While winding up my duties in wintry Warsaw I met three times with the high command of these "Gray Rows" (Szare Szeregi) as they humbly called themselves. Three of those remarkable youth leaders impressed me, "Orsza" (Stanisław Broniewski) in particular, their Commander at the time, the main field inspector "Jurwiś" (Jerzy Kozłowski), and the quiet intellectual "Wacek" (Jan Rossman). They remained in my mind as typical models for future young gentlemen.

I was proud to be entrusted by them with carrying a moving appeal "To All British and American Boy Scouts and Girl Guides so that they could better understand the lofty goals for which Polish Scouting so valiantly fought since 1939. Without mincing words my new friends expressed their great anxiety about:

... the danger of an imminent crisis — the loss of confidence in the Anglo-Saxon world. The youth of the subjugated countries in East-Central Europe, and especially in Poland, builds all its hopes on Great Britain and The United States of America. We were fully convinced in the truth and sincerity of ideals proclaimed by the Western Democracies. In particular we believed that the Atlantic Charter and the Four Freedoms of President Roosevelt, though general in character, were the guiding principles in shaping the true goals of this war. Poles have been fighting with you side by side in defense of Christian Democratic values in national and international life, in defense of the human rights of all nations according to the rules of world justice...

The latest examples of shamelessly opportunistic attitudes on the part of the great powers fill our youth with tremendous anxiety for the future...

Those Scout authorities in Poland advised me to bluntly ask their proper counterparts whether they realize that the Western World will have neither the right nor the chance to bring up their next generations on the same principles which are, to this day, the very basis of education for all true Scouts and Girl guides?

For if we ever replace truth and justice by sheer opportunism and moral cowardice it will be impossible to base education on

143

simple truth and justice as expressed in Christ's teachings...

You have to understand that our young people are ready to undergo painful sacrifices, even to face death, but they resent to die in vain. They have to be able to go on trusting that their long fight was not aimless, that all they cherished and loved will not be given up, that the beautiful ideas in which they were brought up in struggle are still holding fast... if the future of the world is to be decided by force and violence, our generation may well be the last one which is ready to fight and die in the defense of principles which form the foundations of the Scout Movement. We wish to point this out to you, feeling that it is both our good right and our duty to do so, that if you permit your nations to choose the easy path of the selfishness and opportunism you will be responsible for ending the Scout Movement in Europe...

Do not talk and think about us, please, as "poor Poland". We need neither pity nor charity. Being on the front lines we do not suffer from any inferiority complex. We do not desire to be admired or pitied. Our only request is that our hardships, toil and struggle for the common cause be properly understood and not wasted...

Such was the powerful message I was to deliver to topmost the representatives of British Scouting through the intermediary of our exiled Scout leaders in London. I was proud to serve as messenger of the finest youth leaders I had ever met. Many of them, the flower of Polish wartime youth, were killed by Germans during the Warsaw Uprising.[44]

Instead of being properly briefed by General "Bór" or his taciturn Chief of Staff "Grzegorz" (Tadeusz Pełczyński), I was told that the Sixth Bureau (BIP), under "Prezes" (Col. Jan Rzepecki), is preparing mail for the General Staff in microfilms to be hidden in a long cigarette holder. I hated the idea because as a non-smoker I had to yellow my fingers and learn to smoke, which did not appeal at all. In addition, I was instructed by "Dołęga" (Stanisław Kauzik), the Director of the Information Department, that a very confidential letter written by him but allegedly approved by General "Bór" and the venerable Socialist "Bazyli" (Pużak) would be given to me at the last moment before the departure when it will be

144

microfilmed and placed in a long German "Kohinoor" pencil. My intuition warned me that I may be used, when "Dołęga" said that the damn pencil should not be seen by anyone other than the pompous Tadeusz Tomaszewski, Chief Financial Controller in London, known to be the Grand Master of the Copernicus Freemasons' Lodge, which was not even recognized by Scottish Rite Anglo-Saxon Freemasonry. Moreover, I was to keep that special mail out of control of the Prime Minister, which was definitely against my oath of loyalty to the Government in Exile and its Delegate in Warsaw. When I raised objections based on my duties as official Emissary, "Dołęga" could hardly hide his annoyance, but thinking me naive persisted in his demands. Without further argument I left, aware that he had placed me in a difficult position. Reluctant to become a part of any partisan intrigue, I trusted in the sound judgement of my immediate supervisor "Konrad", who had no doubts whatever that our boss was taking me for a ride, knowing full well that no mail of the official courier should remain out of the control of proper authorities. "Konrad" advised me to leave the pencil in trustworthy hands, so that it could be handed to the Delegate with a short explanation note after my departure. This was duly arranged, and the pencil, together with a brief letter was left with my cousin, who was to pass it on to "Basia" with my last mail to the Delegate upon hearing of my safe arrival in England.[45]

Technical preparations for my trip were left in the experienced hands of "Zo" (Elżbieta Zawacka), a daring woman paratrooper. Being in charge of clandestine routes through Germany, Austria and neutral Switzerland, she was admired by all of her colleagues not only for her dedication, but primarily for her calm competence. Originally, according to "Malicki" of the Home Army's BIP, I was to be shipped via the newly explored route through the Latvian port of Riga and the Swedish Gotland island in the North Baltic Sea, but at the last moment it was found by the special "Zagroda" transportation outfit that the Nazis cut that exotic link, and it was determined that I should try the shortest way to the West via Berlin and Paris. As to a personal cover story, the same cell under "Marcysia" and "Zo" prepared a set of six documents for me, all under the name of Johann Schultz, allegedly a *Baltendeutscher* born in Estonia. This was to cover my still inadequate German. I was supposed to be a young scientist involved in production of highly secret rocket weapons of which in reality I knew absolutely nothing.

My handy father devised a pair of hollowed out old shoe brushes to hide all microfilms delivered by the Delegate's Office. They included a substantial number of recent death posters which "Basia"had boldly acquired on my request as the best evidence of Nazi brutality. The Socialist letter to the Labour Party was put inconspiciously in the *Antigrippin* vial and delivered on time. At last the A.K. mail came in the rather conspicious cigarette-holder. I tried my best to be in control of all necessary paraphernalia in those final hectic days.

January 20th was my 26th birthday, but in Poland we used to celebrate only name days, so I did not pay much attention to the event. My travel papers were ready and "Zo' instructed me that I should pretend to be working for German authorities on assignment to the famous Levallois optical factory near Paris. At her hideout I was happy to meet another paratrooper colleague, Stanisław Zaborowski, who was commuting quite regularly as a courier between Poland and Switzerland. He appeared especially to explain to me how to behave in German military trains. Too bad this jovial fellow was soon caught in the service and tortured to death by the *Gestapo*. There was also someone else present for my convenience. "Jan" (Tadeusz Jabłoński) was cheerful but hardly noticeable; "Zo" arranged for him to shadow me all the way across Germany and Belgium to Paris. At the end of this evening's rendezvous, "Zo" embraced me warmly in a sisterly farewell, making the sign of the cross over me.

On January 21, 1944, the day before my departure, I had to organize my mail and make some credible excuses for such abrupt disappearance from my small circle of newly acquired friends. I explained to them that I had to spend some time hiding in the mountains until the *Gestapo* relented in their search for me in Warsaw. That night I slept at my cousin's house at Słupecka Street, and talked without inhibitions with my father, who was soon to be killed by some mad SS men in the Sachsenhausen concentration camp in Berlin, to where he was deported during the Warsaw Uprising in August of that year. "Maria Szara" (Gray Mary) finally came from the Deputy Delegate's office with final instructions from the Delegate. The wretched pencil from "Dołęga" had been delivered earlier, and "Basia" brought the latest radio bulletin with news that were not too comforting. Berlin was being bombed day and night by the RAF and Flying Fortresses alternately. I would be in the midst of these raids in less than twelve hours.

Protected by my new Johann Schultz documents, I could disregard the 8 p.m. curfew for the first time in a year, and on the evening of January 22, 1944, I warmly embraced my father, holding him for what would be the last time in our life, and ran to find a horse carriage. As if with a strange voice I called loudly for the cart, and when it arrived I directed it to the *Hauptbahnhof*. It was a new feeling indeed, to pass Grójecka Street and Jerusalem Avenue when no decent Poles were about. I had been instructed to elude the German control at the Central Station by pretending to catch the suburban commuter train and then moving within the building to the international platform for the Berlin train. I noticed many officers and *Gestapo* dignitaries there, as well as my appointed escort "Jan", who seemed not only unperturbed but quite at home in that intimidating crowd. Whenever he passed by me he maintained a blank expression, but finally asked me for the time in German. We were obliged to look as natural as possible because there were so few civilians on the platform. I took the second Berlin train which arrived from the East as per my instructions. It was designated as a *Fronturlauber*, or the vacation train from the front lines.

First, it was necessary to overcome the objections of the woman railroad attendant by raising my voice in anger. "I am a civilian attached to the Army," I heard myself yelling in German. As usual with the Germans, this pressure tactic succeeded. Shortly thereafter, I was standing in the jammed corridor of that train, the air heavy with the smell of sweat and

147

tired soldiers. Luckily, no one seemed the least bit interested in my presence. We finally got underway and left the darkened Warsaw Central Station at about 10 p.m. As I left that truly heroic city wondering when I shall see it again, I could not help but reflect that an insurrection was inevitable. The population was full of hatred after four and one half years of German oppression, and even children were awaiting the first opportunity for revenge. One the other hand, the Germans were exhausted and sensed that Poland was a powder keg. Both Poles and Germans alike knew that the day of reckoning was near at hand.

I was suddenly roused from my thoughts by the duty officer, his chest draped with the tin half-moon badge of his office. Venting his displeasure at a wretched civilian, he shouted, *"Was suchen Sie in dem Fronturlauber?"* Attempting to seem unimportant but sure of myself, I recited my cover story. As he looked down at me, he voiced his contempt by muttering *"Verfluchte Wehrmachtsangehorigen!"* (Damned army hangers on), but let me go without further questioning. Evidently, they had been so instructed. "Zo" really knew what she was doing when she sent me straight into the lion's den.

Feeling more relaxed now that my first confrontation was over, to avoid unnecessary talk with the soldiers I stationed myself next to the smelly toilet. We were all half asleep when the alarm jarred everyone to his senses. The duty officer's sharp voice resounded through the car, *"Zug im Gefahr!"* (train in danger), and immediately the *"Fritzes"* picked up their machine guns and hand grenades. We were now crossing the Kampinos Forest and heading toward Kutno. This was the area in which a Lwów paratrooper friend of mine, "Lawa" (Tadeusz Gaworski), had managed to derail this very Warsaw-Berlin Express just a few days earlier. Recalling his graphic description of the noises made by the dying and wounded did nothing to calm my nerves at this moment, and as I looked around I saw that my German companions were no less frightened as they looked out at the snow-covered tops of the Mazowian pines. Apparently each time a train came through this area they were put on constant alert due to the possible

Home Army attacks. The thought of being killed by my own colleagues did not cheer me up, but somehow we reached Kutno and passed through the Reich frontier without mishap.

As we stopped at the outwardly teutonized Poznań, a sailor from the *Kriegsmarine* insisted on talking to me, but I pretended to be very tired and he eventually fell asleep on my shoulder. Early the next wintry morning, while approaching Berlin, we saw crowds of workers, clerks, and housewives waiting at the suburban stations for a train to the capital, because staying overnight there was not safe due to British bombings. Passing through the monotonous suburbs my eyes hungrily searched for signs of destruction. From Koppenick onward I saw the ever increasing results of continuous air attacks. The night before our arrival Berlin had been struck again, as was evident from the dust rising from piles of rubble. I had to suppress my malicious glee at the sight, while my companions angrily muttered the word *verflucht* throughout the train.

We stopped at the *Schlessischer Bahnhof* in eastern Berlin, and I was soon amidst the crowd on the platform. "Jan" was waiting for me at the exit to inform me in German that our train to Paris would leave at noontime. We left our baggage at the station office, and "Jan" cabled Warsaw through Vienna from the nearby Post Office to let them know that "Truda" had arrived in Berlin. We spent the next four hours wandering through the city taking in the sights of destruction and noting the ambiance of the city. All the houses near the station had had their windows bombed out. The Berlin *Herrenvolk* looked gray and depressed, even compared to the crowds in Warsaw streets. One could not blame them; instead of the glorious victory promised by Goebbels, they endured increasingly heavy bombing as well as grim news from the eastern front. Even more revealing was the scene of destruction at Alexander Platz, the main square in that part of the metropolis. Olive-uniformed Italians, their former Axis parnters, now as POWs, were cleaning the rubble under supervision of Berlin gendarmes. This reverse of fortunes was a welcome sign to our eyes.

149

Near the fresh ruins of the Exchange Building we bought Berlin newspapers and boarded the elevated train to cross the city. "Jan" sat a few benches away and later told me that with my Tyrolian felt hat I looked like a typical well-fed bourgeois Berliner. On the other hand, "Jan" looked to me like a prosperous prewar Warsaw Jew, with his black overcoat and navy blue hat. He was self composed, and moved among the Germans like a VIP, though he spoke German with a strong Slavic accent. Along with the reports and documents he carried between Warsaw and Paris, on the way home he usually managed to smuggle silk stockings and perfume as well. Once we returned to the railroad station, we parted again and boarded separate cars. Since we arrived early, I took a comfortable seat by the window to avoid any talkative Germans, at least on one side. However, on the opposite side was a SS man who decided to entertain me with sentimental family stories and photographs. At least I was rewarded with *Ersatz* chocolate for my attentiveness. This time my train companions were going back to the front lines from their home leaves. It became quite clear to me that deteriorating food supplies, along with nostalgia for home and family were the basic elements of German war fatigue. I also noticed that the *"Heil Hitler!"* greeting was going out of fashion, but I had to join in the general grumbling against the *"Schwein"* Churchill and that "dirty Jew" Roosevelt, responsible for the destruction of the capital city.

The inspecting officer, an arrogant busybody, decided to move me to a special compartment for civilians, but as soon as I saw him leave the train I moved back to my SS man and the others. At least I could understand their not so complicated mentality, and they greeted me quite cordially. My unusual German accent did bother them a little, and I had to explain that, as a Baltic German from Estonia I had learned the language rather late in life. I also felt quite uneasy around a particular middle-aged sergeant who knew that northern part of Europe from prewar days. I told him that due to many sad memories I preferred not to discuss my homeland. They seemed to sympathize, but at this point became even more inquisitive about the purpose of my trip. I tried to be very clever and dropped a few remarks about science and engineering and "those new weapons" as I cast my eyes toward the ommnipresent inscription, *Feind hort mit* (the enemy listens). I could almost hear them thinking to themselves, "Maybe the Fuhrer was right when he promised those clever weapons invented by brilliant minds, which will change the direction of the war and still give victory to the Third Reich."

Although I was hungry and eager to eat *kiełbasa* and other Warsaw delicacies, I waited until my companions went to the dining car for their *Eintopfgericht,* which was a prescribed meal prepared in one pot as decreed by Hitler. I excused myself from joining them with my very real migraine headache. Everything went smoothly until we reached the documents control station at the German-Belgian frontier in Herbesthal that night. The duty officer flashed his light into my eyes as he asked for my travel documents. Purposely, I showed him the weakest *Ausweis* first, at which time the three Germans proceeded to yell at me until they reached the fourth document. From that paper, the commanding officer, convinced of my importance to the Nazi war effort, saluted and wished me *"gute Nacht"*. This trick , I thought, would not have worked with the Soviet NKWD frontier control, whose suspicions are, as a rule, boundless; but luckily I did not have to deal with them at that time. Casually, I asked whether the British bastards were again bombing Berlin, and the officer informed me with a painful expression: "They flew in the direction of Essen." Showing my "official" document which referred to the new weapons research, I assured him that before long we would be calling the whole of London "Adolf Hitler Platz". Again, I felt more confident, having passed this hurdle and used in public the cigrette holder in which I was carrying messages from the Home Army Commander-in-Chief. As my other mail, the *Antigrippin* medicine bottle rested in my right jacket pocket, pasted with Socialist mail to Vice Premier Attlee, and the shoe brushes containing civilian mail from the Delegate's office had already been used in Berlin by my SS companion for a nice shoe shine. Important as all this material was, the main thing was the fact that my head was loaded with all kinds of messages.

At dawn we passed clouds of coal dust in Liege. I felt much happier on friendly Belgian soil, and as my migraine was now gone, I could enjoy the beautiful rock formations of the Meuse Valley, along with the clean towns and charming canyons of the old Ardennes Mountains. I almost felt like a tourist again, and had to constantly remind myself that not even for a second should I forget my cover as a German engineer working for their war industry. I have to admit that these young, though not overly bright men behaved pleasantly. It was hard for me to understand how the very same people could be as cruel and fanatical as what I had witnessed during my year in Poland. We quickly sped through the picturesque Sombre river valley and reached the Charleroi Junction, where most of the soldiers disembarked for trains to northern France and the Channel *"Westwalle"* forts.

The sentimental Polish heart always beats liverlier on French soil, and once again I enjoyed the sights of cheerful coffee bars, with their huge posters advertising various aperitifs, and old church towers where German *feldgrau* uniforms were the only reminders of the war in an otherwise bucolic countryside. At St. Quentin, the rest of my *Wehrmacht* company left the compartment, and after lots of handshaking, they even turned to wave to me from the platform. I could not supress the temptation, and when I was sure the train had started moving again towards Paris, I opened the window and yelled *"Sieg Heil!"* (To our victory). At last, I was alone and could enjoy the captivating sights of France roll by. However, in Compiegne I was again joined by some boring *Luftwaffe* Corporal. This one insisted on talking politics, even though I told him that I liked to nap after lunch. He asked about my views on the end of the war. Once again I recited my phony story about Estonia, Hitler's new weapons and the dire need for military secrecy. "As for the end of the war, my dear", I said "Don't worry, it is not your headache or mine but the *Fuhrer's*. It is his job to make politics and conduct war. Ours is to keep quiet and do our best in fighting the Russians, Americans, Jews and British."

Surprised by my optimism, he asked how long I had been a member of the Party. "Much longer," I said, "than your service for Göring." My fellow traveler looked to be over forty and was rather pessimistic: "We do not have enough forces left to fight Russia. With more troops, we could chase the Bolsheviks out of Europe; but as things stand, I cannot see an end to the war. My children are waiting at home, and already for the second time I could not be with my family for Christmas. They are drafting older and older people, and your *Fuhrer* has to defend the *Fatherland* with children and old men." Obviously, nothing dangerous could happen to me with this disenchanted veteran, but I was truly relieved when the train came into the suburbs of Paris. "Jan" was waiting at the exit of the Gare de l'Est and informed me that this time he had a difficult time at the border station in Herbesthal. They suspected him of smuggling, but finally let him go. We were both happy to be walking toward the Place de l'Opera after such a nerveracking journey across occupied Europe. I noticed immediately that Paris looked very different from the tragic Warsaw we had just left. Here there were no grim posters fortelling mass shootings, and evidently, on Hitler's orders, at least in Paris the Germans had to behave like civilized Europeans rather than like the barbarians they had become in Eastern Europe.

"Jan" told me to wait at the notorious *"Cafe de la Paix"* while he went as a *Reichsdeutscher* to report to the headquarters of the military government and obtain hotel lodgings. After a while, he returned, happy with his assignment to the old Louvois Hotel, where he took me for the night. With some U.S. dollars which were hidden inside my shaving soap we went to a Spanish restaurant on Rue Montmartre. At the door we were met by a friendly maitre d' who knew "Jan" and asked about the situation in Warsaw. It was a typical Paris scene in that cozy little restaurant with its Flamenco dancer, and the only thing spoiling the atmosphere was a fat, drunken German officer at the table next to ours.

Annoyed at hearing our Polish conversation, he kept looking at his watch and finally yelled, *"Raus! 9 Uhr — Polizeistunde, verfluchte Polaken."* (Out! 9 o'clock - damned Polacks!). This created confusion and the Frenchmen at nearby tables became nervous as he continued, shouting that he would kill us unless we go home to bed at once. Suddenly, I remembered that I had seen this man two days before at the Warsaw station. He must have forgotten that he was no longer in Poland where he could bully people in that fashion. Frightened, the *maitre d'* Antonio came over to us, and I advised him to tell the German police at once about this drunken ruffian. Although it was well before the 11:30 curfew, which we were not technically bound to as Germans, we decided to go back to our hotel. As we were leaving, we noticed the motorcycle patrol arriving, and knew that Antonio had taken my advice. By the same token it became obvious that we were not yet in the free world.

After a restful night in the *Nur fur Deutsche"* hotel, we met "Andre" (Andrzej Kopyto-Renan), a student from Silesia who served as Deputy chief of London's 6th Bureau cell in France. He looked very French indeed in his baret, and proved to be most helpful throughout my stay in Paris. First of all he found a decent room for me through a garrulous Monsieur Robin, an *intermediare commercial,* with M. et Mme Lecomte at 7 Ruie de Bac, just across the Seine River from the main entrance of the Louvre Palace. From their top floor windows the white domes of Sacre Coeur could be seen on the horizon. For the French, I now pretended to be a junior British officer who had just escaped from a POW camp in Germany. "Andre" cautioned me not to roam around the streets during my short stay in Paris, and to avoid trouble for myself or my generous hosts. The next day I was visited by the chief of the Paris post of our General Staff, Capt. "Antoni" (Count Skarbek). Taking advantage of the nice weather he took me for a peripatetic discussion at the nearby Tuilleries Park, showing a fine grasp of the international situation. He was recently parachuted from England, and very eager to learn more about conditions in occupied Poland. I was favorably impressed by this young aristocratic cavalryman, fully dedicated to the cause of allied

154

victory. It was hard to anticipate that soon after he was captured by the *Gestapo* and shot by them in Paris.

Out of great hospitality the Lecomtes became a bit overzealous in catering to my "British" tastes, and twice a day they served me a rather raw *Bifstek a l'Anglaise,* which I had to endure in the name of *l'Alliance Cordiale.* However, the half litre of red table wine with each meal was to my liking, with delicious cream puffs for desert. Quickly I gained excessive weight, as my stay proved much longer than anticipated, due to the fact that some British agents had been caught by the omnipresent *Gestapo* in northern France. The secret night landing "elevator service" of Westland Lysander planes near Angers had to be discontinued to my chagrin. Another effort to get me to England without further delay also failed, though London kept demanding my immediate transfer.[46] "Antoni" tried in vain to arrange for my passage with a British submarine from a Normandy coast secret landing place.

For diversion I had French classics from my hosts' library to ponder over and a fluffy cat "Minou" to play with. Finally, they even let me out occasionally to enjoy Paris. One evening I bought a ticket for the second row of the *Folies Bergere* matinee show, only to find that it was not a bright idea, becaue I had to tolerate the German artillery general in formal uniform just next to me. He was quite chummy, making all sorts of vulgar comments about the semi-nude performers. During the intermission he even invited me to join him in watching a rather disgusting performance of Arabian belly dancers. How glad I was to get rid of him after all was over, the entire program being obviously adjusted to accommodate German taste.

My new documents were brought by "Andre" to testify that I was for a change one Georges Hussler, an Alsatian working in Le Mans. In a nearby neighborhood, a Gaullist conspiracy was uncovered when they met at a ground floor retail store, and all present were arrested. My hosts became nervous lest their deaf *concierge* became suspicious of that strange "cousin" on the fourth floor, so another hideout was provided at 39 rue de Grenelle with a delightful elderly couple, the de

Cortas. Before I moved, though, the happy go lucky Monsieur Robin and his lady friend Mme Menard (who claimed to resemble Mona Lisa of the nearby Louvre collection!) insisted on entertaining me with a typical Normandy dinner, which lasted almost four hours. After emptying several bottles of wine, Calvados and Armagnac, my excited host started shouting *"A bas les Boches! Vive l'Angleterre! Vive De Gaulle!"* I tried to calm him, but the good fellow claimed that the whole rue de Grenelle supports *Le General* and as local *chef de la resistance* he is absolutely sure that there are no police informers in the vicinity. The poor guy was arrested a few months later together with my other five French friends when a British paratrooper of high rank was caught by the *Gestapo* using the same three contacts in the left-bank patriotic district of Paris.[47] The de Cortas were cultural people of a different class. Madame, a Catholic activist, had already spent several months in *Gestapo* detention. Listening regularly to BBC broadcasts in the French language, we heard excerpts of Churchill's cynical explanation of the Teheran decisions concerning the selling down the river of Eastern Poland to Stalin's Russia. My hosts reacted with anger that *"cette heroique, pauvre Pologne"* was clearly betrayed by the *perfide Albion* (the perfidious England). It was exceptionally hard for me to pretend that I was a Scot on faked Alsatian papers, not an enraged son of Lwów. It became suddenly obvious to all intelligent Europeans that Poland was sacrificed by her Western Allies to accommodate Soviet expanionist war goals. I tried to remain stoical, however, and even said a few words in defense of British behavior, though it went against my deepest feelings. They had to be masked under the circumstances.

One other time it was equally uneasy to hide that I was not in fact British. Inez, the seductive daughter of the house, proposed that she give me piano lessons if I teach her King's English. As we were reading through a simple story, she asked: *"Mais comment dit-on grenouille en Anglais?"* My mind was blank, I could not remember the wretched word, and mumbled that I was never too strong in zoology. While worrying through the night that my cover story would not hold anymore, I suddenly discovered the proper translation and told the baffled Inez that morning that "of course" it was FROG. Fortunately, she took it as an example of my English sense of humor in kidding young French ladies. Jokes apart, I was increasingly bored and impatient with the prolonged Paris sojourn.

At last, under Polish pressure in London, the local SOE agent agreed to take all of my mail through their secret submarine service, but because of "lack of space" refused to take me as well. Although I resented to part with those well-hidden microfilms, "Antoni" claimed that he received code instructions from England to speed up the mail delivery. I had no choice, and with an aching heart left in his hands that essential part of my mission. The rest was left in my memory. No longer counting on British promises, I decided to cross the Pyrenees to neutral Spain on foot at the earliest opportunity, the way I crossed the Carpathian Mountains from Poland to Hungary at the beginning of the war. "Antoni" concurred with that resolve, and got in touch with a police member of the French resistance and the middle-aged Baroness "Marie Odille de Savenay" from the Lille region. The latter bragged on being in touch with the American agency in Switzerland which dealt with compulsory evacuation of Air Force personnel, who had been shot down in Europe or had managed to escape from POW camps. She undertook to arrange for my trip across the Spanish Frontier to Barcelona along with a couple of American airmen.

After a night journey in a crowded train I reached Toulouse, where she waited for me with another well-dressed woman. They were discussing the opportunity of getting me on a fast "lift service" by a secret flight to England, but nothing ever developed from this idea. I felt somewhat uneasy with these two ladies, as it became apparent from their dragged out conversation that they were interested in sticking their fingers in too many pies. In addition to her alleged involvement with the Americans, "Marie Odille" tried to impress me with her high-level contacts with the British Intelligence, by the way, taking me for one of them. From Toulouse she took me by local train to St. Antonin, a sleepy little town nestled deep in the gorgeous canyon of the Tarn River. In the vicinity there was a *Luftwaffe* base and an aircraft factory. My companion acquired a detailed map of that strategic area infested with the *Maquis*. We met a group of patriotic engineers, and although they were officially working for the German air force, in reality they were willing to help the Allies in any way they could, as they proudly informed me. Impressed as I was with their eagerness to conspire against the Nazis, I resented being introduced to too many true or imaginary resistance leaders as an important figure in British Intelligence.

When it became clear that there would be no "elevator service" to England, I was taken by bus to Montauban where some time ago "Marie Odille" left the British Capt. Tsudoros for the purpose of awaiting clandestine transport to the United Kingdom. On our arrival at that city my lady guide took me to a girls' high school, where the captain was billeted in the apartment of the principal. Her son, a medical student in Troulouse, walked me to a house rented by a Belgian refugee lady and her daughter. Before the war, the former had been private secretary to Camille Huysmans, President of the Second Socialist International whom I met in London. Her husband, the prominent director of a radio network in Brussels was arrested the previous year by the *Gestapo*. Captain Tsudoros as officer of Greek origin, had taken part in the battle of the Dodecanese Islands in the Aegean, and had been captured. He managed to escape from a POW camp in Bavaria, and was attempting to return to his original base in England. We were to be helped by Francois, the son of the principal who had necessary contacts with the Red Spanish smugglers that crossed the frontier between France and Spain regularly. In spite of harsh winter conditions, we both insisted on using their route across the Pyrenees as soon as possible.

On the way back to Toulouse by train, we met two young, strangely dressed and taciturn airmen. As it turned out, they were to be our future American companions on the way to freedom. Our first attempt to cross the high mountain passes failed because our guide Ramon decided that the snow storms were still too heavy and we had to return to our Montauban hideouts. The next time we were more fortunate. Once in Carcassone, we followed Ramon to a rail bus going up the picturesque Aude Valley to the last station, Quillan. I had now become a Scotsman, George Carson, who had escapted from a POW camp. With my Slavic accent this would obviously not hold water with the American airmen, Lieutenants Casey and Goldstein, nor with Capt. Tsudoros, and I had to disclose my true nationality to them. Part of the way to our destination the rail bus broke down, and all of the passengers had to crowd into the next available bus. As the air inside was unbearable with so many people, the four of us climbed on the roof. The two Americans, unable to speak French, could only smile, and it was the Captain and myself who had to do the talking. Here in the South, the local patois was such that my French could easily pass for Parisian.

We were two hours late in getting to Quillan, and quickly took dinner at the terminal restaurant. Ramon informed us that due to a landslide in one of the canyons, the roads were impassable to vehicles and we would have to march through the night. He assured us that the path was smooth and there would be a "luxurious hotel" at our destination. He moved to the front and the rest of us walked in pairs about 200 yards behind the rascal. Now, as we walked, I had the opportunity of learning more about my companions. Sam Goldstein was from a Jewish family in Philadelphia and had to burn his Flying Fortress after it was shot down near Bordeaux, so that the Germans would not get it; and Lieutenant Casey, a Texan also had a similar experience. They decided to call me "Scottie," and kindly helped me carry my baggage.

Ramon had set a fast pace and we were marching some four miles per hour without stopping, on a rising frosty, cold highway. After three hours we insisted on taking a rest, despite Ramon's protests that we were almost there. The snow was getting deeper with each mile and finally after seven hours Ramon allowed us a break on the hay of an abandoned shelter. The cold made it difficult to sleep though, and we realized that the luxurious hotel was a fantasy. After a short pause, we

159

decided to go on to the village we saw hanging on the steep mountainside. "We are here." Ramon exclaimed, as we began to climb to our supposed haven.

Everybody had a moment of crisis on this journey, and the Captain, who was the oldest tired first. He was revived somewhat, though, when Ramon finally brought us to a huge barn where we were served hot milk and a warm meal by the Spaniard who owned the place. There we slept on hay, and had to wait for two days until the weather cleared enough for us to continue our escape. We then moved on quickly to another village some ten miles away. It was snowing most of this leg of the journey, and ultimately we even had to crawl to reach our new residence. This time it was a cold loft and the conditions were abominable, though we did manage to wash and shave. After about five days in this squalor, one of Ramon's friends arrived and we found that we had to return to our previous barn, where we were to meet up with thirty-four other travelers, who to my amazement, all turned out to be Poles. Two were officers from Poland, and a few were escapees from POW camps, but most of them were miners' sons from northeastern France, who were volunteering to join the Polish Army in Scotland. I continued to pretend that I was a British officer though, telling only their commanding officer, Captain Rozwadowski, of my real mission. I was happy to be with Poles once again, because I knew I could rely on their stamina and loyalty. They also made a very good impression on the Americans and Tsudoros.

After two more days of waiting, we prepared ourselves to travel again. Although the storms had died out, the temperature grew colder and with the snow so packed we were able to cross even the highest passes without skis. We finally left our inhospitable village at dusk, like thieves in the night. Once on the road it began to snow again, but this time not so heavily and we passed on in our determination to conquer the Pyrenees and leave *la douce France* for good. This time we had three armed Spanish guides, all of whom had been pig smugglers before the war; and we were treated accordingly.

After six hours of intense marching the poor British captain weakened and fell behind. We had too keep moving fast, being so close to the German *Alpenjaeger* frontiers posts. We even noticed fresh ski tracks and dog prints in our path, which were obviously made by the German border patrols, who were well-trained mountainers and sharpshooters from the Alps. The Spaniards hit the captain with sticks to keep him climbing; not a pleasant sight, but it saved his life in the end.

At dawn we reached a pine grove at the mouth of the narrowing valley and made three fires to keep warm and cook our food. We would be safe doing so at this spot, since the smoke would be dispersed by the snow which covered the pine branches. With the sunrise and warm food came new energy, and our serpentine formation moved on once more.

The path continually grew steeper, and this time my crisis came, as I fell to the end of the line. A couple of the young Poles slowed down to help me and we managed to cross to the next higher range, moving slowly toward the pass which loomed in front of us. I was once again glad that for the most difficult part of the journey I would be with my compatriots, for if anything happened I would be buried by them in the Catholic tradition.

We were now above the timber line and the cold was formidable. From my skiing experience I was aware of the danger of frostbite, and told my companions to wiggle their toes in their shoes to keep up circulation; but it was too late for some. I was growing weaker in the thin air, and asked the young Grabowski, who had come to my aid, not to leave me for a moment. The Spaniards moved farther and farther ahead as I slowed to a snail's pace; Grabowski walked below in the deep snow to keep me on the path. Without his help I do not know if I would have been able to make this part of the journey. When we finally reached the first divide, I slipped a silver cigarette box into his pocket as a measure of my gratitude. I had brought it from Warsaw, in case I was in need of something with which to bribe the Germans. Losing faith that I would indeed endure the remainder of the trip, I told Grabowski in Polish that he should report to Capt. Rozwadowski that "Jur", the underground envoy, could not fulfll his mission, but his mail was in Paris with "Antoni", to be forwarded to the Commander-in-Chief in London.

As the next pass was reached, I was refreshed by the sharp wind and the sight of a massive snow slide. I was still numb with cold, my legs working mechanically and very slowly. Like my companions, I was a climbing automaton. My intense weakness fortunately had passed as the heart became accustomed to the altitude and the additional effort required for these conditions.

The oldest among us was a Jewish doctor from Drohobycz, and his crisis came just a bit further on. Although his backpack was already being carried by someone else, he weakened and fell in the snow while the other forty of us climbed higher. As a new storm started up, the doctor was left behind. While I remembered what "white death" was from rescue missions in the eastern Carpathians, I knew I was not strong enough to turn back to help him, knowing that this could mean the end for me as well.

Since we had passed the German post at night, the Spaniards paid no attention to anyone except themselves, and even though I was proud of every step forward, I realized strongly the inhumanity of our behavior, with the poor doctor still behind us. The situation was particularly difficult since he was the least popular of our group. He was mainly occupied with himself to the exclusion of the rest of the group, and though his loaded pack was carried for him, he would never share a morsel of food as thanks. I was unpleasantly surprised at how he was able to incite shallow anti-Semitism among these young men.

Even though this hapless fellow was disliked, everyone showed concern, and suddenly one of the youngest, who was not properly outfitted for this winter passage, swore an ugly oath and turned back, followed by his friend; "Come on, we'll bring that SOB Jew up to the pass." With that their silhouettes quickly disappeared across the snow.

While they were gone, we reached the highest pass just as the clouds parted, exposing us to our first ray of sun since the beginning of the journey. In about one hour Andre and Piotr

162

returned with the doctor, and though he was as pale as a cadaver, his eyes were shining with joyous gratitude; he had been saved. Everyone was relieved, and now that the group was once again intact, we began to run down the hill, knowing that on the other side of the lake below was a shepherd's shelter that awaited us. Around dusk we finally reached this windowless, nearly flat structure, covered with deep layers of snow. The Spaniards had started a fire and the first arrivals were already resting on the bunks. We made tea using fresh melted snow and ate some bread and butter. It was much too cold to sleep, so we crowded around the fire, breaking up chairs and planks to keep it going.

At dawn, we moved on towards the Spanish side of the Pyrenees, some fifteen miles away, which we had to reach that same night. At this point even the guides confided that this had been the most strenuous passage they had ever made. During one of our breaks, the Spaniards ridiculed the Anglo-Saxons by pointing out the Poles as examples of soldierly perseverance. Nevertheless, we were all aware that these Spaniards had an interest in the survival of these men, for they were highly paid by the British and American consulates in Barcelona for each airman or secret courier they brought through; and for all we knew they were also paid by Polish authorities.

That evening we rested in the depths of a spruce forest. When the fires were arranged, the Poles began to sing and one of the non-commissioned officers, who had escaped from a *Stalag*, accompanied them on his harmonica.

Our remaining passage was easier and the views were spectacular. I never saw so many wild chamois in my life. Before sunset we reached an inhabited valley. Down by the river were railroad tracks, as well as the highway to Spain. We were thus close to the Puigcerda Railroad Station, after having come through the high pass by Mt. Louis, near the state of Andorra. We waited for two trains to pass through, so that during the cover noise made by the second one we could run across the tracks. We needed this noise so barking dogs would not alert any of the frequent German patrols in this border area. We had to remain perfectly silent and not smoke, patiently watching the first train come and go and then, as the second one departed, the Spaniards signaled and we ran like an avalanche, knowing that the range across the valley was the frontier of neutral Spain. We quickly made it across the highway and up the railroad trestle without seeing anyone, carefully crossing the narrow footbridge over the gurgling river. Then with our last breath, we ran through the fields up to the trees on this final crossing. No one was allowed to rest for even a moment, to insure that we would not be seen and betray the crossing area. Exhausted, we once again traversed through deep snow on the steep northern side. Every few minutes someone fell cursing the Germans, French and Spaniards, but we all fell silent as the whistle of a German patrol filled the air. After one more hour of climbing, we finally reached the frontier and saw the cut in the trees marking the limit of Nazi occupied Europe: a sign which to each of us meant something slightly different. For some thirty minutes we walked along the steep slopes, already on the Spanish side, looking for an easy way down. Continuing through this clear moonlit night we saw in the distance the welcoming lights of Spain. Finally at 4 a.m., extremely tired both physically and emotionally, we were led into a barn, hidden behind a large stone building; this sheep stable was our first shelter outside Nazi territory. A Catalonian *senorita* brought us warm vegetable soup and later more clean hay on which to sleep. The lights were kept lit for the sheep which walked among us all night long. Though it was certainly not the grand hotel which had been promised us, we were thankful to God to be there.

The next day we had to remain unseen as Ramon went along to Barcelona to inform the British consul of our crossing, and to return with transportation. Meanwhile, we washed, shaved and bandaged our frostbitten limbs. The Jewish doctor and a veterinarian were kept busy, as everyone had some medical problem, and a few of them very serious. Seventeen-year old Rex from Lille, for example had to have his feet amputated, while another fellow lost a hand—such was the price of their expedition to the Polish Armed Forces in the West.

Word finally came from our Spanish guides that we would rendezvous at a point some three hours away. We arrived at our destination without incident and hid in a row of haystacks to wait for our transport. A spacious, dilapidated truck covered with canvas pulled up. It used to serve the pig smuggling operation, but we had to play the game and laid down next to each other in the back for the twelve-hour bumpy trip to Barcelona. Although the shrewd driver took only back roads, we were halted by a police patrol. Being packed like sardines, we not even need to hold our breath. What a pity it would have been to have struggled so long in the high mountain snow, only to end up sweating out the rest of the war in the Spanish detention camp of Miranda del Ebro! Our driver must have come up with a good story, no doubt due to his pig smuggling savvy, for we were allowed to proceed without a search. Perhaps the fancy looking gendarmes were simply bribed... ·

Once in Barcelona, we were unloaded in an obscure garage and taken by taxi to a third-rate hotel. After an hour or so, representatives from the British consulate arrived, and a chic young lady welcomed me: "Hello, Mr. George Carson, we know about you. You are awaited with great concern in London." At this point I had to part with my Polish compatriots and asked their commanding officer to apologize for my having pretended to be a foreigner. Along with the Americans and the British captain, I was then taken to H.M. Consulate.45

Back in civilization we were able to relax after our recent ordeal and take showers. We were also given a fresh set of decent clothes, as well as temporary faked documents. After two luxurious days with a Catalonian family at a pension in Barcelona, the four of us were taken by official limousine with a Union Jack to the British Embassy in faraway Madrid. From there I was directed to a hotel, where I stayed for an additional three days, while complicated arrangements were being made through a chain of intermediaries for my pass to leave Spain. When these new papers were ready, I became George Vincent, an airman from South Africa, and was given a permit to travel by train through night and day to the Gibraltar frontier. This was my fifth "nationality" in a span of two months. As arranged at the Embassy, I was met at the San Roque Station by a young man in sporty tweeds and typical English cap. He welcomed me with the "How are you, George?" passwords, and then took me across the frontier to a special SOE station for a night in British territory, full of lonely singing troops. The next evening we went to the Gibraltar airport, the same one at which my boss, Gen. Sikorski, had been killed the previous July, and from there I took a confortable Viking plane, though full of military personnel, across Portugal to southern England.

We had been schedulted to arrive at Hendon Airport in London, but a last-minute change by the RAF resulted in that no one awaited me at the landing area, somewhere between Swindon and Bristol. I reported my precarious status to the airport authorities at once, who in turn contacted London. According to new instructions, I was to take the first train out, and smiling to myself I read the posted warnings, "Is your journey really necessary?" My mission had lasted over thirteen months. It was now March 21, 1944.

When I reached the busy Paddington Station, I took one of the old taxicabs to the Rubens Hotel, which outwardly had not changed much. Once again I felt unimportant among the swaggering General Staff bureaucrats, with their medals and stars for behind-the-desk promotions. Everyone looked well groomed and pleased with himself. They saluted each other while clicking their heels in the prewar Polish fashion. It was not easy to convince the gendarms on duty to alert the Sixth Bureau of the General Staff that Lieutenant "Jur", Poland's secret envoy, had just returned to London. I was looked on as a strange intruder, in the same catagory as the notorious loony who called himself the "King of Poland" and had been pestering exiled Polish officers for several years. After the lunch hour I had better luck, when I was finally noticed in the entrance hall by General Kukiel, the great military historian who was serving as Minister of Defense in Prime Minister Mikołajczyk's cabinet. The tiny old gentleman was delighted to see me again, and immediately sent me to the Sixth Bureau on

Belgrave Square, where I was met by Lt. Colonel Michał Protasewicz and his recently promoted deputy, Lt.-Col. Marian Utnik. The former, who was the senior, obviously approved that I had reported first to his department, which had been responsible for my passage across Europe. I promised to provide his bureau with a detailed report of the trip. Without much delay, he took me by car to my civilian superiors in the Ministry of the Interior at Thorny Court, across from the Kensington Palace Gardens. On the way, he assured me that the microfilmed materials forwarded from Paris had arrived safely and were being developed at that moment. I had come just in time to interpret them. Evidently the headquarters had been concerned as to my whereabouts for the last several weeks.

On the steps of the Ministry's newly acquired building I was recognized by some employees, who warned me at once that relations between the two Peasant Party dignitaries, Minister Banaczyk and director of Home Affairs Siudak were not too good. They were accusing one another, not without justification, of insufficient intellectual qualifications. Someone in the group asked me, "How much of Eastern Poland should we give to the Soviet Union to remain in the game?" Suddenly, I felt more lost in Polish London than I had in those wintry Pyrenees. That same evening, Siudak drove me to Prime Minister Mikołajczyk at the latter's spacious Bayswater apartment. It was not easy to organize my thoughts and summarize my report, but one simple issue, that of Polish-Soviet relations stood out in my mind.

Mikołajczyk had become much more self-confident, having been purposefully described by the *London Times* and British high officials as the "only providential Polish statesman ready for compromise with Stalin." He abruptly asked me, "Why are they, in Poland, so unbending regarding Soviet territorial claims?" Remembering Delegate Jankowski's advice, I retorted, "They see no reason whatever why Poland, who stood alone against German aggression in 1939, should pay any price to Russia, Hitler's accomplice until 1941. The Underground State as a whole, together with the new Council of National Unity (Rada Jedności), the Home Army's Supreme Command, and your own Peasant Party are definitely against any territorial concessions." Mikołajczyk prodded me further: "Don't they realize what kind of pressure is exerted on me by the Churchill Government and even by the otherwise suave Anthony Eden?" "How can they know?" I replied. "As the last emissary from our London government over a year ago, I carried a very optimistic assessment of Poland's position in light of Roosevelt's promises." Mkołajczyk hastened to respond and said, "This situation has greatly changed due to Russia's successes on the Eastern front, and the next emissary, Dr. Józef Retinger, is on his way to explain to the underground leaders the dire need for Polish conscessions. I was under British pressure to send this controversial man as your successor, although I do have some doubts about his loyalty. But how do you explain the far from realistic stance of the underground leadership?" I answered without hesitation:

They consider it their primary duty to supply the Government in Exile with strong arguments on behalf of the Polish cause by their everyday efforts. When I left Warsaw they were still deeply convinced that you, over here, are proceeding according to the well known original war goals, consistent with our raison d'etat. *But all of them, including your own Peasant Party, complain about insufficient communication from London, for which the Ministers of Information and the Interior are mainly resposible. For instance, it was not until I arrived in Paris in February, that I heard the unambiguous statement made by Churchill after Teheran, which contradicts the reassuring evaluation presented, Mr. Prime Minister, in your own radio speech.*

I then went on to report on the divergent views in the Underground. "Besides the small communist group of PPR and its new satellite, RPPS (Workers' Polish Socialist Party), only two men of note expressed opinions differing from the majority. The director of the Department of Foreign Affairs, Roman Knoll, recommended the exchange of Poles for Ukrainians and Byelorussians across a new demarcation line which would leave Lwów, Wilno and the Borysław oil fields in Polish hands. Dr. Widerszal of the Home Army's BIP staff, on the other hand, held that we should place our total trust in British foreign policy and accept their advice on Polish-Russian frontiers."

Finding insufficient support for his conciliatory policy in my report from the Polish underground, the Prime Minsiter concluded our first conference with the reassurance that he would do his best to save Wilno and Lwów. But, anticipating an Anglo-Saxon war against Russia within twenty to thirty years, he was in the meantime determined to show a willingness to compromise with Moscow in order to save as much of Poland as possible from sovietization and biological annihilation. "It is therefore imperative that, in the face of the increasing pressure form the Big Three, we show good will toward our powerful eastern neighbor in order to remain in the game," he concluded.

I was shocked. The unyielding stand of the underground leaders seemed to me more realistic than Mikołajczyk's poker game with Churchill, Roosevelt and Stalin. Nevertheless, I made a last, bold attempt, purely on my own initiative. "Won't you consider parachuting with me to meet on our own soil the entering Red Army as Prime Minister of the legal Polish Government?" He demured, though much later he did prove great personal courage by opposing the Communists in the 1945-1948 period, after he had returned via Moscow to liberated Poland, as leader of the anti-Communist opposition. It was now very late, however, and we finally shook hands in a businesslike farewell. Driving with Siudak to his distant apartment in Mill Hill, and completely exhausted by all that had happened that day, I watched the dawn reveal the fresh, green leaves of London's early spring.

Following that first visit with the Premier, I began a long series of reporting conferences with the not too bright Minister of the Interior, Władysław Banaczyk. He was quite chummy, and without even knowing the details of my experiences, assured me that he would personally see to it that I receive the highest Polish war decoration, *Virtuti Militari*. However, I would first have to submit my own application, listing "a few heroic deeds." It seemed absurd to me and I told him,

169

exaggerating somewhat. "Most of the time I was scared to death. I would have to write a whole book, not just an application, about the thrilling everyday events of those thirteen most important months in my life." He replied matter-of-factly. "Then we would not have sufficient evidence for awarding you the Cross." In vernacular Polish the word "cross" also means "spine", so I responded, "Thank God I returned with my own 'cross' intact." So it happened that, because of my big mouth, I am the only Polish emissary not to have been awarded that most precious blue-black ribbon. Perhaps someone in the next century will consider this account as a belated fulfillment of Banaczyk's tasteless request.[48]

The President of the Republic Władysław Raczkiewicz was informed at once of my arrival, and he graciously invited me for lunch at a secluded British club in Mayfair, where by chance we met Churchill's right hand man, General Hastings Ismay, who was polite but noncommittal.[49] While being driven back to the Ministry of the Interior, I confided to the President two sensitive requests from the underground. The first had to do with their demand that Dr. Stefan Litauer be immediately removed from office, because they strongly suspected him of being a Soviet agent. Despite the remonstrances of Litauer's boss, Professor Kot, President Raczkiewicz fully shared the suspicions of Warsaw leaders and promised to support my mission in that respect. The second, more delicate matter had to do with the dual designation of the President's close political associate, Gen. Sosnkowski, as his constitutional successor, in addition to his position as the Commander-in-Chief of the Polish Armed Forces. Party leaders at home requested that the General resign from the "Vice-Presidency". Though he was highly respected for his analytical intelligence and military virtues, he was suspect for his prewar affiliation with the anti-democratic "Sanacja" establishment, and should not be in the position of holding so much power. The underground leaders were planning to appoint Tomasz Arciszewski, the veteran Polish Socialist leader, and were soon to try to send him to London. The President seemed to be aware of the problem, but confessed that he could not do much until the new

170

candidate actually arrived, though he did comment favorably on the selection.

I anticipated to be called in to report to General Sosnkowski. Indeed the rich material from the BIP, brought in that cigarette holder (now preserved in the General Sikorski Historical Institute in London), had already been developed, decoded, and read by the General Staff. But the request which I had conveyed for removing the very touchy General from his purely political position as successor to the President had enraged a number of his sycophantic assistants, and for the time being must have antagonized him as well. Consequently, I was barred from seeing him. The Commander-in-Chief himself was a fine erudite gentleman, frequently out of town for important military inspections. Considered by the fanatics who surrounded Sosnkowski as "General Sikorski's man", I was thus neither admitted to Sikorski's successor nor promoted to Captain from Lieutenant upon completion of my assignment. I approached one of the junior officers of the "in" group to explain that such a one-step promotion would greatly facilitate my forthcoming lecture tour of His Majesty's Armed Forces. According to British tradition, it is only from the rank of Captain that an officer may carry the lifetime name. He replied that as too close a friend he could not push such an action on my behalf, though within a matter of weeks he showed fewer scruples about accepting his own promotion for loyal bureaucratic performance in recruiting prospective paratroopers.

The general atmosphere of Polish London obviously had deteriorated during my absence. Despite his shortcomings, the late Gen. Sikorski had indeed been the undisputable leader of the free Poles, the last of that category during World War II. I also realized that though the main center of Allied operations was still in London, Churchill no longer called the first shots. Britain was now being overshadowed by Washington and Moscow, whose actual roles in defeating both Germany and Japan had tremendously increased, while England had exhausted her own resources during this long struggle. Regardless of that obvious shift in importance in the interallied relationship, our ultimate Polish goals and the duties of my fighting generation remained unchanged, although they now had to be carried on differently in more adverse circumstances.

About one month after my arrival in London came the first secret night landing of a British plane, a Dakota, bringing new envoys straight from occupied Poland. This group included: Zygmunt Berezowski, aging Secretary General of the National Party; "Stanisławski", (Stanisław Ołtarzewski), personal envoy of Delegate Jankowski who had originally been sent before me but was stranded in Budapest; General "Tabor" (Stanisław Tatar), Operational Chief of the Home Army; Lieutenant Colonel "Hańcza" (Marian Dorotycz-Malewicz), Chief of "Import", who took care of the reception of parachuted weapons and people; and the brightest of them, the eloquent Lt. "Dowmunt" (Bohdan Sałaciński), from the BIP. Their journey had taken only a few hours as compared to my two months of hardship; but I was not jealous at all of their much faster trip to England. We badly needed such representatives from the Polish underground in this wavering London scene, and each new envoy who came intimately knowing the Polish home situation could more adequately reflect the needs of the Polish nation.

Prof. Kot, though unhappy with the crticism of his Ministry I had conveyed from Poland, kindly invited me for a Sunday stroll through the blooming Kew Gardens, along with his wife and my prewar friend, Franciszek Wilk, who was now secretary of the National Council. Kot remained calm until I mentioned the Litauer case, at which point his unpleasant sarcasm came to the fore: "As Minister of Information, I am certainly aware that Litauer is a Soviet agent, but knowing that much, I prefer to control him in my own way." Unhappy with this machiavellian response from the otherwise likeable scholar, I repeated the demand by the underground authorities that Litauer immediately be dismissed from his position as head of wartime propaganda.

My role in informing the Western public of the plight of Poland started with a press conference arranged by Litauer's

172

Polish Telegraph Agency (PAT). Two American war correspondents and representatives from the Swedish and Swiss press were present. At once they asked about the underground's attitude to the Red Army entering Poland from the east. I responded by telling them of the strategy formulated jointly by Delegate Jankowski along with General Bór-Komorowski, the Home Army Commander, and the clandestine Council for National Unity headed by Pużak. It consisted of appointed regional representatives of central underground authorities to meet the commanding officer of Red Army units with Red and White Polish flag in hand, they would welcome the "allies of our allies" to the Polish territory and express both hope and promise for effective cooperation in the struggle against the common enemy. The main thrust of my press statement, however, was a passionate plea for more weapons to be parachuted into Poland.

Early next morning I was called by an excited Stanisław Paprocki, of the Ministry of the Interior, who told me that his wife had just heard on the BBC Polish morning program, that emissary "Jur" appealed to the entire Polish underground to welcome with Polish flags the Red Army and to join forces under Soviet command. This vicious interpretation of my message also appeared in the *Polish Daily*[40] In a flash, I called the amiable director of the BBC Polish section, Karol Wagner, and asked him to stop the dangerous nonsense of completely twisting the meaning of my words, which in this case sounded like prodding that the Polish underground was to come completely out into the open regardless of the risks involved. Mr. Wagner, an unusually scrupulous gentleman, explained that in his absence, one of the night editors had received and immediate broadcasted the statement, attributed to me from PAT. He assured me that this program would not be repeated.[51] Unfortunately, the implication of an enthusiastic reception of the Red Army had already been made. General Bór, doubting my complicity in this distorted report, sent a cable demanding punishment of the culprits.[52] It should be noted that the American, Swedish and Swiss press reported my statements without distortion. In addition to their intent to

173

provoke, the villains at our Ministry of Information also endangered the personal safety of my family in Warsaw. Contrary to all the rules of conspiracy, my real name had been disclosed by PAT officials, and to this day, I still wonder to what extent the later deportation of my poor father, and his subsequent death, could be linked with PAT's indiscretion.

Professor Kot nominated a well known opportunist Mr. "X" to investigate and concluded that Litauer and his Deputy Director Mieczysław Obarski had accurately reported my statements at the press conference, and that I was lying. Knowing how inconsiderate some of the London bureaucrats were, I settled on the most direct approach in dealing with the situation. I publically slapped the culprit in the face as he went down on his knees, to apologize for his false report. Another frightened journalist, Jan Meysztowicz, witnessing this confrontation, ran to warn Litauer as soon as I asked of his whereabouts, and he was escorted down the back stairs before I could administer my version of justice to him. Dr. Kot was enraged by my handling of the situation and spread the word that my hard experiences in Poland evidently affected my mental balance. I responded by telling a mutual friend that Professor Kot should also be careful, for if what he said was true, my condition might lead me to attack him as well. The tension was finally diffused when President Raczkiewicz intervened by firing Litauer, who, after all openly collaborated with the Soviet officials.[53]

Kot was also critical of a speech I gave at a large meeting of the Association of the Eastern Lands of Poland. In accordance with my instructions from Poland, as well as a personal attachment to my native city, I made a very strong plea for the unity of the home and emigre forces in denying Soviet appropriation of those definitely non-Russian territories. Apparently, Kot and Mikołajczyk had already made up their minds to cede the eastern half of Poland to Russia, yielding to pressure from Anglo-Saxon leaders. As a result, for my loyal adherence to the underground's policies, I paid with the cancellation of my upcoming trip to America, which had been suggested by Ambassador Jan Ciechanowski at the instigation of Jan Karski. The latter had fruitfully spent one busy year lecturing in America, and had also been the guest of President and Mrs. Roosevelt. His revealing book, *Story of a Secret State*, with a generous assessment of Jerzy "Jur's" role was then about to be published.[54] Concerned about American ignorance of Eastern European affairs, he wanted me to provide a sequel to his thrilling speaking engagements, and by writing my own account of Poland's struggle for survival. However, another representative of the Polish underground, General "Tabor" (Tatar), accompanied Premier Mikołajczyk on that trip to Washington instead of me. Only a few of us knew at the time that this otherwise brave man had actually been sent abroad by Underground authorities because they wished to be rid of a person with his pro-Soviet tendencies. Courageous as he was, Gen. Tatar was thus definitely not a political spokesman for the underground. In London, however, he had become a convenient echo of Mikołajczyk's policy of surrender. So it was that my own written account of the strife-torn Polish Secret State had to be postponed for many years.

Meanwhile, I was called before the Government Committee on Home Affairs to give a full report of my mission. For the most part, I addressed the same men who had dispatched me to Poland some fourteen months earlier. At this time, I was also invited by Judge Franciszek Wójcicki, to speak before the National Council and answer their numerous questions, including those of Dr. Isaac Schwarzbart about the Jewish situation. They all treated me with respect and courtesy, for which I was very grateful, and in return I tried, as faithfully as possible, to render the feelings and views of the underground leaders.[55]

The fate of the Polish Socialist Party's letter to Clement Attlee and the British Labour Party was rather peculiar. It had reached PPS authorities, but as I was later informed by Adam Ciołkosz, due to the vanity of Vice Premier Kwapiński, the specific recommendations of underground leaders were disregarded, especially the one which stated that I should personally go to Attlee and give him first hand interpretations.[56] Instead, they rushed ahead without me as an

175

eyewitness, and were thus less effective. However, I did have a good session at Stratton House with the Foreign Committee of the PPS, among whom I sensed a growing split between those who remained faithful to their adamant comrades inside Poland and those who saw themselves as the "wiser" advocates of the reconciliation with the Communists.

One of the latter group, the dwarfish Jan Stańczyk, Minister of Labor and Social Welfare, left the debriefing session early, but insisted that I visit him at his Melvyn House apartment in Chelsea later that night, so that he could be "inspired" by my report on the eve of his departure for New York. Tired as I was, I went to see him at about 10 p.m., having been warned by his neighbor, Kwapiński, that I should not trust the "scoundrel." Stańczyk was very hospitable, receiving me in his long red robe, and excitedly explained how he would finally heal the breach in the United States labor front. He had reserved a large suite at the Waldorf Astoria and would first invite William Green, President of the American Federation of Labor, for a drink. The next day, the same privilege would be extended to Phillip Murray, President of the Congress of Industrial Organizations. As a former Polish miner and trade unionist, he would then appeal to these two American "comrades" that they should be ashamed to keep the two organizations separate. On the third day he would invite them both for dinner and could thus preside over the unification of the two factions. He gave me no chance whatsoever to "inspire" him with my reports from the underground labor leaders. Anxious to catch the last underground train, I could only briefly comment that, that if Green and Murray were ready for unification, they could manage it without his mediation. It was not a nice way to speak to a "statesman", but I was fed up with his egocentric self-importance.

Ciołkosz and his dedicated staff at Liberty Publications did their best to include me in their campaign to inform the public of events in Poland. Similarly, the British Department of the Polish Ministry of Information and Documentation used me as a public speaker for the growing network of Anglo-Polish and Scottish-Polish societies. From the British viewpoint, perhaps the most important was my debriefing luncheon session at Chatham House with some twenty inquisitive members of the Royal Institute of Foreign Affairs. They were all well-informed people, but evidently without sufficient influence on the Cabinet level. I also enjoyed a night conference at the Euston Square headquarters of British Quakers. Though fundamentally pacifist, The Society of Friends were, at least, deeply concerned about humanitarian aspects of postwar reconstruction including the Soviet Zone. Anybody who wished to seriously listen to my message seemed important as the target of my "Tell the West" mission... Before long, I was approached by the British Ministry of Defense to become an official lecturer, touring their Armed Froces with a talk on the achievements of the Polish underground movement. I repeated my speech so many times in one day on the ships at the Rosyth naval shipyard that were preparing for departure for the Pacific War Zone, that I lost my voice.

Important seemed to be my discussions with the specialists of the British Foreign Office, McLaren, Osborn and Winch of the Political Intelligence Department. They were trying to squeeze as much information out of me as possible. Inviting me to their private homes, they asked numerous questions about the attitude of Poles to Russians, the Poles' readiness to give up eastern Poland, and their attitude toward conciliation with the Communists. These men obviously wanted to get a true picture of the complex situation for their superiors.[57]

However, due to the new circumstances of the London-Moscow war alliance, unlike my predecessors Karski and Nowak, I was not admitted to the VIPs of the British Cabinet, and had to do my best instead to disseminate fresh information on Poland's struggle through the media with the help of friendly members of the Parliament. The spring of 1944 witnessed a vicious anti-Polish campaign, launched by some pro-Communist Jewish circles. They accused the Polish Army in the West of rabid anti-Semitism and many Jewish soldiers who had been saved in General Anders' mass exodus from the Soviet Union were allowed to desert in British controlled Palestine, among them Corporal Cadet Menachim Begin. Soon the free world press was repleted with false accusations of fighting Poles, and General Kukiel, the Minister of Defense, had his hands full. I was asked by Prof. Kot to meet with several of those anti-Polish members of the Parliament. The two who appeared for the meeting were Thomas Driberg and George Strauss, while Mr. Mack preferred to avoid me. My strongest line of approach in such cases was to express serious doubt as to whether thousands of Polish families, including my own in Warsaw, would continue risking their lives to hide Jews if the harmful anti-Polish campaign on the part of some Jewish members of Parliament continued. I had a particularly difficult time with Driberg, who later openly joined the Communist Party. His mind was completely closed, being less interested in saving Jewish lives in Poland, than in persisting in a sort of vendetta against anti-Soviet Poland. However, George Strauss and I became friends, and he introduced me to Aneurin Bevan, the towering Welsh figure in the Parliamentary Labour Party and fiery editor of the *Tribune*.

With growing Anglo-Saxon pressure on exiled leaders for concession to Russia and the possibility of a political split in our ranks, suspicion was mounting that Premier Mikołajczyk, with the backing of his exiled Peasant Party and some of his Cabinet ministers might surrender, retreating from initial Polish war goals. As instructed by Warsaw leaders, I sided with those who were adamant in their uncompromising stand of Poland's independence and territorial integrity. We opposed those, both in the civil service and the military, who were already to bow to foreign pressures. A two-pronged semi-conspiracy developed in Great Britain, emulating the highly admired underground movement in occupied Poland. Career officers of the younger generation created the "Sovereignty and the Armed Forces" (N.I.W.), while patriotic civilians of my generation formed the nucleus of the future Polish Freedom Movement "Independence and Democracy" (NiD).

To counteract propaganda fed by the Soviet Union to the western media that our underground movement was ineffective, operation "Jula" was coordinated between Warsaw and London. The stunning result was the simultaneous demolition of several railway bridges on the key East-West railroads in Poland on April 4, 1944.[58] To congratulate the legal Polish authorities in London for such a successful operation, Lord Selborne, the elderly Minister of Economic Warfare in charge of subversion, hosted a reception for our Premier, Commander-in-Chief, and recent envoys from the Polish underground at his country residence. Prime Minister Mikołajczyk invited me to attend the affair with him, and it was then that I realized the personality clash between the Prime Minister and Gen. Sosnkowski was escalating into a major conflict.

On the way back to London, Mikołajczyk confided that everything must be done to get rid of Sosnkowski as Commander-in-Chief, because the British claimed that they could not deal with that stubborn anti-Soviet figure. I tried to impress Mikołajczyk with the importance of unity among the Polish leadership in exile, but he seemed determined to make Sosnkowski the scapegoat for the Polish exiled government's deteriorating relations with Allied leaders.

In the meantime, various people were coming up with ideas on how to best use my services as a public speaker. Over a pleasant dinner, I was asked by a city banker, Mr. Andrews, to give a talk on May 3rd, Polish National Day, at the recently opened Allied Circle. As chairman of that planned homage to Poland, he had one reservation, however, that I do not attack the Soviet Union or even use the word "Russia". I had strong doubts whether, under such restrictions, I could honor his request, and told the old man bluntly that all through my war experiences I had thought we were fighting for freedom of expression in order to establish democratic institutions. Rebecca West, Andrew's wife and a prominent writer, took advantage of her husband's absence from the table and advised me to accept the conditions as far as my speech was concerned. She assured me that she would organize pointed questions on the subject of Soviet aggression. Having just read her fascinating book on Yugoslavia's resistance, *Black Lamb and Gray Falcon*, I trusted her promise. My trust was rewarded when several people, among them a Polish American WAC,

179

bombarded me with questions on Soviet-Polish relations, including the taboo issue of the Katyń Forest massacre of Polish officers. Great Britain was, after all, still a free country!

The young barrister Harold Dunkerley, of the Liberal Party, became interested in my story and invited me to dinner the evening of the day in mid-May I was to move from Gustaw and Patricia Gotesmans' flat at Shepherd Bush into a lovely house at 12 Stanhope Gardens in Kensington. Since I had to hurry to meet him at his Temple office, I deposited my belongings in the basement of my new rented lodgings without unpacking. When I returned at night after the "V One" bombing attack I was flabbergasted that the house had virtually disappeared, hit by one of the rockets. Doubly lucky, I found that my suitcases did surive admidst the rubble. Our charming Foreign Minister, Tadeusz Romer, was wounded in his nearby residence during the same raid. Even in London we were not quite out of the woods yet. Judge Korboński, brother of my Warsaw friend, died in a hospital as result of another bombing just after my visit at his bedside. I saw Mr. Romer with his head bandaged in the Prime Minister's office, and was told by him that I need not travel to Rome to complete my special mission for the Polish clergy. Their requests would instead be delivered by our Ambassador in the Vatican, Dr. Juliusz Papee. According to Romer, there was a fairly good chance for implementation of those *desiderata* with the aid of Monsignor Montini, one of the Undersecretaries of State in the Roman Curia (the future Pope Paul VI), who was already known to be well disposed toward our tormented country. I was disappointed with the decision of our Foreign Office, being particularly eager to visit my family serving under General Anders in Italy. Basking in the glory of the Monte Cassino capture, our Second Army Corps was about to move northward and I was counting on meeting my mother, stepfather and half-brother in the Cassamassima Hospital near Bari.

My brother Jaś, an eighteen year old cadet Officer, was determined to earn the famous *Virtuti Militari* Cross, and indeed did so with his foolish bravery. Having taken a Nazi bunker by tossing hand grenades through a narrow window, he jumped ahead to repeat the crazy performance. But the ploy did not work as well again, and he was left bleeding heavily on the steep slope of the ravine. Thanks to the assistance of another wounded soldier from Lwów, Jaś was taken on time to the first medical aid post, where the doctors recommended immediate amputation of his left arm. My stubborn brother insisted, however, that such a major operation could only be performed by his father. The latter saved his arm miraculously, and our mother, who worked as a nurse, had the unique opportunity to spoil the young hero, before sending him off for full recovery to Scotland.[59]

My busy lecture schedule followed in the footsteps of Jan Nowak's excellence performances. Like Jan Karski before him, Nowak was demonstrating his amazing talents in the public relations field on behalf of the Polish cause. I was told for instance by Mrs. Beaty of the Chester Anglo-Polish Society that never before had they heard an equally forceful speaker. He recommended me more than once to various organizers of British-Polish friendship associations. We were also asked to appear together before the Polish exiled community in London, under the auspices of the Journalists Union at the "Polish Heart" (Ognisko Polskie) on June 13th in Belgrave Square. Speaking under the chairmanship of the witty writer Zygmunt Nowakowski, a member of the National Council, we decided to strongly emphasize the dire need for national unity and total devotion in the freedom struggle, instead of dissipating our potential strength with personal intrigues and irrelevant party squabbles. We were both enthusiastically applauded by the elite of "London Poles" as we laid out our message on behalf of all those who sent us from fighting Poland, and the organizers later entertained us at a lively dinner in the White Eagle Club in Knightsbridge. We were lavishly praised for our well orchestrated oratorical performance but could not help wondering how long they would remember our appeal for being in tune with our comrades-in-arms at home?

Nowak and I had a lively discussion with the Honorable Arthur Greenwood M.P., Parliamentary Chairman of the

Labour Party, famous for his September 1939 support of Poland's lonely defense against the Nazi *Blitzkrieg*. I had met that moderate leader of the British working class a few years earlier, and had always been truly impressed by his sincere friendship for Poland. Again, he accepted without fussing my invitation to the Brown Hotel for afternoon tea, and openly criticized Churchill's new policy of accommodating Stalin. He told us how much he disliked the Prime Minister's high handed *modus operandi*, which caused his resignation from the Coalition War Cabinet.[60] Soon after, Nowak was called for duty as our Commander-in-Chief's special envoy to Warsaw.

After an emotionally exhausting round of reports and lectures all over the island, I badly needed complete rest, having none for over a year. So, early in July, I gladly accepted a non-business invitation to a peaceful Devonshire farm near the town of Exford. Fully relaxing with a kind and uncomplicated English family in the rolling countryside, I enjoyed building a dike across a brook, which was reminiscent of my boyhood vacations in Zakopane. But prescribed rest did not last long because the long expected news of the Normandy invasion reached us one day in these Arcadian surroundings.

Rushing back to London, I was fortunate to encounter our splendid First Armored Division under the legendary General Stanisław Maczek. This was the most competent unit I had ever seen, which made me somewhat jealous that I could not join those zealous colleagues of mine, who had come as volunteers from all over the world and had prepared for years to proudly participate in the forthcoming liberation of the European continent. After a rescheduled lecture at the British scientific war research center in Farnham, I managed to spend a few hours with my former anti-aircraft artillery regiment in Evshott near the Aldershot War College.[61] Lt.-Col. Olgierd Eminowicz wanted me back as his regiment's education officer for the "crusade," but my duty now lay with the Ministry of the Interior as prospective courier to occupied Warsaw, although I could not disclose this to my friends. They kept asking me about my last mission to Poland and the whereabouts of other members of the unit who had left with me in 1941. The next day I had to report at Thorny Court, and thus bade farewell to those dear people with whom I wanted to be when their finest hour struck at last.

I arrived back in London, only to pack up for a series of lectures in Scotland, my favorite part of the British Isles, which had been arranged by the British Division of the Polish Ministry of Information. At one of my first press interviews, I was asked an embarrassing question. An impertinent reporter for the *Glasgow Bulletin*, Mary Crawford, inquired how, in view of grave food shortages in Poland, I could return so fat. "Every single meal," I retorted, "I considered as perhaps the last one in my life." We became close friends after this bit of repartee, and she later married my brother. I was kept busy that whole summer lecturing to the British Armed Forces, Polish-English Friendship Societies, Quakers, Trade Unions, numerous Rotary Clubs and other similar groups all over the island. Some days I had to speak twice, and by the end of July, I had logged some fifty speeches in English and at least twenty in Polish. The last tour of the places where I had been stationed in 1940 I was able to make in the company of Jaś, who had just arrived, all smiles, from the Italian front, his arm still in a sling.

Another important arrival was to affect my life at this point. Just before the outbreak of the Warsaw Uprising, the British were able to land one of their Dakota planes at a clandestine landing spot in southern Poland to pick up a group of underground leaders, including Tomasz Arciszewski, Dr. Retinger, and an intelligence officer who was bringing essential parts for one of the V-1 engines.[62] I was particularly excited to meet "Stanisław" (Arciszewski) at a small gathering organized by Adam Ciołkosz, at the offices of his Liberty Publications at Knightsbridge. The old man had been disignated by the Underground Council of National Unity as constitutional successor to the Presidency of the Republic, to replace General Sosnkowski, who was conspicuously absent from London at the outbreak of the Uprising, having spent this period on the battlefront in Italy with General Anders. Arciszewski shook my hand firmly, remembering our January meeting in Warsaw.

In the meantime, I was able to fulfill the last of my Warsaw tasks, the publication of the thrilling underground text *Stones on the Rampart; The Story of Two Lads in the Polish Underground Movement* (With a foreword by Percy Hugh Beverley Lyon, M.A., Headmaster of Rugby School), by "J. Górecki". To make the arrangements, I visited the headquarters of World Scouting, and delivered the text to Lady Baden-Powell, the widow of the Association's famous founder. I was still quite busy with American and British journalists who were clamoring for additional news features on the Polish underground. My first such interview on April 12, 1944, appeared in the London daily *News Chronicle*. It had been conducted by the ranking commentator, Vernon Bartlett, later an independent Member of Parliament. The deputy editor of *Time and Tide*, Freda Bruce-Lockhart, became deeply involved in Polish matters as well, and suggested that I periodically pass on pertinent material to her, not only on the Polish war performance, but also on our problems with the Soviet Union. She had a green light from her editor Lady Rhonda, to publish regular pieces reflecting the Polish viewpoint in that respectable London weekly. Gradually, I established other valuable contacts in the Parliament and press, and though not sufficient to turn the course of events, they proved helpful in battling deteriorating relations with British officialdom.

Another of my assignments was to help the secret ŚWIT (Dawn) radio station which operated out of a spacious farmhouse near Bletchely Park in Buckinghamshire. It was important for the staff to know as much as possible about the current situation in Poland, including the linguistic changes during the occupation. The station was closely supervised by the Political Intelligence Department (PID) of the Foreign Office, and on the spot by Major Charles Brysson.

Fascinating as this type of public relations work was, I was longing for active involvement on the battlefront and was contemplating a return to the anti-aircraft battery regiment in the First Armored Division, which was moving quickly through

184

France, after having closed the Falaise Gap in Normandy. Another alternative was to join my family under General Anders in the Second Army Corps fighting in Italy. However, the most probable and exciting prospect was a return trip by air to Poland. British experts from SOE asked the Polish authorities to assign me to help in the training of new paratroopers, promising they would soon recommend my next parachute drop behind enemy lines. I thus spent the last weeks of July at one of the training stations, for those who were about to be sent to our Italian base for flying to Poland. Then early on August 2, 1944, came the long-expected news of the outbreak of the Warsaw Uprising. I was called back to London immediately and went to a briefing at the Sixth Bureau, called by Chief of Staff Gen. Stanisław Kopański. Those of us who were considered efficient among the British media and politicians, were given well-prepared instructions to alert the British authorities and public opinion to the dire need for immediate support of the Home Army insurrection, particularly through substantial weapons and supplies by air.

That Saturday, canceling my social plans for a relaxing weekend with a sophisticated lady friend, I met instead with Adam Ciołkosz, that most resourceful Socialist, at his apartment in Golders Green to prepare a press release. We were to blitz the Socialist press and parliamentary leaders with the first reports from Warsaw. Ciołkosz wrote a strong piece and asked me to take it right away to Aneurin Bevan M.P., the left wing Welsh editor of the *Tribune* at 222 Strand Street, with whom I established good relations some time ago. A heavy drinker, Bevan was sitting red-faced at his desk. Without comment, he read our text intensely and entitled it "Who Deserted Warsaw?" for the front page of the next edition.

My fate took a new turn at this point, when in the midst of the uprising I was sent to exquisite Edinburgh as Director of the Scottish section of the Ministry of Information at Charlotte Square, to intensify there our propaganda efforts during the most critical period of the war, thereby replacing Jan Roehr, an ailing ski acquaintance from Lwów. I would now be closer to Jaś, who had just begun his senior year at the Polish High school in Glasgow. As I had promised my parents to take care of him, I could more easily do so from this close proximity. Having excellent help in the office, I was able to produce quite a number of letters to editors, including those of the Edinburgh *Scotsman*, the Dundee *Inquirer*, the London *Tribune*, the *Sepctator*, and even the *New Statesman and Nation*. My staff included a bright Scottish couple, the Luke Parsons, Dorothy, the pregnant Canadian wife of the brilliant editor of the *Scotsman*, Wilfred Taylor, and two dedicated Polish secretaries. I was able to continue my intensive lecturing as well, mainly confining myself to Scotland, but also fulfilling pervious commitments in such distant English towns as Plymouth and Leeds.

Thanks to especially good relations with Sir George Waters, the retiring editor-in-chief of the prestigious *Scotsman*, and his successor, Mr. Watson, I was able to publish a number of articles on Poland's plight as an anonymous "Foreign Correspondent". As a matter of fact, I do not know of any other top ranked daily newspaper in British Isles which was so consistently supportive of our cause during those critical times. I had great satisfaction in using as sponsor of my public lectures numerous Scottish-Polish Societies, and helped organize Polish language classes for most of some three thousand wives of Polish soldiers. They, in turn faithfully provided useful network, by watching the press and initiating numerous cultural activities throughout bonny Scotland.

Before the capitulation of Warsaw in early October, with the help of influential local Scottish friends, I was also able to get a huge window on Princess Street in Edinburgh, to exhibit documents and photographs of the amazing Warsaw struggle and other important events in Poland. This, in turn, led to the arranging of an exhibit in Aberdeem on Polish Freedom Fighters. As representative of the Mikołajczyk Government in Scotland, I thought it was important to set up close ties with our military establishment through Generals Janusz Głuchowski and Mieczysław Boruta-Spiechowicz. With the help of the charming Major Kornel Krzeczunowicz, I organized in my office periodic meetings of ranking Poles in Edinburgh, at which we discussed various aspects of the deteriorating political situation.

When Gen. Sosnkowski returned to London from Italy later in August, he issued a pathetic condemnation of the insufficient Anglo-Saxon response to the Insurrection, squarely putting the blame on London and Washington leaders for Poland's tragic isolation. This "Order Number 94" was not very helpful when all our efforts were needed to obtain as much assistance as possible. Moreover, it gave Prime Minister Mikołajczyk a good excuse to pressure President Raczkiewicz into relieving the Commander-in-Chief of his duties for good.

With Sosnkowski's forced resignation, the problem arose as to whether the position of Commander-in-Chief should be filled at all. Our NiD movement, not in the open, was convinced that the Constitution of the Polish Republic should be respected in its provision for the wartime position, and at a conference arranged by Dr. Bronisław Jedlewski, personal physician to the President and member of the NiD, we were able to convince the latter that he should not give in on his vital matter. It was clear that Mikołajczyk was willing to eliminate the office altogether. Our idea was to appoint, *in absentia*, the heroic commander of the Home Army, Lieutenant General Tadeusz Bór-Komorowski, as the new Commander-in-Chief, leaving the actual functions in London to be performed jointly by the closely cooperating Chief of Staff, General Kopański, and Minister of Defense Gen. Kukiel, both intelligent commanders of good will.

Sometime in October, Mr. Arciszewski visited Glasgow and Edinburgh, and I arranged meetings for him with the respective mayors of these two cities, Sir Patrick Dolan and Sir William Darling. Through my efforts, he also met with the pro-Communist president of the Miners' Union, Mr. Moffat, as well as another influential Labour Party leader, Pethick Lawrence, the latter promising to support Poland against Soviet greed. Somehow I always trusted Scots more than the English and felt more at home there than in the South of the island, but my days in Edinburgh were counted.

CHAPTER V

THE PRIME MINISTER'S SECRETARY

Late in November, 1944, a deep political crisis unfolded among leading Poles in London, the third one in exile. Upon his return from Moscow, Mikołajczyk recommended that we abandon our defense of the eastern lands of Poland and accept a compromise formula as suggested by the Ambassador of the United States in Moscow, Averell Harriman, who promised to continue negotiations for Lwów only to remain within Polish borders; otherwise, the 1920 Curzon Line should serve as the definite Polish-Soviet frontier. Premier Mikołajczyk did not have sufficient support in his cabinet for acceptance of this proposal and hence, had to resign. The task of forming the new government was given by President Raczkiewicz to the Deputy Premier, Jan Kwapiński; he failed, however, to get the necessary support of all the coalition partners.[63]

The next to try was Arciszewski. With his recent underground mandate, he was more successful, though the majority of Mikołajczyk's influential Peasant Party refused to participate. I considered it my duty to phone Prof. Kot for instructions, and he told me that, regardless of his own and the Prime Minister's resignation, I should continue my work for the Arciszewski Government in Scotland, and that he hoped his Peasant Party would soon return to the wartime coalition. He thanked me for my efforts on behalf of his Ministry in Scotland, and despite our differences, behaved in an exemplary way, that of scholar and gentleman.

A few days later, I was called for a conference with the entire staff by our new Minister of Information and Documentation, Prof. Adam Pragier, a brilliant Socialist dialectician. He was not happy with my article in the *Scotsman*, in which I

189

described the composition of Arciszewski's Cabinet and mentioned his own Jewishness in order to assure the Jews in Great Britain that Soviet accusations of Polish anti-Semitism were not well founded. Dr. Pragier claimed that his name simply indicated he was descendant from a pretty Jewess from the Praga suburb, who had been the mistress of the last King of Poland. He felt completely Polish, and did not like being singled out as a Jew. At the same time, however, he asked me bluntly if I would consider returning to London to help the new government. This was followed up a few days later by an official call to accept the position of private secretary to Prime Minister Arciszewski. The old man needed to have someone he trusted from the Underground. Fully aware that politically we were fighting a losing battle, I could not refuse that request, though it meant a lower salary, less independence, as well as parting with my brother and leaving attractive Edinburgh, of which I had grown quite fond; but I packed up my belongings once more and bade farewell to Jaś, to continue my service in London.

On December 14th I started the last and emotionally the most difficult chapter in my wartime story, when I arrived at 18 Kensington Palace Gardens. No, I was not looking forward to living again among quarrelsome "London Poles," but I had to keep my Warsaw promise to the Polish Socialist Party. Mikołajczyk's competent Secretary, Judge Mazur, proved to be very helpful during the transfer of his duties, and introduced me to some of the tricks of this new job. As soon as *"Pan Tomasz"* (Prime Minister Arciszewski) arrived, I became more comfortable in accepting this uneasy task. I took a convenient room on the ground floor of a small hotel at Collingham Gardens in Kensington, to be within walking distance of our office at "Ambassadors' Row."

A few days after my arrival, I was alarmed by a gendarme on duty at the Premier's office building; early that morning he had chased away some Polish intruders who had opened the safe in the basement and left with boxes of stolen documents,' but were unable to close the safe properly. It was soon established that all confidential papers dealing with the tense situation inside Poland were missing. A trustworthy employee, Krystyna Piotrowska, informed me without hesitation that it was her immediate boss, Dr. Franciszek Szeląg of the Peasant Party, who had used his special keys to transfer those valuable materials to the Barrie House apartment in Bayswater where he lived with ex-Prime Minister Mikołajczyk.[64]

Deeply annoyed, Arciszewski ordered to change all locks in the huge building. I found a reliable locksmith in the person of Air Force Sergeant Cieślik. When the Premier saw the man fixing the lock for his mahogany desk, he eagerly took the tools himself, only to be reprimanded by the good mechanic, "better for you to take care of our politics and leave the locks to a specialist." The old man replied with a twinkle in his eye, that "you were not even born when I was making my living as a locksmith."

My predecessor warned me that they were no less than three paid informers planted by British authorities in our office, including one of the butlers and one of the switchboard operators. It became important at this point to reassure the Prime Minister, who was by nature very suspicious, that he would have only trustworthy people around him. His own background was that of a manual laborer without higher education, despite the fact that he was descendant of impoverished nobility in Byeolorussia. His working habits made him a night owl, and it was necessary to help at his home late at night. He lived with a trusted Doctor, Józef Rosenberg, and his wife. Their Georgian apartment was at 26 Park Crescent, about four miles from our office at the attractive entrance to Regent's Park.

My work as Arciszewski's translator began with a near disaster. Various press commentators, curious about the new Government's attitude towards the Soviet Union, asked for a briefing conference. The American correspondent, Ferdinand Kuh, began with a loaded question, "What does the Premier consider more important for Poland, the eastern lands with Lwów and Wilno, claimed by Stalin, or the western territories with Wrocław (Breslau) and Szczecin (Stettin), to be recovered from defeated Germany?" My straightforward boss answered promptly, despite my signal of a possible trap. "Wilno and Lwów are historical cities with predominantly Polish populations, so it is my Government's duty to protect them rather than to overreach for the German dominated territories far in the West." However, he made, a qualifying remark that, for the security of Poland's access to the Baltic Sea as a recompense for the horrible destruction by the Nazis, Poland should obtain the entire East Prussian enclave with Królewiec (Konigsberg), and it would be essential to shorten the border in western Pomorze (Pomerania). Similarly, the entire mining region of Upper Silesia (Górny Śląsk), together with the Polish populated Opole district should definitely become part of the Polish state.

My intuition warned me that Ariszewski's answer might be interpreted as our disinterest in the important cities of Wrocław and Szczecin. I tried to cover his statement with a less specific version, not knowing that Kuh understood Polish. As a result, I was challenged with the request for a literal translation by someone else. Dr. Tadeusz Lutosławski then replaced me and his exact version was used. The *Sunday Times* (December 17, 1944) for instance, printed a report that the new London Government was not at all interested in the western territories with Wrocław and Szczecin; and soon after, poor Arciszewski was attacked by the Polish Communists as a traitor; the Party's First Secretary Bolesław Bierut even expressed his surprise that the Prime Minister, "...spoke from London and not Berlin."[65] One should understand, however, that the Russian-German battlefront followed the Vistula River, at that time in mid-Poland, while Hitler's army in the west had just begun its counteroffensive in the Ardennes. It was not easy to foresee that millions of Germans would soon flee from what are today's Polish regained territories, in fear of the Red Army's vengeance. However, Lwów and Wilno were still predominantly Polish cities, to be protected as such by Poland's spokesman.

One of my first tasks was to help the Prime Minister in preparing his policy platform to present to the National Council. The initial draft was done by Prof. Pragier; but the

Premier did not like to deliver anyone else's text, preferring to carefully think over each formulation. He asked me, along with his Socialist comrade, Bronisław Skalak of Lwów, Acting Chairman of the National Council, to help in drafting the final text. The new government would function as a continuation of the wartime policies of Sikorski and Mikołajczyk, but there was to be a special emphasis on a nondeviating line in defense of Poland's sovereignty and territorial integrity, while maintaining the 1939 Paris admendments to the April 1935 Constitution, which substantially democratized the Constitution by limiting President's executive power. Arciszewski's Cabinet fully embraced the progressive socio-economic programs formulated in 1944 by the Underground Council of National Unity. One of the results of this new policy was that the political parties of the Coalition would have more say in the decision-making process.

The three of us worked until the early hours of the morning on the following text:

The Polish Government residing in London is the only legal representative of the Polish Republic as far as the Allied Nations and Neutral States are concerned... Furthermore, we are basing the entire system of Foreign Relations upon formal alliances and links of friendship which were at the root of our 1939 decision and foremost upon our alliance with Great Britain... The Government sincerely wishes that it be of the sort which will not evoke feelings of harm and injustice in the Polish Nation.[66]

This statement did not satisfy those members of the National Council who were in favor of the more elastic policies of Mikołajczyk, which made it necessary for the new Premier to appear again, at a secret meeting on December 19th, to answer questions and interpret his position. The old man was upset, so we had to spend another night in preparation for the heated debate. His new explanation was as follows:

My accession to this office was received in an unfriendly manner by the British press. It was no surprise to me, because the true measure of our policy cannot be merely the reaction of world press, but rather the interests of Poland. This response was, however, further proof that the previous govenment, even though with the best will, evoked excessive hopes for an attitude of compromise on the part of the Poles; hence the current disillusionment. I have decided, therefore, to stand firm until the world is resigned to the fact that there are limits to our concessions and that the Government will resist the demands directed against the independence of Poland.[67]

The London press was, indeed, not kind to us. Particularly venomous was the masterful cartoonist, David Low of the *Evening Standard*, who presented Arciszewski as a sort of mad Santa Claus, preventing Stalin and Churchill from embracing each other. Another commentator specializing in anti-Polish vitriol was A.F. Cummings, of the ultra liberal *News Chronicle*. The worst, however, was the Jewish-Polish journalist, Isaac Deutscher, who had access to various Polish politicans in his hunt for indiscretion. This correspondent for the influential *Sunday Observer* and London *Economist* had betrayed his former Trotskyite comrades and coined the asinine slogan about "Good Uncle Joe" (Stalin), praising the Generalissimo's unique sense of humor. We also had to face attacks from the myopic "Parlor Pinks", snobs and various Soviet agents. Among the former, the most damaging was Kingsley Martin, the erudite editor of the *New Statesman and Nation,* who reminded his readers of the 1916 Balfour Memorandum, which declared that an independent Poland was not in the interest of the English. Instead, the Poles should be satisfied with autonomy within the framework of the Russian Empire, as recommended once by the anti-Polish Marxist Rosa Luxemburg.

With a growing public relations problem, I considered it my duty to continue writing letters to the British press and speaking with influential commentators and politicians whose mentality I began to understand better than most of my emotional compatriots of the older generation. First we invited to the Prime Minister's office a group of Catholic leaders, including the Archbishop Griffith of Westminister and the Apostolic Delegate Archbishop Godfrey for lunch. They were surprisingly warm, though they must have been aware of Arciszewski's earlier involvement with the atheist movement, as President of the Freethinkers' Association in prewar Poland. Actually the English Catholics never let us down, nor did the Irish.

Christmas neared and Mrs. Rozenberg, the kind Jewish landlady of the Prime Minister, decided to arrange for him a traditional Christmas Eve dinner, for which she invited me, my brother Jaś and Chairman Skalak. Beginning with the traditional red borsch with mushroom filled raviolis *("uszka")*, we had the symbolic dishes, sang carols and then the old man started to hum revolutionary songs of the Polish Socialists. No one but that veteran anti-tsarist workers' organizer could have still remembered those lyrics and melodies from the end of the 19th century. Too bad I didn't tape them before it was too late.

We had promised to attend Midnight Mass at the Rectory at 2 Devonia road, but the Premier wanted to visit "comrades" Adam and Lidia Ciolkosz on the way, making us twenty minutes late due to terrible London peasoup-fog. The good Monsignor Staniszewski delayed Mass, and received us warmly at the church door, softly telling me that, "It does not often happen that the Prime Minister of Poland, an ex-atheist, wants to greet the newly born Christ child." From that time on Tomasz Arciszewsski began visiting the Rectory more often, although he still did, somewhat reluctantly, maintain his contacts with the Copernicus Great National Lodge of Polish Freemasonry under the gavel of its Grand Master, Dr. Tadeusz Tomaszewski. The latter called one day in January to remind the Prime Minister of a "tea party" to be held that coming Sunday. When I repeated the message, I noticed that Arciszewski was not enthusiastic. That Sunday, Grochowski, the official chauffeur, must have been off drinking, for he forgot to pick him up. Accordingly, I called a taxicab and escorted my boss to 55 Princess Gate, at the meeting place on the top floor. To my amazement, there was a small crowd of dignitaries of various political affiliations, including Foreign Minister Adam Tarnowski, Minister of Information Adam Pragier, and a number of high officers of our Foreign Office. Most importantly, among the formally dressed men I saw the former Minister of Foreign Affairs and actually the influential

Chief of President Raczkiewicz's Civil Chancery, August Zaleski. The host looked at me with horror, since I was not one of the initiated "brothers". He suggested that I go to a movie and Arciszewski would be driven home by someone else. I left the meeting angrily, knowing I was not at all welcome, but certainly did not go to a movie either.

A few days later, opening as a matter of routine the Premier's mail at his home, I read a note about my "intrusion", written by Professor Nagórski, in the Grand Master's name. While recognizing my war record with approval, they, nevertheless, expressed their surprise that Arciszewski had selected me as his secretary instead of one of their own, such as Sylwester Karolus. Deeply hurt, I instantly wrote a letter of resignation, asking to be transferred to one of the fighting units in Europe. I reminded Arciszewski that I had never asked for the position as his secretary, and was sorry that some of his intimate friends did not trust me. I left the letter on his desk and the next morning was requested very firmly to withdraw my resignation. "I know you from Warsaw and trust you completely. I have never met Karolus and cannot allow those Freemasons to interfer with my personnel or dictate whom I should choose as my closest assistant." Although I never mentioned the incident again, I noticed that from that time, the Prime Minister began avoiding Sunday "tea parties" and sought more frequent meetings with Monsignor Staniszewski and Bishop Radoński.

Arciszewski was very sensitive to the need for strengthening ties with genuine Jewish leaders, which resulted in our spending some evenings at the hospitable home of the Sokołow family, the children of Nahum, the late president of the World Congress of Zionists. Dr. Celina Sokołow introduced us in turn to other influential people, concerned about Soviet expansionism and the Communist threat to Jews and Poles alike. Similarly, as a Socialist, Arciszewski maintained close contact with the Bund representatives, Emanuel Szerer, Rafał Bluth, and Leon Ohler.

On January 6, we learned that Moscow had definitely recognized its own stooges from the "Lublin Committee" as

196

the new Polish Government at home. Arciszewski's Cabinet reacted through the PAT Telegraph Agency:

Official Soviet recognition of the temporary government in Lublin, its own agency, constitutes a violation of the fundamental right of the Polish nation to true independence, free from foreign intervention. It also violates Poland's right to arrange its State according to its will.[68]

This firm stand evoked an enthusiastic response from many Poles all over the world. We received hundreds of cables and letters of support from various organizations. It looked for a while from these numerous messages that Arciszewski had become the most popular Prime Minister since the 1920 Government of National Unity under Wincenty Witos.

At the same time, the Polish Workers' Party Communists increased their attacks on Arciszewski, "the arch traitor." Similarly, in the free world, efforts were redoubled to split the Poles and undermine the pre-eminence of the Government in exile. The fact that it allowed the participation of the National Party, known for its virulent prewar anti-Semitism, fueled accusations against the legal authorities of Poland. This propaganda campaign had some success, not only in Jewish circles, but even among prominent Poles of Jewish origin, for example, Antoni Słonimski, an erudite poet and editor of the *New Poland* monthly, Dr. Mieczysław Szerer, former editor of *Dziennik Polski i Dziennik Żołnierza (Polish and Soldiers Daily)*, and Dr. Ludwik Grosfeld, former Socialist Minister of the Treasury. In the lesser ranks were a substantial number of Jews employed in various ministries, most of whom decided to support former Prime Minister Mikołajczyk in opposition to Arciszewski. From my boss' point of view, the particularly painful aspect of this situation was the growing split in the ranks of his own party, the PPS, though the Underground WRN movement, the clandestine continuation of the PPS in occupied Poland, remained united. However, the newly created "Transitional Government of Poland" in Lublin claimed to have the partial support of the socialists, even though none of the prewar elected leaders of that Party had expressed approval for that Communist controlled body officially chaired by their Prime Minster Edward Osóbka-Morawski of the splinter RPPS (Polish Workers' Socialist Party).

Another propaganda ploy on the part of the Communists was directed against the underground's Home Army. An absurd rumor was spread that the Home Army had assisted in the Nazi Holocaust against the Jews. Prime Minister Arciszewski, in an interview with Joel Cang of the *European Jewish Observer*, announced firmly, "If the Jews are to profit in a future Poland with equal rights, as is our sincere wish, they must have guaranteed access to all positions in economic and political life. My government will definitely stand against any discrimination. The Jewish people must be employed wherever they want to work. In the future Poland, there will be no racial separation or any sort of ghettos." In answer to Cang's question regarding the three "Endek" members of his Cabinet, Berezowski, Folkierski and Demidowicz, Arciszewski responded, "Representatives of the four coalition parties signed a binding declaration to the effect that the Jews should have equal rights. This charter of freedom was also endorsed by the National Party."[69]

Prospects grew even bleaker with the preparation for the forthcoming Big Three Conference at Yalta, actually an implementation of the secret decisions undertaken at Teheran. The Prime Minister spoke to a number of press correspondents, stressing the need to use the Atlantic Charter's principles in solving the Polish-Russian conflicts. In his interview, published in the *New York Times* on January 24, 1945, Arciszewski said, "The main fear for Poland is the prospect of being made a sort of vassal state by the Big Three verdict. Poland's independence could become fiction." He called the Lublin regime "nothing but a tool of foreign power." While stressing that he would gladly welcome into his Cabinet representatives of the Peasant Party with Mikołajczyk, he saw no chance whatsoever of forming a coalition with the Provisional Government of Lublin, which was clearly patronized by the Soviet Union.

Arciszewski tried to draw the world's attention to the wave of arrests of members of the Underground by the Soviets, and their enforced enlistment into the Red Army. This all happened despite the fact that the A.K. strictly followed the directives of January, 1944 from the London Government to resist only the Germans and not fight the Russians. Demanding implementation of the principles of the Atlantic Charter, especially the principle of self-determination, the Prime Minister stressed that if only the Soviet Union would stop insisting on an immediate change of borders, the complicated territorial problems could be justly resolved by following the will of the local population, expressed in unfettered voting under Allied supervision.

Arciszewski claimed that "Poland's fears regarding the Soviet Union's designs result from the Stalinist policy of the *fait accompli,* such as mass deportations, increasing incarcerations, concentration camps, rescinding of freedom of speech, the calling into being of fictitious puppet parties, creation of the Lublin Committee, and signing of an international agreement with this Committee." The Premier concluded the interview by emphasizing that his government was ready to "start negotiations with Russia and deeply wishes to establish normal neighborly relations with her. Poland is ready to cooperate with Russia, but refuses to become the new Soviet Republic even under the designation of independence."[70]

In the same spirit, he appealed to the Polish people over the BBC on January 19, 1945 and stretched his hand to the Russians once more with some hope that it would not be refused. This important message read as follows:

...I extend my hand to the Soviet Union... I do it in the name of the Government, in the name of the exhausted Polish Nation, in my own name as an old fighter for a better future, and not just as a gesture of temporary reconciliation but to reach a permanent understanding and a lasting, honest cooperation.

From the botton of my heart I believe, despite all that has been said and done, that such an agreement can be achieved. Geography and History speak for such an understanding. We do not want, nor can we want, anything from Russia. She needs

199

nothing from us. Poland fought with Czarist Russia for independence. The Russian revolution carried liberation to the enchained nations under the despotic Tsardom. In the year 1938, Hitler's proposal for joint attack on Soviet Russia and a sharing of the booty was rejected by the Polish Government with contempt.

We extend our hands to Russia and cannot believe that we could be rejected. The right for true independence of our nation—that is the whole of our platform—this is all that we aim for. Such a right, though not by the bayonet, even one covered with glory, should dictate who shall govern the country. Freedom means not only the liberation from Germany slavery, it is personal freedom, of speech and thought, press, association, trade unions, religion; it is government not imposed by force, but created with democratic elections without foreign pressure.[71]

Unfortunately, Arciszewski's hand was extended in vain, and our channels to the leaders of the Anglo-Saxon governments were blocked as well. Despite many efforts of our experienced ambassadors, we could only reach President Roosevelt and Prime Minister Churchill through diplomatic notes. On January 22, 1945, the Polish government solemnly warned the three powers against any bartering with Polish independence.

...the Polish government foresees that questions pertaining to Poland will be dealt with at the announced meeting of the leaders of the Great Allied Powers... The Polish Government wishes to take this opportunity to stress the following:

Territorial matters should be settled only after the cessation of hostilities... The Polish Government will not recognize any one-sided decisions, keeping in mind that Poland, belonging to the United Nations in the joint struggle for freedom of the entire world, made huge sacrifices of its most precious resource, losing almost one fifth of her population, killed on the battlefields, murdered in concentration camps, ghettos, prisons, in exile and in labor camps...

The Polish Government thus has the right to expect that the governments of the United States and Great Britain will not take part in any decisions pertaining to the allied Polish Government

200

without the participation and approval of that Government. The Polish Government expects that the governments of the United States and Great Britain will respect its decision on the nonrecognition in Poland of the fait accompli *and in particular of the puppet regime. Recognition of such a regime in Poland would amount to the writing off of Polish independence in support of which the war began.*[72]

We knew, however, that even our best arguments would likely fall on deaf ears, so, in those last days before Yalta, we accelerated our mobilization of friendly support in the United States and Great Britain. Besides our diplomatic and propaganda agencies in the United States, the main political activity in that crucial country was conducted by such patriotic Polonia leaders as: Charles Rozmarek in Chicago, Franciszek Januszewski in Detroit, and Maksymilian F. Węgrzynek in New York, along with the support of a dozen Polish-American congressmen.[73] In London we could always count on Catholic intellectuals such as Douglas Woodruff, editor of the *Tablet,* Freda Bruce-Lockhart, associate editor of *Time and Tide,* besides Frederic Voigt of *Nineteenth Century and After* and Elma Dangerfield publisher of *Whitehall News.* Our most vocal friends organized at that time the League of European Freedom, under the leadership of the aging "Red" Duchess of Atholl ("red" because she was known for vigorously supporting the anti-Franco elements during the Spanish Civil War). They held a public meeting in Caxton Hall in mid-January 1945, at which the League's goals were defined as: support for the regaining of real freedom and independence by all smaller European states which had existed in 1937, prior to the annexation of Austria, proclaimed in accordance with the Atlantic Charter principles; and to counteract Soviet deportations while securing the return home of all dispersed populations. Following the position of the Polish Government, the League for European Freedom stood firmly against any territorial changes under foreign occupation, unless they were undertaken with the full agreement of all interested parties. Among worthy friends we could also count on former Chairman of the Labour Party, George Dallas of Nottingham, and a few important Labourite members of Parliament mainly of Catholic-Irish origin.

Though the anti-Soviet group of Tory backbenchers were the main nucleus of the oppostion to Churchill, we did not lack understanding of British friends in other circles. In his House of Commons speech, Professor Douglas Savory, representing North Irish universities, quoted the ranking Oxford historian H.A.L. Fisher, who called the 18th century partition of Poland "the most shameful event in the yearbooks of European history." Speaking on behalf of Polish rights to Lwów and Wilno, he appealed to the British Parliament not to permit the ceding of these two important, non-Russian towns to the Soviet Union. In support of his argument, he quoted the 1920 document signed by Lenin and his Foreign Commissar, Gregory Chicherin, "The true border which Russia will draw with representatives of the Polish Nation will run to the east of the borders designed by London and Paris imperialists."[74] We also had the support of Socialist Leftwinger George A. Strauss, M.P., who wrote an article in the monthly *Left News* entitled, "Poland: Frontiers and Independence", strongly bolstering the idea of the Atlantic Charter as the only just basis for future peace.

An unexpected blow to our cause was the pro-Soviet policy of the ungrateful President in Exile of Czechoslovakia, Dr. Eduard Benes. Forgettig that the pro-Czech Sikorski government had been the first to recognize him in 1940 as head of state after his capitulation in Munich, he rushed to Moscow and on January 1, 1945, recognized the Communist regime in Lublin. Arciszewski reacted on February 1, by severing relations with the sneaky Benes crowd.

At the same time, countless Polish organizations in the United Kingdon, United States and elsewhere publically expressed their support of Arciszewski's resolute stand against Allied concessions to Stalin. The largest meeting was held in a large hall by the Westminster Catholic Cathedral under the auspices of the Eastern Land Associations of the old Polish-Lithuanian Commonwealth. Representative spokesmen from all political parties in exile repudiated any forthcoming territorial changes in favor of Soviet expansionism.

When the Prime Minister was inspecting our cruiser *Conrad* stationed in Portsmouth, Ambassador Raczyński called, relaying a British emergency request for disclosure of the underground chain of command. Suspicious about the real intentions of the move, I contacted the Premier, who decided to cut his tour short and called a special session of the Cabinet in that delicate matter.

In the meantime a dramatic act was taking place in Poland as Brigadier-General "Niedźwiadek" (Leopold Okulicki), the last Commander-in-Chief of the Home Army, gave final orders under duress, releasing all rank and file from their A.K. oath and disbanded its units in view of the Red Army's occupation of the country. Issuing that pathetic last order, he urged the men and women of A.K. "to be from now on your own individual commanders in further service of Poland's ultimate victory."[74] And I, for one, consider this call of my senior paratrooper colleague still binding. Our propaganda activities during that critical period were substantially strengthened by the fact that my dear friend Jan Nowak, the first eyewitness and participant of the Warsaw Uprising, reappeared in London with his newly-wed heroic wife "Greta" (Wiśka), after crossing European battle lines in thier new mision to the West. He became immediately the most effective spokesman on behalf of Home Army fighters, not only in the Polish milieu but especially among the British, and later Americans.

Anxiously we were awaiting news from the Yalta Conference of the Big Three. During the late hours of February 12, 1945, the Foreign Office handed Ambassador Raczyński the official text of that outrageous "executive agreement." There could be no doubt anymore that what actually was Adolf Hitler's War would end after six dreadful years of holocaust, with the one-sided success of Stalin's Russia. As happened *mutatis mutandi* with the Congress of Vienna in 1814-15, the vexing Polish problem again took much more time than any other issue discussed. The unhealthy compromise reached in the Crimea Conference strictly followed the secret Teheran accords of the ailing American President with the ruthless Soviet dictator. It amounted to an Anglo-Saxon capitulation to Soviet expansionist goals in East-Central Europe, as originally formulated in the treacherous Ribbentrop-Molotov deal of August 23, 1939, and ultimate betrayal of the faithful Allies, Czechoslovakia, Poland and Yugoslavia.[75]

As soon as the Prime Minister heard the grim news, he told me to invite President Raczkiewicz, all the Ministers and the Chief of Staff for an emergency session to be held on Thursday, February 13th in his office. I was required to stand by at my desk for instructions resulting from that historic meeting. After several hours the committee of three Ministers, Berezowski, Pragier and Tarnowski, handed me the outline of a communique to be polished and translated into English. I was given handwritten points dealing with the violation of the Atlantic Charter, mainly with regard to Poland's territorial integrity and sovereignty. It did not take me long to realize that this draft lacked a clear formulation of the Polish Nation's position concerning vital decisions about her future, taken without her participation. As a prewar international law student under Professors Ludwik Ehrlich and Stanisław Hubert I was sure that the fundamental principles of that law had been outwardly violated. Without much ado, I added in red pencil the subordinate clause of the following sentence: "The Polish Government declares that the discussions of the Conference of the Three pertaining to Poland cannot be recognized by the Government, **and cannot bind the Polish Nation.**" The six underscored words were approved by the Council of Ministers and thus became my own contribution to the historical protest.[76]

Proud of taking some part in this most important act of Arciszewski's Premiership, I was well aware that we could not be satisfied with protests, or falling asleep in the glory of wartime banners. It had become clear by the end of that long day that with our public defiance we had actually challenged the mightiest powers of this merciless world in defense of our sacred rights and national dignity. In particular, we had to prevent any irresponsible reactions among the two hundred thousand-strong Polish armed forces, still very much involved on several war fronts in land, air and sea hostilities against Nazi Germany. After all ours was the fourth largest Army in the allied camp...

Minister of Defense Gen. Kukiel and Chief of Staff Gen. Kopański recommended that in spite our bitter grief, we remain exemplary faithful on the Allied side until the very end of hostilities. Prime minister concurred and a directive to that effect was drafted that same night appealing to all commanders and soldiers, "to fulfill your duties and maintain the brotherhood of arms with the forces of Great Britain, Canada, the United States and France, in view of so much blood already shed in the common struggle."[77] Frankly, I was not happy with the prospect of more Polish blood being shed after Yalta betrayal, but I was too small a fry to have much to say in that policy matter.

Greatly perturbed I walked home empty headed reaching 25 Collingwood Gardens around midnight. Having almost automatically unlocked the hotel entrance, I noticed a bright light under my room door and realized how absentminded I have been. A gorgeous English girl whom I just started to consider seriously as my life companion was sitting there since 7:30 p.m. for a dinner date in nearby Gloucester Street restaurant. I found her pale with justifiable anger. My Yalta excuses with sincere apologies and jeremiads about the division of European continent were of no avail. Since "X" proved to be completely insensitive to my grievances against Churchill it became obvious to both of us that we are definitely not destined for each other. Despite her shock that proud daughter of Albion somehow managed to survive our parting and so did I...

Anyhow seeing how much my boss needed assistance I decided soon after that incident to move to 26 Park Crescent to be under the same roof with him. His tired mind worked best after supper. Moreover, not to lose precious office time, it was better to brief him during breakfast on the latest war news and editorial comments of the morning London press. I rented, therefore, a small study on the mezzanine of that same house. At this historical junction, our salvage effort became by far more important than all the beautiful women of the British Commonwealth.

First of all, we had to be prepared for negative reactions from British authorities to our widely publicized protest. Among possible reprisals we expected confiscation of our offices, archives and radio communications. One had to always be on guard against surveillance of our movements and phone tappings by Soviet Embassy personnel. Their premises faced us across the street, with one of the buildings being just next to ours. Evidently we had to be neighbors, even at London's Ambassadors' Row!

Though well aware that London was no more the proud capital of the Western Alliance, with the center of gravity shifting to far away Washington, D.C. we kept well in mind the August 25, 1939 British-Polish Treaty of Mutual Assistance, the initial cornerstone of the wartime alliances. The chairman of the Parliamentary Committee of the Friends of Poland, Captain Alan Graham, M.P., invited Tomasz Arciszewski on Thursday, February 15th, to explain his Government's adamant rejection of the Yalta decisions. This was preceded by a lively luncheon presentation of the Warsaw Uprising plight by Captain Nowak and his wife, who had participated in that lonely, 63-day long struggle. As usual, I had attempted to draft the Prime Minister's speech, but he seemed to be in a bad mood and rejected all proposals. Since Ambassador Raczyński was to translate the Premier's address paragraph by paragraph in Westminster, I informed him that we might be in trouble, having no written text.

That difficult-to-pronounce name, "Arciszewski" began to symbolize an uncompromising stand against Soviet expansion for British politicians, and many were curious to meet the feisty old man. The ancient reception Hall was filled to capacity with some one hundred members of both Houses and the press corps. Thrilled by the firsthand report of the Nowaks, the distinguished gathering was now ready to listen to my boss. He moved together with our popular Ambassador to the middle of the Hall, and before long I was happy to find that my concerns about the Prime Minister's presentation had been unjustified.

He first stressed his awareness of speaking under the roof of the Mother of Parliaments of the world, and went to emphasize that during the long war years the Poles, under ruthless German occupation, had never lost faith in British democracy and fairplay. It was one of the basic tenets of the Resistance of which he was now the main spokesman, that the British leaders would surely abide by their public commitments to defend the fundamental principles of justice and decency in international relations. Arciszewski ended his brief address with a moving appeal to the democratic conscience and world-recognized integrity on the British Parliamentarians, who should keep in mind that there, in underground Poland, their words, spoken in this House, are weighed on a scale of pure gold, as the voice of a free tribunal representing all brave people who fought not only against Nazism, but any form of foreign oppression. The Prime Minister was spontaneously applauded and even embraced by some of the listeners, including the Chairperson of the Labour Party, the tiny Eileen Wilkinson.

Our next maneuver on the same battlefield was the long-planned debate of the Polish Socialist leaders with the influential Parliamentary Committee of the British Labour Party. Official invitation was signed by Charles Johnson, M.P., its Secretary. Although in the wartime coalition dominated by Winston Churchill the Labouraties played only second fiddle, especially when it came to matters of foreign policy, they were sincerely concerned about Poland's independence and democracy. Our delegation was composed of Tomasz Arciszewski, Emanuel Freyd, Jan Kwapiński, Dr. Adam Pragier, Bronisław Skalak, and myself as translator-recorder.

After an introduction by Arthur Greenwood, Chairman of the Parliamentary Labour Party, Arciszewski explained the leading role of PPS in the underground Polish State. Based on his own experience, he gave a short survey of the struggle against the Nazis and the new state of affairs under Soviet rutless occupation. He succinctly presented numerous attempts of his Government to resume relations with Moscow, and ended by explaining the Polish stand on the Yalta decisions. The Prime Minister was followed by Jan Kwapiński.

who gave examples of the extermination policy pursued by Soviet authorities in Poland, supplying them with information dealing with the deterioration of Polish-Soviet relations during the preceding period, when he served as Deputy Premier under Mikołajczyk. Professor Pragier stressed that the Crimean decisions were at variance with the basic principles of international law, and ably summarized the Polish arguments which had been provided by our Government for the British and the United States Governments before that fatal Conference. He tried to prove that Soviet Policy had already demonstrated Stalin's goal of full domination of East-Central Europe, thus eliminating British influence in that area.

On the Labour Party's side, the most articulate spokesman was the radical firebrand Aneurin Bevan, M.P., known for his sharp criticism of Churchill's policies. According to him, one had to distinguish, in the whole complexity of Polish-Soviet relations, two major issues: the future Soviet-Polish border and the question of Polish sovereignty. He felt, and his comrades agreed, that in the first matter our position was weak, especially from its ethnic aspect, regardless of the legal arguments about the so-called Curzon Line. He did not believe that it would be possible to change the Yalta conclusions concerning territorial questions. But the second issue, the Independence of the Polish State being more essential, the policies of British and Polish Socialists should be directed at supporting the Arciszewski Government in London. Being a practical but honest politician, Bevan asked us for specific suggestions as to what they, the British Socialists, could do to help in that crucial matter.

The Premier replied with his usual dignity, that neither his Government in exile nor the Polish Socialist Party could give up half of the prewar Polish State to the rapacious Soviet Union against the principles of the Atlantic Charter and other binding treaties with the Allied Nations, particularly with Great Britian, at the expense of Polish and non-Polish populations living there for many centuries. Such territorial problems should be settled in a civilized way, in accordance with international law and the free self-determination of the people concerned, and

208

not by the one-sided dictates of a foreign power, though unfortunately it seems acceptable as a reasonable compromise by the two other Allied Powers. It was clear to us that the Labour Party was not willing to confront Prime Minister Churchill and Foreign Secretary Eden, but would do their best to ensure the democratic character of the postwar Polish Government based on free, unfettered elections, implemented by an Inter-Allied Committee for Polish Affairs. The Yalta Agreement would stand for a long time, it looked, though it could eventually be treated as not properly consummated and therefore invalid.

Skalak argued that the most effective action on the part of the Labour Party would be its firm opposition to proclaimed policies of both Anglo-Saxon governments, who ignored Poland's legal authorities in London. Their current policy, he averred, was tantamount to abandonment of Poland's legal Government for some chimeric creation of a puppet, Communist-controlled regime.

Richard Stokes, M.P., a Catholic Labourite, then asked whether the Poles would accept a plebiscite solution of the territorial dispute in the eastern half of the country. Pragier replied that, until the return of millions of its deported citizens, and as long as Poland was occupied by the Red Armies, such a referendum would not truly reflect the actual will of the people. Moreover, previous sad experiences with similar referenda under Soviet domination left Poles more than skeptical of such one-sided solutions.[78]

After these two major attempts in Westminster, it remained to mobilize as many Members of Parliament as possible to voice their support for Poland's right to independence based among others on our fine war record as an Ally. With a group of NiD activists, I became very involved for at least a week in preparing information packets for all those honest members of Parliament who were ready to stick their necks out against the domineering Premier of Great Britain.

The longest debate on Poland ever held in the British Parliament began on February 27, 1945, and lasted three full days. I obtained passes from Ivor Thomas, M.P., of the

Labour Party, which enabled me to watch our parliamentary friends in their uneasy efforts to challenge the official policies of the Big Powers. Of course, numerically they lost heavily, but their names will go down in history of British-Polish relations as those who nobly stood up in our darkest hour; and their arguments will one day help to renounce the Yalta division of Europe.[79]

At the same time, our government was once again exploring official channels of communication. Ambassador Raczyński saw Foreign Secretary Eden on February 20th, when the Minister of Foreign Affairs Tarnowski prepared a lengthy memo directed to British Ambassador Sir Owen O'Maley. Eden seemed to understand that elections in the territory occupied by the Red Army were of dubious character, but he closed his mind on the issue of Lwów and Wilno. Deceitful, he tried to convince the sensitive Ambassador Raczyński that the Yalta decisions were not really Soviet successes, nor did they threaten Polish sovereignty. Particularly brutal were Premier Churchill's discussions with Gen. Anders, acting Commander-in-Chief of the Polish Armed Forces. Churchill told the victor of Monte Cassino, "We have enough armed forces of our own. We no longer need your help, and you can withdraw your divisions." General Anders stoically endured this undeserved rudeness and continued to defend Poland's interests along the lines set out by Arciszewski's government.[80]

In his introduction to the Polish debate, as expected, Churchill divided the problem into two allegedly unrelated matters, frontiers and independence. In the case of the former, he supported the 1920 proposal by Lord Curzon. With typical fervor, he claimed that the Yalta decisions would guarantee Poland full independence through free elections, soon to be held under the direction of the provisional government, called into being after consultations among Ambassadors Harriman, Kerr and Foreign Minister Molotov. But Churchill also stated that postwar Poland would have to be on good terms with the Soviet Union, implying however, that the assessment of such a "friendship" would be up to the Soviets alone. With astonishing shortsightedness, he claimed that he left Yalta with

the firm impression that Stalin and the entire Soviet leadership
"...nourished their bond to Poland" and felt "... that their
word was binding."

The first to challenge Churchill was the never failing Arthur
Greenwood. Focusing on the issue of Poland's sovereignty,
Greenwood reproached the Prime Minister for improper
treatment of Arciszewski's allied government. He also claimed
that the cardinal sin of the three super powers had been their
decision on the future of Poland with no representation of the
latter. The next of the thirty speakers was Lord Dunglass (the
future Prime Minister Lord Hume). As the prewar
Parliamentary Secretary to Prime Minister Chamberlain, he
reminded the House that Great Britian had a binding
obligation to her faithful first ally, which was fortified by the
principles of the Atlantic Charter. With unusual foresight,
Lord Dunglass characterized the Russian attitude regarding
Poland as symptomatic of her expansionist intentions towards
other smaller nations. As a sort of chief of staff for the
"Westminster Operation," I had passed on to Lord Dunglass,
through our mutual friend Zymgunt Nagórski, Jr.,
documentation of mass arrests and deportations of Home
Army soldiers, which he used in the debate. The earnest
Scotsman did not hesitate to defend our eastern territories,
ceded at Yalta.

Despite the wishful thinking of Anthony Eden, who claimed
that everything would soon be in good order in Poland, twenty
five backbenchers voted for the anti-Yalta amendment, which
had been presented by Major Petheric. Eleven members
abstained from a vote which would have supported Churchill,
among them the Parliamentary Secretary for Town and
Country Planning Prof. Harry G. Strauss, who subsequently
resigned from Churchill's government in protest. In all, thirty-
six members of the House of Commons chose to be loyal to
their Polish ally rather than their highhanded Premier.[81]
Obviously, it was quite a shock to Churchill, as evidenced by
the chapter in the last volume of his war memoirs, "Deep
Anxieties about Poland."[82]

This extended debate ended with the subject of the jailing of

Melania Arciszewski, the wife of my boss. She had been working for the Polish Red Cross when, in March 1945, she was arrested in Kraków in reprisal for her husband's intransigent stand againt Yalta. The Prime Minister was very uncomfortable about my plan to raise the matter in the British Parliament, as he was against bringing any of his personal affairs into the political arena. However, I finally convinced him that such a humanitarian interposition might be helpful in the final phase of the debate. I sought the aid of the Cambridge don, Dr. Kenneth Pickthorn, a Tory Member of Parliament who was known for his dry sense of humor as well as for his antipathy to Churchill. He was quite amusing when he spoke to me of being concerned primarily with the past and future of his native East Anglia. But he had to admit that, after all, that region too depended on Great Britain, whose future in turn hinged on the situation in Europe, including Poland. By such syllogisms, he admitted that he must also care about the fate of East-Central Europe, and therefore, agreed to intervene on behalf of Mrs. Arciszewski. He suggested, however, that it would be more effective to approach the leftist Welsh Member of Parliament, Rhys Davies of the Labour Party, which I did.

Answering for the government, Eden confirmed the disquieting news of Mme Arciszewski's arrest, promising that he would intervene directly with the new authorities. Professor Pickthorn pointed out Churchill's amazing naivete regarding Stalin's promises, as evidenced by Malenia Arciszewski's incarceration. On March 6th, seven other members of Parliament asked for strong intervention on her behalf. Most witty were the comments of Austin Hopkins, who alluded to the redundant peregrinations of Mrs. Churchill in Russia, asking Foreign Secretary Eden about the security of wives of other prime ministers. That side issue was resolved happily when His Majesty's Ambassador to Moscow reported the release of Mrs. Arciszewski the day after the question was raised in the House of Commons.[83]

Several months later, I went with the Prime Minister to meet his wife at Croydon Airport and was proud to hear her firsthand report. The day after her imprisonment was

212

discussed in Westminster, her situation suddenly improved. She was informed by her jailers of developments and shortly thereafter was released on condition that she sign a statement agreeing never to return to Poland. This particular case shows how sensitive the Soviets were to any well-founded criticism of their human rights violations. Naturally, we sent proper letters of gratitude to all those Members of Parliament who had graciously helped in her release.

Despite the growing popularity of Arciszewski with the Armed Forces and in Polish communities the world over, we were no longer united in London. Besides the regular Communists, British authorities too were sowing dissention for various reasons among Polish exiles in London. We were reminded of the prophetic words of the late Marshal Piłsudski, "In times of crisis, beware of foreign agents." Some Poles decided to abandon the committed Arciszewski camp. There were, in addition to opportunism, also the natural considerations of family reunification and of taking up the necessary work of reconstruction back in the homeland. At the same time, it was crystal clear from the dialectical viewpoint that there should remain some nucleus of respected Poles outside Kremlin's control. Such undefeated Poles must continue the negation of the Soviet agency operating under the name of the Polish Government. It was, therefore, obvious what role the Prime Minister and his team should play in the future. As chairman of the Polish Socialist Party, he would lead the Free Poles in their unfinished crusade.

There were serious splits in the Polish community immediately after Yalta, the most important person involved in the conflict being former Prime Minister Mikołajczyk. Pressured by the Anglo-Saxon governments, he had decided to accept the Yalta decisions as the basis of his own and his Party's hopeful cooperation with the "Lublin Communists." Although Arciszewski and those who worked closely with him were bitterly critical of Mikołajczyk's policy and the anti-government editorials in *Poland's Tomorrow (Jutro Polski)*, the Peasant Party's organ in exile, we did not for a moment consider any of these people Soviet agents, but simply deplored the fact that under foreign pressure they gave up on Poland's sovereignty, while trying to preserve whatever possible of its biological and cultural identity.

Siudak, who had recruited me into the Secret Service back in February of 1940, now invited me for lunch at a small Church Street restaurant. Speaking for his chief Mikołajczyk, he hinted that I should seriously consider going with them to Soviet occupied Poland to help the leaders of the Peasant Party in their difficult struggle for democracy and human rights. I asked him directly, "How do you envisage your cooperation with the Communists backed by the Soviet Union?" His answer was rather simplistic: "Stalin will have to rely on the support of the true representatives of Poland's largest class, the peasants, and that is why Bierut and Gomułka will have to accommodate the democratic *desiderata* of Chairman Mikołajczyk." "Fine", I replied, trying to reason with him, "but what will happen even if your Mikołajczyk does become Prime Minister? You can be certain that the Communists will take the key positions of Ministry of the Interior and Defense. How will you deal with the situation, under the ever watchful eyes of the NKVD?" Siudak said, "I anticipate that the Communists will be a small minority in the Cabinet and will be easily outvoted." My reply was that, "You mean, it's like making a lady just a little pregnant." The poor man blindly believed in Mikołajczyk's acumen and the latter, in turn, optimistically relied on the promised support of Churchill and Roosevelt. Overestimating the political might of Polish peasantry, he even told me that, with common shrewdness, they could manage to take the Polish Communists for a ride. "That's lovely, but," I asked, "do you really think that you can take Beria (head of the secret police) for a ride too?" We parted politely, but somewhat coldly. His "take them for a ride" theory ended with his jailing in Stalinist Poland, along with his brave but hopelessly naive friends.

Part of the blame for this shortsighted policy might be placed with the learned editorial writer of the *London Times*, Professor E.H. Carr, one of the crucial members of Chruchill's unofficial "Kitchen Cabinet". While berating Arciszewski and likeminded Poles for "lack of political wisdom" in their adamant stand against Stalin's demands, Mikołajczyk was simultaneously praised, for his readiness to compromise, as the only statesmanlike Pole. Unfortunately, such compliments from the Anglo-Saxon establishment were bound to turn some heads. Nevertheless, I got in touch with his secretary, Witold Kulerski, to arrange a strictly confidential conference between the former and the present Prime Ministers, on the eve of the latter's departure for Poland via Moscow. The two met without witnesses and, though unable to give any account of what transpired, I am convinced that it was a deadly serious exchange of views between the two leaders, who with all good will, had chosen different paths in their struggle for Polish democracy. To repeated suggestions that I abandon Premier Arciszewski and return to Warsaw with Mikołajczyk, I responded with a lenghty open letter to the latter, published in the Polish papers of the free world, in which I outlined our past relations and strongly reproached him for abandoning the policy of his own Peasant Party at home, which demanded full independence. I wrote of an emotional attempt to bring him a handful of Polish mud from Warsaw and said that, as a Lwów man, I was more than glad to deny him the control of even that small a portion of Polish soil. I also reminded the former Premier that my readiness to illegally return to Poland was to have been again by parachute, as an agent of the legal government, but never as one of the co-sponsors of the political shareholders who were helping to liquidate Poland's independence. I ended this uneasy letter with an expression of hope that I might be wrong and that, at some time in the future, Polish children would remember his name with respect, not shame. I wished him godspeed in his difficult task and stressed that I was writing as a private citizen, and not in my capacity as secretary of the Prime Minister.[84]

Worse than opposition from Mikołajczyk and his followers were the regular opportunists in our ranks who behaved like the proverbial rats abandoning a shinking ship. At least Mikołajczyk was going to use the Yalta stipulations to try to win elections, even if the price was very heavy. Each political party was undergoing painful divisiveness. Even the Peasant Party was not entirely united behind Mikołajczyk. Particularly distressing to Arciszewski was the split among the Socialists. The minority group decided to back Mikołajczyk and returned with him to Poland to serve in a coalition with the Communsits. Some of them were simply homesick for their families, while others claimed that they had to support the venerable President of the trade unions, Zygmunt Żuławski, who indeed distinguished himself later by his outspoken statements in defiance of Communist totalitarianism. But quite a few of those returnees proved later to be real scoundrels.

I was personally involved in trying to save the small Democratic Party, being asked by its two prewar vice-presidents, Stanisław Olszewski, who was then in Palestine, and Bolesław Zubrzycki in Canada, to definitely keep it in the anti-Yalta camp. However, the London group led by Dr. Witold Langrod denied me, by a small local majority, the right to vote in the name of the Palestinian members, and I spent two exhausting days at the end of March, 1945, losing the battle to save the organization from drifting into the Mikołajczyk camp. I also failed in my attempt to unite the Democratic Party with the newly created anti-Soviet "NiD". Frankly, I became more and more irritated with futile exile politics, in which opportunism, fanaticism, and personal vendettas were so often manipulated by external influences.

Morale was still higher among the armed forces, but even there Mikołajczyk got some support from its generals and colonels. There were also deep splits in the ranks of writers, and editors of the pro-Yalta *Nowa Polska* monthly who decided to return to Soviet dominated Poland. Most reprehensible were the defeatists among high level bureaucrats. Three cases exemplify these opportunistic characters. There was the former Piłsudskiite, Tadeusz Kochanowicz, a smart man who had served as one of the editors of the Dawn *("Świt")* Radio Station. He came to tell me that he was abandoning Arciszewski's team to return with Mikołajczyk and Grosfeld for the work of reconstructing Poland. Kochanowicz wrote a nasty little book once he was back in Poland in order to ingratiate himself with the Communists; and not only did he twist my arguments and attack the venerable Prime Minister as a man allegedly seeking comfort outside Poland under British protection, but he also insisted that the interests of Poland must be inevitably linked to our eastern neighbor, the USSR.[85]

At the end of May, 1945, I was invited to a "soul searching" discussion with Dr. Tadeusz Bronstein-Łychowski, a specialist on trade treaties who had served all the Polish governments for the previous fifteen years. Speaking for himself, Dr. Czesław Bobrowski, and a number of friends from the Ministry of Industry and Commerce, he began with flattery: "There certainly is a need in the West for uncompromising young politicians like you who have recent experience in Poland and a good command of English." But the situation for architects, civil engineers, educators, physicians, and economists was different, according to Dr. Łychowski. They could only serve Poland well by returning to work for reconstruction, which sounded logical in the given circumstances. He, for instance, would really be of help to his country by negotiating new trade agreements profitable to her. I was almost convinced, and promised to tell the Prime Minister of his reason for returning. However, three years later I witnessed a humiliating scene at the Palais de Chaillot in Paris during the UN General Assembly debate over Dr. Jan Papanek's case. The latter, a Czechoslovak diplomat served as a high functionary at the UN but sympathized with Jan Masaryk, who had just been "defenestrated" in Prague by the Communists as Foreign Minister of his country. The Soviet Bloc diplomats insisted that Dr. Papanek should be dismissed at once from his position because they could not rely on him. Łychowski, as temporary chief of the Polish delegation, played a disgusting role in this debate, performing slavishly under the baton of the Soviet representative Andrei Vyshynski. Such was the "constructive" service he rendered Poland during her reconstruction and I could only spit when our eyes met for a moment.

The most despicable of all, however, is the story of our expert on German affairs in the Ministry of Congressional

Affairs, the conservative journalist Józef Winiewicz. It was the sad day on which representatives of the British and United States governments delivered official notes of diplomatic severance to the Polish government in exile, when Mr. Winiewicz came, insisting on seeing the Prime Minister immediately. As his secretary, I said that the Premier was too busy that day with foreign envoys. Winiewicz claimed that he had matters of the highest importance to reveal to Arciszewski and persisted in his demand to be shown in. Unfortunately, at the moment the Premier passed through the outter office on his way to the toilet. Waylaid by Winiewicz, he agreed to hear him out briefly in an adjoining room. A few moments later, I was told to call the Minister of Finance. Kwapiński was then instructed to pay three months advance salary to Winiewicz, who reported in Paris the following day, for service in the Communist government. He eventually became the regime's Deputy Foreign Minister and its obnoxious ambassador to the United States in Washington, D.C. I still do not understand how a suspicious man as my boss could have been so eaily taken in by such a turncoat. Along with the bemedalled General Gustaw Paszkiewicz and the treacherous ex-Minister of Labor, Jan Stańczyk, "His Excellency" Józef Winiewicz was one of the most despicable characters among the returnees. Doubtless they performed useful services for the new masters of Poland, but what can one build on such scum?

These were most painful days for all of us, but it was particularly hard on the Prime Minister who now looked angry and depressed. We decided to arrange for him to tour our armed forces. On March 19, 1945 we visited the famous airborne brigade which had been stationed in Stamford in Lincolnshire since the costly "one bridge too far" battle at Arnheim in Holland. We were greeted at the camp entrance by the new brigade commander, Lt. Colonel Antoni Szczerbo-Rawicz. I was moved to see their standard which had been stitched together in my presence in 1943, by Polish ladies in Warsaw. The brigade had lost 23 percent of its officers and 22 percent among the rank and file in the senseless debacle at Arnheim in Holland.[86] But it was once again prepared for the

218

final showdown against the Nazis. There were some 250 officers and 2,919 soldiers, including 1,800 new recruits. originally conscripted in western Poland by the occupying German army. They had later deserted or allowed themselves to be taken prisoner by the Allies in order to serve in the free Polish forces. Originally, the brigade had been trained for the purpose of supporting the uprising in Poland. As such, it was an elite unit. The Prime Minister addressed them, stressing the need to fulfill our duty to the very end, giving ourselves at least a clear conscience when we demanded that our Allies remain loyal to us. He was still hoping that somehow a joint military and political effort would pave the way for Poland's freedom and independence.

Similarly, in the first days of June, 1945, we traveled by night train to visit the First Army Corps in Scotland. We were greeted at the railroad station in Perth by Generals Gluchowski, Maczek, Glabisz, and Dworak. Again, many of their soldiers had been recently recruited from Silesian Poles' forces to serve in the German army. The Prime Minister was honored with a last military parade of the Fourth Grenadiers Division in Forfar, where the famous First Armored Division under Gen. Maczek was initially formed. The Premier, aware of the warm relations between the Scottish people and the Polish soldiers, thanked the local notables for thier lasting hospitality, proposing many "Long Live Scotland" toasts. At each station, he assured the soldiers that his government would never compromise on Poland's sovereignty and integrity. He was enthusiastically received, and the next day, after a brief rest in the Caledonian Hotel in Edinburgh, he visited the Podolian Uhlans Regiment in Galashields, the heavy artillery regiment in Selkirk and the Staff Officers School at the Peebles Resort. At this last stop, he told the assembled fifth "Scottish" class that though the political situation was extremely grave, his Government's main responsibility was to history and the future generations of Poles.[87]

The last day of our stay in Scotland, I arranged an interview with the new editor of *Scotsman*, Mr. Watson. Arciszewski was especially careful to deny the malicious rumors that the Polish

Army in Great Britain was being prepared to fight the Russians. He explained that if the Poles take occupational duties in Germany, the Americans and British could be relieved to concentrate on thier unfinished struggle with Japan. The Premier complained that foreign correspondents were not being admitted to Soviet-occupied Poland and claimed that their respective governments should insist on having first hand reports of the events there. After a dinner sponsored by the generals and other high commanders, we regretfully left friendly Scottish soil. These were the few happy days for Prime Minister Arciszewski before the final debacle.

The war with Germany ended on May 9, 1945. The Prime Minister addressed Poland over the BBC and summarized our contributions, "in the air, on the sea and on land... We fought twice in France, Norway, in the Battle of Britain, in Africa, Italy, Belgium, Holland, and Germany. But first and foremost, we fought for six years on Polish soil. We fought almost beyond our human strength for our freedom and that of all the allied nations."

Our last feeble hopes rested, during those final days, on the sense of honor of the formidable conqueror of Germany, Prime Minister Churchill. The latter ignored Prime Minister Arciszewski and his Government, dealing only with Mikołajczyk and forcing him to accept the Yalta verdict. The President of the PPS was not too fond of the arch-Tory Churchill, on ideological and other grounds. Nevertheless, he agreed to send a congratulatory message on the fifth anniversary of Churchill's Premiership. Together with other leaders of the allied governments, Arciszewski received an invitation to the ceremony in St. Paul's Cathedral. The service was held early in the afternoon on Saturday, May 12, 1945, V.E. Day. I accompanied the Prime Minister and Foreign Minister Tarnowski to the Cathedral, mingling with the crowd of lesser officials outside as the two entered. I remember that I spoke with a bright American woman in the uniform of a lieutenant colonel. She was on the staff of General Carl Spaatz, Commanding Officer of the United States Air Force in the European theater. It was heartening to find that she knew of the Polish air force and their contribution to the victory over the Third Reich. On the whole, however, we were feeling increasingly left out of the prevailing sense of uplift at the war's end.

After a couple of hours, the dignitaries emerged. Mr. Tarnowski, usually slowed down by his Parkinson's disease, was very agitated and rushed over to tell me this story: "During the thanksgiving prayers offered by the Archbishop of Canterbury, Churchill turned around to get a look at the crowd. Sitting in the prescribed alphabetical arrangement, Arciszewski was right behind his British host. The two men locked glances, and then the British Prime Minister, a few years younger, bowed his head in respect. They knew well what to think of each other." Our black limousine, with its red and white national flag waving above the Prime Minister's name plaque, moved in to pick us up. We heard from the crowd spontaneous shouts of "Long Live Poland!" along with growing applause, as we made our way through Fleet Street, the Strand, Trafalgar Square and the Mall. The cars were moving in slow procession behind the Royal couple. At last, the London cockneys had paid us our due. A few days later, we also received the first message ever from Prime Minister Churchill:

"His Excellency Monsieur Tomasz Arciszewski:
I thank you most sincerely for your kind message of May 10. In reply, let me express my deep admiration of the great part which your countrymen have played in the attainment of our victory and my pleasure that out of this struggle in which they and we have fought side by side, there has grown a bond of friendship between Britian and Poland which I hope will endure through the years that lie before us."

W.S.C. May 15, 1945[88]

A few days later, I attended a Victory party with some English friends in Chelsea, when suddenly we heard by BBC radio Churchill's hoarse voice announcing *urbi et orbi* that the "Iron Curtain" has fallen upon Europe. Well, I thought, Mr. Prime Minister, you have contributed quite a lot by your pro-Stalin myopia to that tragedy... Didn't you?

221

The next and last official communication we received from Whitehall dealt with the ultimate withdrawal of British diplomtic recognition. Dated July 5, 1945, it marked the sad end of almost six years of a close British-Polish alliance during World War II. Ever since our Yalta protest, we had been aware that sooner or later the recognition would be withdrawn, and the confiscation of our government documents could follow, perhaps by the British, or more likely by the Polish Communist government. The Prime Minister gave his authorization to hide selected materials. and so, when we learned that London and Washington were about to recognize the puppet regime of Edward Osóbka-Morawski, I asked Krystyna Piotrowska to sort out valuable papers and pack them up as inconspicuously as possible. I transported them by regular taxi as I did not want to confide this secret mission even to the Prime Minister's personal chauffer, and took them to the apartment of a former British girlfriend, at 35 Redcliff Terrace. She was vacationing in Brighton and had kindly given me the key to her home in the event that my family should arrive from Italy. She was totally unaware of the political use I had decided to make of her residence. After a few days, the heavy packages were taken to the General Sikorski Institute in Gask, Scotland, and eventually transferred to the Polish Institute and General Sikorski Museum at Princess Gate near Hyde Park in London. At least something was saved from the overall calamity.

Fully aware that official protests would not be effective, the leaders of the just publically established Polish Freedom Movement "Independence and Democracy" (NiD), of which I was one of two recently elected vice-chairmen, launched a campaign among the younger generation to mobilize all dynamic elements in the armed forces and civilian agencies for a long-range political struggle.[89] President Raczkiewicz was informed of our plans by his personal physician, Dr. Bronislaw Jedlewski, who on April 24, 1945, submitted our blueprint for a political action based on the fundamental division of tasks between the capitve nation at home and the exiles in the Polish Diaspora. We called it the "concert on two pianos." The campaign was started by a series of public meetings in London. Under the chairmanship of our senior Professor Zygmunt Szempliński, Andrzej Pomian (Bohdan Sałaciński) and I addressed this first large gathering at Caxton Hall on April 30th. We both still carried a fairly fresh mandate from the A.K. Underground, and as such were attentively listened to by the emigre audience. As a grim reminder, well prepared Pomian soberly analyzed 25 years of Soviet policy towards the Ukrainian nation. My role was to give the NiD program for future Polish action. I entitled it "The Homeland and the Emigration.". As such it was soon published by "NiD" in Polish on the front page of its first official statement "Kraj i Emigracja."

The next NiD rally, held on May 30th, was organized to protest the Soviet kidnaping of the sixteen top leaders of the Secret State for a Moscow trial. Rowmund Piłsudski, the sophisticated NiD chairman, sketched at that occasion the ambitious concept of "the nation in exile", appealing for a mobilization of millions of Poles in the free world. Early in July, together with Captain Bolesław Łaszewski, I was sent to Scotland to address the Polish communities there, to explain our new duties according to the National Anthem's motto that "Poland is not yet dead as long as we remain living!" A number of appropriate publications were initiated by NiD in these days of growing confusion. Besides a profound exchange of ideas by Dr. Stanisław Gryziewicz and Zygmunt Szempliński (W tej Walce chodzi o Sprawę Człowieka — A struggle for Human Rights: Letters to a Friend) there were also guidance brochures by Adam Rudzki under various pseudonyms, and popular leaflets dealing with the new tasks facing political emigres. Trybuna, a lively monthly ably edited by Stefan Gacki, became our effective organ. Thus, along official protests of Arciszewski's Government, the new blueprint for the 1945 political emigration began to take shape.

It was impossible, however, to arrest the process of decay in various ministries. Communist agents Juliusz Katz-Suchy, Karol Lapter, Stefan Wilimowski and others whose names were not disclosed, penetrated the Polish community, agitating against legal authorities. Then there were the so-called "Yalta Cavaliers," articulate followers of Mikołajczyk's capitulation and truly homesick people, not ready to face the hardships of Poland. A couple of Bank of Poland directors for instance, transferred our Government's substantial gold reserves, against Jerzy Nowak's opposition, to Lublin regime's disposition depriving us of the much needed funds for essential activities abroad.

But, the most important underground leaders, free and jailed, remained absolutely faithful to the concept of a Sovereign Polish Republic for which they fought for six years. So did the overwhelming majority of exiled politicians. I was proud to be among them when we celebrated on July 3, 1945, in the Prime Minister's Office the second sad anniversary commemorative of my first boss, Gen. Sikorski's death in the Gibraltar "accident." The notables who solemnly gathered for the occasion were: President of the Republic Władysław Raczkiewicz, the entire Cabinet of Tomasz Arciszewski, Ambassador Edward Raczyński, former Foreign Ministers August Zaleski and Tadeusz Romer, Generals Bór-Komorowski, Haller, Kopański, Kukiel, Pełczyński, Ujejski, Admiral Świrski, Judge Franciszek Świetlik from Milwaukee, Wisconsin, representing American Polonia, and Mrs. Helena Sikorska, the late Commander-in-Chief's widow. They all seemed to appreciate the last speech I helped prepare for the Prime Minister, giving a panoramic survey of Gen. Sikorski's impressive contributions to the Allied Cause during the first four years of the just ended war in Europe. Surely it was rather that distinguished gathering than the Lublin regime of Stalins' nominees that still represented true Poland. Nevertheless, only two days later, the latter crowd of dispicable traitors were recognized as the Government of Poland by our Western ex-Allies. Our Government was officially notified of that fact by British Ambassador Sr. Owen O'Malley and Americn charge d'affaires Rudolph E. Schoenfeld. While their personal feelings were masked by polite smiles, they did not express any sorrow. A pitiful performance by otherwise charming men.

The Arciszewski Government fulfilled its sacred duty in

protesting the betrayal of Poland in official notes delivered by our Ambassadors in London and Washington. They concluded with the following solemn pledge: "Notwithstanding the recognition by other powers of its present subjection, the Polish nation will never give up its right to independent existence and will never cease to struggle for it.[90]

No Poles were invited to the San Francisco opening session of the United Nations. Only maestro Arthur Rubinstein remembered to play the Dąbrowski Mazurka (Polish National Anthem) at the Gala Concert, and kept the VIP audience, including the stony-faced Venceslaus Molotov, standing in honor of the nation which had the guts to be the first to fight the Nazis in September, 1939, and which lost more people in proportion to its prewar population than any country ever lost in any previous war.[91]

As soon as recognition was withdrawn, the British authorities began systemtically closing down our operations. This moribund task was assisgned to the Interim Treasury Committee for Polish Affairs with a token Polish staff under Ambassaor Raczyński assisting the British personnel. The offices of all Polish ministries were to be closed and their work wound up within a matter of weeks. Tomasz Arciszewski never returned to his office at 18 Kensington Palace Gardens. While he continued his Prime Minister's work at home, my little room at the *entresol* of the same building had to serve as the busy secretarial office for a month or so. One of the few kindnesses extended to the veteran Socialist leader by the newly elected Labour Government was their assistance in freeing Mrs. Arciszewski from the Montelupi jail in Kraków and providing her with a special British visa. I scouted for them more spacious lodgings, and was happy to negotiate their move into a charming house of old Lwów friends at 12 Gilston Street in Kensington. The Premier had to give up his business car, and from then on had to use public transportation just like any ordinary Londoner. I was a little annoyed when several years later old Frank Savery of the Foreign Office, the man still in charge of Polish affairs in the United Kingdom asked me ingenuously at his home if "Monsieur Arciszewski" was still around?...

On V.J. day, to celebrate the surrender of Japan, London went amok with joy once again. Just as on September 1st, 1939, when it had all begun in Poland, the skies were cloudless. But the heroic Polish airmen of the Battle of Britain were forgotten so as not to antagonize "good uncle Joe" in Moscow. They were not invited to march in the final Victory parade. I was so depressed by this shameful ingratitude on the part of the country which I had so long admired, that for the first time in my turbulent life I seriously contemplated suicide in front of Buckingham Place, having written a brief message of protest to His Majesty King George VI. Before going through with this melodramatic gesture I wished to keep an appointment with my close friend, Tadeusz Horko, editor of the *Polish Soldiers' Daily* in London. It was essential for proper post-morten publicity. Heading towards the Allies' Club at Picadilly, I passed the crowded Green Park lawns, amazed at the hundreds swarming couples celebrating the end of hostilities in an open orgy. When I introduced Tadeusz to my grim plan at the Club's bar, his healthy cynicism came to the fore. Ridiculing my sense of drama, he asked: "And what kind of contribution to the history of British-Polish relations do you propose to make with such a senseless act? Better give them hell and write a book of your war memoirs instead. Anyhow, England is on her last legs by ceasing to be the largest colonial empire and even one of the leading world powers." *Quod erat demonstrandum.*

Indeed my friend convinced me that I could do much more for our cause as public speaker, teacher and writing scholar. So, I decided to enroll for the Fall Semester at Oxford to finish my interrupted studies before embarking upon the new phase of my unfinished crusade.

226

CONCLUSION

As a person who has had a unique experience of intimate relationships with all three wartime Prime Ministers in exile, I was often asked to compare them as political leaders. Now, from a perspective of almost half a century of experience of professional historian, I feel obliged to leave the readers of these personal memoirs with a clear impression on how those three prominent Poles actually dealt with their extremely difficult tasks.

Unlike World War I, when Poland was blessed with exceptional statesmen of international repute, Roman Dmowski, Ignacy Jan Paderewski and Józef Piłsudski, during World War II there was no one who could aspire to the same category, if by a statesman we mean an influential politician with a rare sense of foresight combined with executive ability to perform accordingly to reach such long-range goals.

For a while it looked like the Polish Nation had found such a providential leader in Prime Minister and Commander-in-Chief Gen. Władysław Sikorski. After the 1939 debacle of the prewar military and civil authorities, he was widely acclaimed in the Western world and very popular at home. But his star shone brightly only for eight months, until the collapse of the French Third Republic, which proved to be a shocking surprise to him. A gifted military organizer and a bright, though somewhat vain charmer, Sikorski was, despite his constructive intelligence, not strong enough to withstand political pressures of the Allies, particularly with regard to Soviet, anti-Polish designs. He lived to witness Stalin's high-handed severance of dyplomatic relations with his London Government over the Katyń Forest crisis, but was soon abruptly eliminated in the Gibraltar plane disaster, two years before the war ended.

His hard-working successor, the self-made Peasant leader Stanisław Mikołajczyk, lacked international experience and was ultimately used by the Anglo-Saxon war leaders to accommodate Stalin for implementation of the latter's goals, formulated at the Teheran and Yalta Conferences. Because of his readiness to abandon the initial Polish war goals, Mikołajczyk was unable to lead the Polish Armed Forces in the West in his ultimate capitulation to the Big Powers' pressures. He was opposed both by the potential leaders of the younger generation in exile, and by most of the older representatives of the traditional political parties in London, though he managed to retain his stronghold over his own Peasant Party and most of the faithful followers of late General Sikorski.

The third and most serious crisis in exile politics occurred late in November, 1944, when the Cabinet majority rejected Mikołajczyk's plans for substantial territorial concessions to Russia, and the Socialist envoy of the underground Secret State Tomasz Arciszewski formed a new coalition Government. This uncompromising Social Democrat, however, could only perform one symbolic duty of national protest against the Yalta selling out of Poland. A lovable but unsophisticated old fighter for Freedom and social justice, he was unable to communicate with Anglo-Saxon leaders without translators, being rejected by them from the beginning of his historic mission.

While in the Monte Cassino victor Władysław Anders, as well as in Dr. Tadeusz Bielecki and Adam Ciołkosz we did have astute leaders of the second echelon abroad, it was rather in occupied Poland that one would have to look for potential statesmen. Too bad that most of them had been gradually eliminated by either Nazi or Soviet genocide. During my year long underground experience, I was particularly impressed by three outstanding personalities, namely the charismatic Commander-in-Chief of the Home Army (A.K.) General "Grot" (Stefan Rowecki), the level-headed Chief of the Secret State "Sobol" (Jan Stanisław Jankowski), and the tough-minded Secretary General of the Polish Socialist Party (PPS-WRN) "Bazyli" (Kazimierz Pużak), who became Chairman of the underground Rump Parliament early in 1944. Of the three, the first was murdered in a Berlin prison during the Warsaw Uprising, and the other two were treacherously kidnapped by Soviet authorities to undergo a trial in Moscow which led to their subsequent deaths in Communist jails.

The crux of the matter was that no one, even a genius, could have saved Poland from her gravest predicament ever. It was humanly impossible to overcome dire geopolitical handicaps by winning against mortal enemies and trusted friends alike. Karl Marx, who never was a supporter of Russian imperialism, warned the International Workingmen Association (The First International) in his London speech in 1864:

...the policy of Russia is changeless... Its methods, its tactics, its maneuvers may change, but the polar star of its policy — world domination — is a fixed star... Poland is the great instrument for the execution of Russian designs on the world, but it is also an invincible obstacle to them, until such time as the Poles, worn out by the accumulated betrayal of Europe become a whip in the hands of the Muscovite...[92]

For us, the Poles, the much maligned "Cold War" started long before the "Hot War" with Hitler's Germany was over. And who, if you please, has any moral or other right to blame us that we tried to disprove Marx's gloomy prediction? I am inclined to believe that in adverse circumstances we have all done our best in paving the way for the next generations, including the amazing Solidarity movement of 1980-1981, to regain Poland's rightful place in a free and undivided Europe.

THE END

APPENDIX

DOCUMENT 1 (translation from Polish).

"The note deals with Second Lt. Jan Karski's memo to Gen. Sikorski, who is leaving for Poland in the capacity of Political Courier.

In the next few days he is flying home. I think that he could play a useful role in the transmission of the General's materials: 1) for the country in general, 2) for those persons and groups from whom I delivered to you the political material. I am sure that it would be very useful for the Cause if you would be willing to accept him before his departure and then to use him in *this or any other* character. I have known Second Lt. Lerski for many years, he is one of the noblest and wisest men I have ever met. He is discreet, well-oriented in political situations, he has an unusual sense of duty, is not bound to any political center, is enthusiastic about his mission, and I am convinced that he would well perform his assigned tasks in *enlightening* or informing the Country of specific people.

They know in Poland that I have reached London, and thus understand as well that I have delivered to you, Sir, all materials that I had to hand officially or discreetly. I allow myself to ask you, Sir, that Second Lt. Lerski could take with him at least the confirmation of the receipt of the above materials by you, General. By this occasion I permit myself to mention that I have not yet passed to you all the material.

February 5, 1943   Jan Karski
                                                    (signature)"

DOCUMENT 2 (translated from Polish).
To The Executive of the
British Labour Party,
c/o Deputy Prime Minister
C.R. Attlee

Dear Comrades,

We decided to write to you once more at this juncture, when the plans of the future organization of the world are being shaped and defined. Your friendship and sympathy have been to us, throughout the war, a source of comfort and encouragement to persist in our flight. To you, therefore, we address ourselves and beg you to be willing to be the spokesman of our aims and desires.

We are deeply disturbed by tendencies showing in political discussions in Britain, which, to our mind, may have fatal consequences for Europe, opening a period of anxiety and troubles all over the world. Our anxiety over the future of our nation and of the central and eastern European regions increases with the growth, day by day, of the danger menacing our country.

We write our letter to the awe-inspiring cracking of the guns of the German squads carrying out public mass executions in the streets of our towns. Since October, when this method of terrorism and extermination had first been applied, 'til the 1st of January of this year, 950 hostages seized in the streets or dragged out of their homes, have been shot in Warsaw only, in groups of 10 to 100, publically, in the squares and streets of the city. This happens in many other towns and villages. Simultaneously, the killing of prisoners continues as before. There is no doubt that the Germans will go on killing our youth, our workers, peasants, and educated classes right to the end of the war, chosing the best people, the most valuable and forceful individuals with the aim of weakening and disabling our nation to the utmost degree. And, parallel to this mass-murder — round-ups and raids go on night and day, and hundreds of our men, women, and young people are being arrested. Transports to concentration camps continue in endless procession, and in these camps the Germans have brought to perfection their bestial tortures from which there is not escape but death. The crematories in the camps burn day and night.

In this fight against the Polish people the Germans use every available means, including lethal gas. In Oświęcim, Bełżec, Majdanek, and Treblinka they have built special gas chambers to destroy prisoners wholesale. The Germans already embarked on gas warfare in this war! Not yet on the fronts — but hundreds of our fellow-citizens perish in gas chambers daily, serving at the same time in tests for various kinds of gas.

Our losses have mounted to 5-6 million dead — of whom 2.5 million are Polish citizens of Jewish faith, who were murdered last year for the simple reason that they were born Jews.

The holocaust of millions of Polish people has already destroyed the majority of social and political leaders, scientists, scholars, technicians, and a multitude of ordinary working men and women, whose only fault was that they remained Polish. Add to this over two million women and peasants deported to the interior of Germany and over a million driven into Russia, of whom only a small number succeeded in getting out to the Middle East, while the great majority gradually passed away in the frightful conditions of the Soviet "penal labor camps." The most active elements, the most useful and vigorous were chosen, so that they should not stand in the way of the aims of another age-long aggressor against our country and our freedom.

This is the price we have already paid for our decision to fight tyranny.

We know how difficult it is for you to believe that all of this has really happened. The idea of cruel biological extermination of nations is so foreign to you, that your imagination simply does not grasp such a terrible picture, which we face every day, and which reminds every one of us that it is only by chance that the life of this or that man will be saved.

And the final act is still to come. Himmler already decided and Frank already sent instructions as to the evacuation of Polish territories. The educated and professional classes, and all unable to work are to be destroyed. Those fit to work physically will be deported as slaves in the wake of the retreating German armies. We know how these orders were executed in the Ukraine. We have no illusions. The Germans will execute the orders in Poland with the same meticulous thoroughness.

We do not complain. We want, however, the world to know of our fate, so that the sacrifice of our people shall not be in vain. We do not despair, but get ready to face the new horrors. The world may rest assured that before we die we shall fight first. But let it be known that we shall die in thousands and tens of thousands in our fight against the Nazi hordes, their tanks and airplanes, their automatic

233

guns and pistols — ourselves equipped only with the most primitive weapons. We are disarmed. We clamour for arms. The degree of our resistance will be measured by the level of our armaments. We can get that assistance from you, from Britain only. As, according to your letter to us, it is impossible to paralyze the murderous activities of the Germans by retaliations from the air, there remains nothing for us but to hope for salvation through the speeding up of military operations and delivery of arms to us.

What our Home Forces, with which we closely cooperate, received, has become a serious factor of defense. But it is inadequate, especially in view of German evacuation plans. Our first request to you is, therefore, to multiply the arms deliveries for our Home Army.

Permit us, however, not to confine ourselves to this only. In spite of our losses, our political life continues, and if only for the sake of a historical record, let us state that the working classes of Poland preserved all their spiritual fortitude, and that every gap torn in our ranks by the terrorism of the invader is quickly filled by new men, ready for work and sacrifice. Our organizations to an ever-increasing degree embrace all the working people. The political, military, and special organizations of our Party and of Trade Unions work ceaselessly. As representatives of this vigorous and undaunted movement we have the right and the duty to present to you our political standpoint.

Until now, despite our tragic conditions, we felt certain that our sacrifice will lead to a victorious end for us as well, to the reconstruction of an independent and strengthened republic, in which the workers and peasants in brotherly union with the non-manual workers will be able to realize the ideals of liberty and social justice.

Our hope is now shattered. That hope gave us 'till now the strength to face death steadfastly. Today, however, there is fear in the eyes of our fellow citizens, fear caused by increasingly growing symptoms of a return to imperialistic methods in international relations. Doubts enter our hearts, and a painful thought hurts our brains, that our people who were honoured as "the inspiration of mankind in the fight against Nazism" weakened and bled in the unceasing struggle and perhaps laid prostrate tomorrow, are being sacrificed by the great powers to the insatiable greed of Russia. Where conscience raises its voice the conservatives will silence it by an appeal to "statesmanship," while the so-called progressive elements will feel absolved by the partnership with Soviet Russia, which for the ignorant and snobs of all kinds has become a symbol of progress.

How well we Poles know this situation. Our history is full of analogies. Had not the three partitions of Poland been executed by Prussia in partnership with Russia, in the same fashion as the fourth partition of 1939 by the Nazi Reich and Soviet Russia? Was not Catherine, Empress of Russia, the personification of progress for the European snobs of the XVIII century? Was not she the Semiramis of the North and defender of dissidents? Diplomacy watched with indifference the destruction of a nation — for that was "statesmanship."

You do not know, however, the communists and communism. You know how they tried to weaken the British people's will to fight nazism. How much, by spreading cowardice in France, they were responsible for the capitulation of that country. You know that communism in Russia is a disguise for old imperialism, which always tried to devour its neighbours.

We consider ourselves to be members of the western European family of nations. We want to live and to progress together with other European peoples. We have once overthrown the Moscow yoke, and we are ready to give our lives once more in order not to be under that yoke again, even if for a transitory period. Even a temporary occupation of Polish territories by the Soviets will magnify the calamities caused by the German occupation.

You may not know and perhaps you cannot understand the tragic fate of our officers — mainly of the reserve — who surrendered to the Russians after the September campaign. But you do know the fate of Alter and Erlich and you will not think that we exaggerate when, after what we have experienced in our relations with Russia throughout these long years, we expect from a Soviet occupation nothing but a final destruction of the active elements of our nation, in the first place of the socialist movement, which will not agree to any compromise with Soviet tyranny, and will not betray its ideals of freedom.

Trust us. We do not hate Russia. We want to live on the friendliest terms with her. In the interest of peace, of our economic development, and of the general progress of our country, we want a peaceful and friendly cooperation with Russia. However, our generation still bears in mind the Tsar's predatory attempts to russify our country — and now, after a short respite granted to us by the Russian revolution, we face again the violation of solemn nonagression pledges and undisguised tendencies to grab a part, if not the whole, of Poland.

Absolute certainty that the sovereignty of the two countries, Poland and Russia, will not be impaired, is a condition of a friendly and peaceful relationship. Without that certainty, Russian nationalism and imperialism will always look on Poland as its ready prey on the road to further conquests in the West and South of Europe.

Security and a lasting peaceful settlement in the eastern part of Western Europe are indispensible, not only for the welfare of Poland, but also for the good of Russia, in order to rid her of imperialism and agressiveness for the good of Europe, to guarantee her against Russian imperialism.

The fate of Estonia, Latvia, Lithuania, and Poland, the territorial integrity of these countries and their security through an international organization, will determine the fate of a future Europe. And concession to Russian imperialism will serve as an encouragement and a prize for Russian nationalism and chauvinism.

We are well aware how little moral values count in international relations. However, leaving in the hands of Russia even the smallest bit of land which the Soviet Union acquired through her alliance with Hitler, directed against the entire democratic world, would absolve the USSR of her policy in 1939-40 and would amount to approval of that policy. If Russia will not comply with the will of the world to restore the independence of those countries, overpowered by Hitler, where it has been done with her cooperation — then the future may indeed bring an intensification of the danger from that most powerful empire.

That is why we reject categorically Russian annexation plans as regards our eastern territories and demand that the pre-war Polish-Russian frontier be maintained. That is why, in full agreement with our party, the Delegate in Poland of the Government of the Republic has ordered that in the event of the Russian armies entering Polish territory, the population not only must remain on the spot and resist the German evacuation, but also reveal to the Soviet armies the fact that a Polish underground administration exists on all territories legally belonging to Poland.

We know that we shall not be strong enough to assert ourselves. It will depend entirely on the Soviet Union how we shall have to treat their armies — which we, as the appeal of the Government's Delegate put it, will meet as the "allies of our allies" — and whether we shall have to regard them as the new invader.

236

When we were signing the peace treaty with Russia in Riga, we had left beyond the frontiers of our Republic two million Polish people, who for centuries lived on Ukrainian and Byelorussian soil. Where are they now? Remnants could be traced in official Soviet statistics, dispersed in the remotest parts of the Soviet Empire. Yet, we kept silent for the sake of maintaining peaceful relations with Russia. We have no claims on Russia now, but we cannot agree to any attempts at weakening us today, when the biological war waged against us by Hitler is devastating us to the extreme.

The Polish people for centuries have lived with the Ukrainian and White Ruthenian peoples on the confines of our Republic. Our Party has always been the most loyal friend of Ukrainians and White Ruthenians during the lifetime of the Polish Republic, and we always protected them against the abuses of bureaucracy. More than once they have elected our comrades to represent them in the Parliament, thus demonstrating their confidence. We do not hesitate to tell men and women all the world over, and especially you, comrades, that the heart of the masses of the people of those areas is filled with fear at the prospect of incorporation into the USSR. The fraudulent comedy of the so-called "elections for self-determination," when people were compulsorily driven to the polls and no political group but the communist party had the right to nominate candidates — was a nauseating exhibition of cynicism of both the authors and actors.

We are all the more entitled to take such a stand, that the major Polish parties, which support the Government and cooperate with it both at home and in exile, have solemnly adopted the principle of full equality of all Polish citizens regardless of their faith or nationality. This found its expression in the declarations of the Government and guarantees for the future that the national minorities and the Poles will henceforth live together in full harmony and friendship on the basis of "equals with equals and free with free."

It is, therefore, the duty of our allies to safeguard the rights of the Polish state on the territories which may be occupied by the Soviet armies pursuing the Germans westward. It has come to our knowledge that the Moscow conference made decisions regarding the obligation to withdraw forces from foreign territories on the cessation of military operations in particular areas. If this is not to remain a hollow promise, conditions must be created for the work and activities of the authorities set up by the government of the country. The Soviets, paving their way for "faits accomplis" have

237

broken of diplomatic relations with our governments and have created puppet Polish formations in Moscow. It is, therefore, imperative, that at the time the Soviet armies will be crossing the Eastern border of the Polish Republic, political allied missions should be present there, with the mandate to cooperate in the establishment of a loyal relationship between the onmarching Soviet troops and the recreated Polish authorities, to safeguard the lives and liberties of Polish citizens and to prevent further accomplished facts.

This is a most acute problem. A satisfactory solution of that problem will serve as a basis and a precedent for future general political settlements.

As to those future settlements, we must categorically protest against, and oppose any tendencies to establish a Russian sphere of influence over the Baltic States, Poland, and the Balkans. These countries wish to and can develop as independent units. Even the most backward of them are havens of civilization compared with Russia. The creation of a "sphere of influence" would amount to forcing that European region at least a century back in the development of its civilization. We fully appreciate Russia's effort in her upward drive. We wish her a speedy progress. But the world should be aware that to place any non-Russian areas under Russian influence would retard the development of Russia herself. It will open new sources of national antagonism — for none of these nations will agree to Russian supremacy without resistance — it will foster Russian nationalism and divert their efforts from urgent problems of internal reconstruction and progress to a struggle against these nations rising against being forcibly placed under Russian tutelage.

This is not what mankind expects from an allied victory. All human beings the world over are yearning for a life of peace, for socially organized creative work, for a development of the civilization of various nations and the pooling of its efforts in one world civilization, embracing all mankind. That is why we aim at a closer union with our neighbours in the north and the east on the basis of uniting "equals with equals, free with free." That is why we cherish the ideal of a Central European Federation, the foundation of which was laid by our government in the Polish-Czechoslovak confederation agreement. Yet, hardly born, that scheme had to face a formidable enemy, Soviet Russia. The Soviets spared no efforts to prevent that scheme from materializing. They attacked it by diversive activities of communist bands in Poland, who fight the Poles rather than the

238

Germans; they torpedo the Federation with the help of a group of Czech exiles. How significant it is! Will this scheme of a new organization in Europe not materialize for the sole reason that it may guarantee a full independence of Central Europe from both Russia and Germany, an independence which is a prerequisite of international cooperation? We shall fight to the end for that idea. We are convinced that the entire socialist movement of Europe will fight for it and that you, with all your force, will be in the forefront of the fight.

Such voluntary regional federations will form the foundations of a Union of the Free Peoples of Europe, friendly cooperating in full security, having at their disposal a military force, which will be a guarantee of that security. Russia and other great powers should also be members of that Union. A far flung international cooperation will develop in this union, as well as the consciousness of a European unity and solidarity, and of world citizenship.

We are fully aware that we may be told reproachfully how little we can materially contribute today to the realization of our ideas. But the very fact that we daily face death, that in the nearest future we shall be faced by an even greater tragedy, moves us to express to you our feelings, to inform you of our aims and ideals which give us the necessary strength to persist in the uneven struggle. And who can know our situation better than oursleves, as well as the situation of that strip of Europe on which our people have lived for a thousands years?

The knowledge that our ideals will be realized in this war, and the assurance that our sacrifice will not be in vain, enable us to follow the path we had chosen and increase tenfold our strength in our struggle.

This knowledge and this assurance we shall derive from a clear stand of the governments of Great Britain and the United States of America as regards our basic aims:

To secure our territory against the prospects of a Soviet occupation.

To take into consideration in the operational and strategic plans of the Allies the use of our forces in exile in such a way, that they should reach their homeland in the shortest possible time.

Finally — to equip us with arms and munition, so that we shall successfully resist the German evacuation plans.

This would again create an atmosphere of confidence and security so badly needed in a country which is being ruthlessly devastated.

We write to you in the conviction that our thoughts and aims will be properly reflected and expressed in your political activities.

Central Executive Committee
of the Polish Socialist Party.

Warsaw, 10th January, 1944.

DOCUMENT 3
To All British and American Boy Scouts and Girl Guides.

The chief authorities of Scouts and Guides in Poland asked me through the National Commissioner with whom I had three conferences in January 1944, to take the following message to world Scouting.

The Scout authorities in Poland desire that the Supreme Council of the Association of Polish Boy Scouts and Girl Guides should convey this message to British Scout and Guide authorities.

The National Commissioner emphasized that the Supreme Council in London should do its best to fulfill the wishes expressed in the message.

1. Scouting in Poland fully realizes how strong the bonds of international scout brotherhood are. It believes that the scout movements in all the countries form one family. They were brought up on the same unaltered scout principles. All these movements share the responsibility for international scouting as well as for each separate movement in every country; they should not limit themselves to their mother country alone.

2. The educational ideal on which the Polish Scout movement before this war was founded was based on the Law and Promise as given by Lord Robert Baden-Powell.

We always stood firmly by these principles. Inspite of the difficult circumstances of nearly five years, underground fights, our educational ideal became now ever more faithful to B.-P.'s principles.

3. Polish Scouting believes that it is its right and its duty to speak for the scout movements of other countries of East-Central Europe. While they desire true liberty, they are not able to defend their own rights sufficiently, and besides, they are not in such a close contact with Great Britain and the United States of America, as Poland is.

4. Scouting in underground Poland points out with great anxiety the danger of an imminent crisis — the loss of confidence to the Anglo-Saxon world. The youth of the subjugate countries in East-

240

Central Europe, and in Poland especially, builds all its hopes on Great Britain and the USA. This youth was fully convinced about the truth and sincerity of the ideals proclaimed by the western democracies. It believed that the Atlantic Charter and the 4 freedoms of President Roosevelt were the guiding principles, and though general, the true aims of this war. Poland has been fighting with you side by side in defense of Christian democratic principles in national and international life, in defense of the rights of all nations and respecting of international justice.

We undertook this fight alone, against overwhelming forces, on September 1st, 1939. It is for the same ideals that we have been fighting for nearly five years under the most cruel, organized oppression.

The latest examples of an undoubtedly opportunistic attitude of the great powers fill our youth with greatest anxiety.

The scout authorities in Poland told me to ask all sister-guides and brother-scouts whether they realize that the Western World will have neither the right nor the possibilities which are, to this day, the very basis of education of all youth and especially Scouts and Guides. For if we replace truth and justice by opportunism and lack of courage, it will be impossible to base the future education on the truth and justice as expressed in Christian teaching.

Scouting in Poland, which every day is paying immense sacrifices of toil and blood, asks whether it is possible that these moral values gained in the struggle should be wasted.

You must understand that people are ready to undergo most cruel suffering, to face even death — but nor do they want to die in vain. They must be able to go on believing that their fight was not aimless, that all they loved and cherished will not be given up, that the ideas in which they were brought up are still holding fast. After all, it is for this that they die. Our young generation is fully aware of the fact that if the future of the world is to be decided by force and violence, our generation may well be the last one which fights and dies in the defense of principles which are the very basis of the Scout Movement. We want to point out to you — and we feel that it is both our right and our duty to do so — that if you allow your nations to take the easy path of selfishness and opportunism, you will thus put an end to the Scout Movement in Europe.

5. Scouting in underground Poland has been informed about preparations of post-war help for the youth in the occupied countries of Europe and about the part of British Guides and Scouts in this

action.

This help will be of an utmost importance, and besides, it is a valuable, practical test of a real, international scout brotherhood. But we want to stress it as strong as possible, that in spite of all its importance, material help is only a secondary problem.

We want you, above all, to bring us that for which we have been longing so much for years — give us true freedom and independence.

This is our first and greatest need. Do not talk and think about us as "poor Poland." We want neither pity nor charity. We are in the front line and those in the first lines have no inferiority complex; they do not need to be admired or pitied. They only wish that their hardships and toil should be understood and not wasted.

6. Polish Scouting wants the youth of the whole world, and scouts and guides above all, to be informed about the unyielding, stubborn fight, the hard fact, the anxieties and hopes of Polish youth. Together with the whole nation, Polish Scouting has voluntarily and spontaneously undertaken the great burden of this war; and it did it with full consciousness and a firm conviction that it is the right path to follow, not only for our own sake, but for the good of other nations as well.

Trying to let you know about the fight, the everyday life and the thoughts of Polish Scouts, we sent to London a book: *Stones On the Rampart* published underground.

We should like the book to be translated into English and distributed amongst your boys and girls.

Scout authorities in Poland request the British Scout and Guide authorities to take it in hand, and if possible, to write a foreward to it.

DOCUMENT 4 (translated from Polish of a radio cable #210/K, received in London at 1410 on January 29, 1944 from Warsaw).

I/21 sending to Janka [Paris] emissary of the Delegate's Government Jur. In view of the elevator's elimination, let Ziomek [Capt. Skarbek] transfer him without delay to Waleriana [Spain).
1. Do it either using our own routes of the cub scouts or the old Spanish one. Inform friends in Waleriana and Liza's contacts.
2. Either use the Wera-Weng route, which Lubiewa discussed with Grzegorz, let Wera radio us and Ziomek the point in Klara, to send her Jur in order to transfer him directly to Waleriana.

I am sending directly to Wera on mechanical exchange of II/2 the photo and the biodata for visa to Waleriana. Jur carries the mail of the Government's Delegate and that of BIP [Home Army-A.K.]. Years 27, height 173, grey eyes, blond hair, oval face, small hands, small scar by the right eye. For Waleriana his pseudonym is George Carston [sic].

For Ziomek Jur is guided by Jan. Without Jan Jur will look for contact through Żarnowski on the Quai de Bourbon.

Lawina [Gen. "Bór"] 102 22/I/44

DOCUMENT 5 (translated from Polish of a radio cable 785/TJN.4 [confidential].

attention if possible, send this cable immediately. January 31.

For ZIOMEK   v.urgent

Jalina [Gen. "Bór"] sent to you on I/21 emissary Jur with mail accompanied by Jan.

Without Jan Jur will look for Żarnowski Quai de Bourbon. Send Jur urgently to us via Spain. Data of Jur, 27 years, height 173, grey eyes blond hair, oval face, small hands, small scar by right eye, pseudonym for Spain George Carston [sic].

RAWA 785 [Lt. Col. Michał Protasewicz]

DOCUMENT 6 (translated from Polish of a radio cable from London). Staff of Commander in Chief, 6th Dept. 785/TJN.44 [confidential] January 31, 1944

most urgent

To Colonel Perkins

We received a cable from home about sending emissary pseudonym "Jur" who will be transfered from France to Spain. In Spain he will use the name George Carston [sic].

I respectfully request you, Sir, to inform British posts on Spanish territory and for assistance in possibly quickly expediting that courier to Great Britain.

George Carston is 27 years, height 173 cm., grey eyes, blond hair, oval face, small hands, scar (small) by right eye.

Chief of Special Department of Staff of C-in-C
Lt. Col. Protasewicz

243

DOCUMENT 7
Gen. S. Kopański, CB., CBE., DSC.

55 Hallowell Rd.
Northwood, Mddlx.
May 25th, 1949

TO WHOM IT MAY CONCERN

On the strength of a statement issued by General Bór-Komorowski, formerly C-in-C. Polish Home Army, I hereby confirm that Lt. Jerzy Lerski was dropped by parachute in Poland on February 19th, 1943, as an emissary of the C-in-C Polish Armed Forces under British Command, and that he remained with the Polish Home Army until March 21st, 1944; when he reported to the Polish General Staff in London on his return from Poland.

Lt. Jerzy LERSKI fulfilled with great efficiency the tasks and the mission he had been entrusted with and merited the highest praises of his superiors.

(signature)
S. Kopański

DOCUMENT 8
May 8, 1985

Dear Prof. Lerski,

I have the pleasure to inform you that the Special Commission for the Designation of the Righteous, at its session of 14.1.1985 decided to confer upon you its highest expression of gratitude: the title of Righteous Among the Nations.

This honour entitles you to a medal and a certificate of honour and the privilege of having a tree planted in your name at Yad Vashem, Jerusalem. These awards will be subsequently forwarded to you at a later date.

Please accept our congratulations and best wishes.

(signature)
Dr. Mordecai Paldiel

DOCUMENT 9 (translated from Polish).
The Emissary Who Returned from Home:
"We Need More Weapons"
The Polish nation united as never before awaits orders from London.
(PAT)
The Government's special envoy, sent some time ago to Poland,
retured with important instructions to London. He brought with him
the first reports concerning the Russian armies' entrance into eastern
Poland, which occurred, as is known, in the first days of January of
this year.

Jerzy Jur-emissary pseudonym—shared with PAT's correspondent
his impressions from his sojourn in Poland, where he was sent still
during the life of the late Gen. Wł. Sikorski. Jerzy Jur then took with
him instructions to the Delegate of the Government functioning at
home as the Deputy Premier of the Government of the Polish
Republic, also to the Home Political Council (KRP) composed of the
four political parties of the ruling coalition. After his landing in the
country, he worked for several months in one of the departments of
the clandestine home administration.

"What does the country need from the Allies in its uneven
struggle?" we asked the envoy from home.

His response was emphatic: *"We need more weapons. We do not
have enough weapons over there. This is why delivery of such weapons
by the Allies is of utmost urgency, on which depends the chance of the
Home Army's (AK) expansion of activities.* The spirit of the population
is splendid: everyone wants to fight the Germans. In each district of
Poland there are organized operational units which either are
already fighting, or are prepared for struggle. The remaining men
able to carry guns form a reserve in anticipation of being armed."

From October, 1943, the new wave of Nazi repressions increased
in Poland. This remains mainly as their reaction to the growth of the
Home Army's activities. The Germans publically announce the
names of the executed Poles, whom they in most cases call members
of: "Polish Union of Insurrectionists in England's Service," at the
same time they spell on the posters the names of hostages *to be
executed if the Home Army does not cease its operations.*
"Long Live Poland!"

Jerzy Jur eyewitnessed such an execution performed in October,
1943, at Puławski Street, in the district of Mokotów. *It was a public
execution, and to terrorize the Polish population, the Germans forced
the Mokotów residents to attend it and watch.* The place of execution

245

was fenced by cordons of S.S. German police detachment, when the covered trucks with hostages arrived. All had their hands tied in the back. They walked to the place of execution, stumbling from exhaustion, *because on the eve that day the Germans took the hostages' blood for wounded German soldiers.* The hostages were only in their underwear and barefoot. In view of the fact that during preceding executions those to be shot shouted *"Long Live Poland!"* or *"Long Live Freedom,"* etc., which made a great impression on the people forced to watch the execution, the Germans tapes their mouths. Those executions are performed by German police by hand machine guns. *The hostages were brought for execution in my presence in a group of 100 people, shot in three groups.* Those who had to wait in the second and third groups had to watch the execution of the preceding victims.

Attempts at Contacts with Russians"

About the entry of Russian troops into Poland, Jerzy Jur relates as follows:

The first units of the Red Army entered during my stay in Poland. Following the orders from London, the Polish Undergroud organizations in the Eastern Borderlands disclosed their existence to the Soviet miliary authorities. Delegations of local Home Army units were arriving at the headquarters of the Russian commanders with their white-red flags. The Polish commander handed the Russian commander a sealed document containing the declaration of cooperation already known from the press. In such a way the cooperation of the A.K. units with Russian troops in various localities were initiated.

Simultaneously, a substantial increase of the Home Army's activities was evidenced in eastern territories at the rear of the withdrawing German troops. The Home Army cuts supplies which adds to the chaos in rallying centers, forcing the Germans to keep stronger units in the rear to fight that diversion.

Jerzy Jur confirms the news about German action aimed at winning Polish support to fight the Soviets. They are trying to initiate this type of action everywhere, in towns, townlets, and villages, under the slogan of *"Fight Bolshevism."* They try to penetrate every social group, equally using persuasion as they use menace, temptation and terror. "The attitude of the entire Polish population to the Germans is to hostile to be changed. So the German initiatives will undoubtedly come to nothing. The spirit of the Poles is great. Never were they so united at home as they are now. The Polish

246

nation awaits orders from London to rise for the final and decisive struggle with the Germans. *"Nothing can shake the Poles' faith that the moment of German collapse and the Allied victory is approaching."*

DOCUMENT 10 (translation of the late Karol Wagner's statement deposited on May 10, 1949 in "Studium Polski Podziemnej" LDZ 287/49/76).
Paris, April 8, 1949.

On the request of Mr. Jerzy Lerski, I am submitting the following statement: From July, 1943 to July, 1945 I was in London in charge of the broadcasting department of Ministry of Information and Director of the "Polish Radio" subordinate to the same Ministry. In contrast to the Polish broadcasts of BBC being the English institution]. By the end of March, 1944 Emissary of the Underground Polish authorities, Mr. Jerzy Jur (Lerski) arrived in London from Warsaw. In the middle of April I received from the Polish Telegraph Agency (PAT), directed by Dr. Stefan Litauer (future "Plenipotentiary Minister of the Communist Warsaw Regime"), a communique about the press conference of Mr. J. Jur, to be broadcast to Poland. According to this communique, Mr. Jur allegedly declared that Polish Underground organizations were coming into the open with their national colors to meet the Soviet forces entering into the eastern lands of Poland. After the first broadcast of that communique, I received a telephone call from Mr. Jerzy Jur informing me that he did not make such a statemet to anyone, as it is false. He demanded the immediate withdrawal of that PAT communique from broadcasting, which I did on his request. At the same time, he informed me that he is protesting at once the PAT abuse with the top government authorities through the Minister of the Interior to whom he is answerable as political courier, because his statement for the press conference with American newsmen was definitely twisted.

The above statement of mine is submitted as an enclosure for proper filing in the Historical Office of Underground Poland.

(signature)
Karol Wagner

247

DOCUMENT 11 (translated from Polish of a radio cable 693 from Wanda 7 [Warsaw], received on April 24, 1944 at 16:37 in London)

Commander-in-Chief

The BBC broadcast of April 12 contains a paragraph allegedly based on Jur's reports in presenting the meeting of A.K. units with the Soviet army in such a deceitful and senseless way that the only result of such broadcasts is the loss of face of the government and its propaganda in the eyes of the population and the Bolsheviks.

Also, the BBC communique of April, 1945 hrs., broadcast deceitful information that the command of the Red Army in Moscow received a response to Gen. Sergeiev's proposal. This deceives the commanding officer of the Volhynia district, who conducts these discussions. Because it is natural to supposition that presenting any A.K. activities in government bases them on my reports, therefore such pronouncements are undermining my authority, causing the disorientation in A.K. rows.

I ask for prevention of such propagandistic broadcasts. If they repeat, I would have to disavow them in the clandestine press at home.

Lawina 693 [Gen. "Bór"]
IV/15, 1944

DOCUMENT 12 (Inter-office correspondence between Mssrs. Osborne and Roberts from the Political Intelligence Dept. of the Foreign Office).

Frank Roberts, Esq.,   3rd April, 1944
Foreign Office

Dear Frank,

I am enclosing a brief report of a conversation with Mr. Lerski, the most recent arrival from Poland to this country, which may be of some interest to you.

Yours sincerely,

(signature)
Harold Osborne

DOCUMENT 13.

Position of the Polish Underground Movement and attitude re the Curzon Line Settlement.

Encloses a report of a conversation with M. Lerski, the most recent arrival from Poland. He discussed the attitude towards Russian proposals, and the post-war Poland.

He emphasized the tragic lack of weapons and money in the Polish Underground Movement.

This all rings true.

(signature)
D. Allen?

DOCUMENT 14.

This is worth reading. It confirms our view that the real Polish fears do not so much concern the Polish Curzon Line frontier as ultimate Soviet intentions regarding the future Poland. Oddly enough the Polish Socialists are the most extreme anti-Russian elements in Poland.

(signature)
Frank Roberts

DOCUMENT 15.
MEMORANDUM   MOST SECRET
**Attitude of Polish Underground
to Curzon Line Settlement**

The following is based upon a conversation with Mr. Lerski who left Poland in Janaury, 1944. Mr. Lerski was trained by us and during his stay in Poland was head of the Information Department of the Propaganda section in the Polish Underground Movement. He is very frank and I think perfectly honest.

1. He does not think that there iwll be any serious fighting against the Russians on a Curzon Line issue.

2. If the Russians attempted to impose a communist or a pro-Soviet regime, otherwise than through the existing Underground Movement, he is convinced that it would lead to some degree of civil war.

3. He is quite certain that the Underground Movement in Poland, both the leaders and the younger element, are even less disposed to agree to the Curzon line than the Polish official set-up in this country. He gives the following reasons, which may be interesting:

a. The Underground Movement does not believe the Soviet demands would be satisfied by a Curzon line frontier. As he put it "the part of Poland which remained west of the Curzon line would never be allowed to interfer with Russian foreign policy or to act as a serious ally of the Western Powers if their interests clashed with those of Russia."

b. They are seriously afraid of a powerful Germany, communist or otherwise, arising in the not very distant future, which would demand back ceded territories in Silesia and elsewhere.

c. Quite apart from the question of ceded territory, the Curzon line is more unwelcome than any other possible line to Poland because they know that Great Britain has once declared herself in favour of it and are afraid that if she does so on a second occasion it will be quiet final.

d. The underground organization realizes the necessity of maintaining the morale of the Polish people and of maintaining its own prestige with them. Acceptance of the Curzon line frontier would seem to the population at large to be a betrayal by the Underground Movement of what they have been resisting and suffering for and would seriously weaken its position with the people.

e. Mr. Lerski emphasized that there is no nationalistic megalomania now in Poland and that the people are much more realistic there than here. Their refusal to consider the Curzon line is based upon a realistic consideration of Poland's post-war position. They do not consider that Poland will again become a great European power; but they feel that she must become a power of sufficient strength to maintain dignity and to play a part in the establishment and maintenance of European peace and not to be merely a pawn between the two great powers Russia and Germany.

f. There is also a moral consideration, particularly among the younger elements and youth movements. They believe that although the White Russians and Ukrainians do not like the Poles or Polish overrule, they would prefer this to Sovietization and that the Poles are morally obliged to refuse to abandon these Polish citizens to Soviet Russia without protest.

4. Mr. Lerski agrees with other witnesses that hatred of the Germans is growing more intense and more universal in Poland. He

says, however, that they still do not desire to kill all Germans. They intend to kill all Gestapo and all Party men, the young Party members in particular, all German police and all German minorities in Poland. The Operation of vengeance against the Germans will not obscure the Russian problem.

5. Mr. Lerski emphasises the tragic lack of weapons and money in the Polish Underground Movement. He says that our failure to supply arms and money more than anything else is causing the genuineness of our support and sympathy to be doubted.

DOCUMENT 15 (article in *The Edinburg Scotsman*).

Some time ago this column alluded to the exciting adventures of an Allied agent who travelled through Germany disguished as a member of the "Luftwaffe." It may now be disclosed that the agent was Mr. Jerzy "Jur" Lerski, who is now Director of the Polish Ministry of Information in Scotland and who is to talk on his experiences in the Usher Hall next week.

Mr. Lerski who is still under 30 does not look at all like what one thinks of as a secret agent. He might easily pass for a studious undergraduate. Before the war he shared his interests between sport and political science. One effect of his secret journeys was to put a terrific strain on his memory as so many of the messages which he carried were to dangerous to commit to paper.

The other day Mr. Lerski was reunited with his younger brother. His brother, at the age of 18, has added the "Virtuti Militari" to the family's decorations. This he won by his bravery in assuming command of a unit at the storming of Monte Cassino when all the officers had been killed.

FOOTNOTES

1 Cf. Jerzy Lerski, "Lwowska Młodzież Społeczno-Demokratyczna, 1937-1939" ("Social Democratic Youth of Lwów, 1937-1939") *Zeszyty Historyczne*. Paris: Instytut Literacki, 1979, No. 47, pp. 149-182.

2 World War II thus started with the Polish resistance to the Nazi onslaught on September 1, 1939, and not as British writers like to claim, on September 3, when the United Kingdom declared war. See e.g., Anthony Carter-Brown, *Bodyguard of Lies*. Newhall: Bantam Books, 1978, p. 23.

3 Cf. Robert M. Kennedy, *The German Campaign in Poland*. Washington, D.C.: Department of the Army, 1956, pp. 84-85.

4 Cf. General Wacław Stachiewicz, Chief of General Staff, Polish Armed Forces in 1939. *Pisma* (Collected Works). Paris: Instytut Literacki, 1979, vol. II, pp. 172-193.

5 Cf. Roman Buczek, *Stronnictwo Ludowe w Latach 1939-1945: Organizacja i Polityka* (The Peasant Party: Its Organization and Politics). London: Jutro Polski, 1975, pp. 20-23.

6 Władysław Anders, *An Army in Exile: The Story of the Second Polish Corps*. London: Macmillan and Co., Ltd., 1949, pp. 1-20.

7 Jan Karski, *Story of a Secret State*. Boston: Houghton Mifflin, 1944, p. 102. This, by the way, is the first account of the Polish underground movement in the English language. It was selected at the time of publication as Book of the Month choice.

8 Jerzy "Jur" Lerski, "Kurierski Turniej" (Jousting Tournament). *Wiadomości*. London: Dec. 15, 1946, No. 37.

9 Cf. Józef Białynia-Chołodecki and Stanisław Rachwał, *Jan Lerski Uczestnik Powstania Styczniowego, Porzemysłowiec, Obywatel i Radny m. Lwowa* (Jan Lerski, Participant of the January Uprising, Industrialist, Citizen, and Counselor of the Town of Lwów). Lwów: Drukarnia Piotrowskiego, 1926. I found this brochure in the Hoover Institution collection at Stanford, California.

10 Quast, "Szmaciany Gmach" (The Rag House). *Dziennik Polski*, London: Sep. 30, 1940. The reporter changed my name from Lieutenant Lerski to Relski in order to avoid reprisals against my family in occupied Poland — such were the rules of self-imposed wartime censorship.

11 For a better account of that West Slavic Movement, see Jerzy "Jur" Lerski, "Szkocka Kontrofensywa Zachodniej Słowiańszczyzny" (Counter-offensive by the Western Slavs in

Scotland). *Symposiones.* London: Univeritas Polonorum in Exteris, 1981, pp. 159-179. See also Sarah Meiklejohn Terry, *Poland's Place in Europe: General Sikorski and the Oder-Neisse Line, 1939-1943.* Princeton: Princeton University Press, 1983, p. 305-316.

[12] Numerous recent monographs deal with that intricate decoding process, e.g., Richard A. Woytak, "The Origins of the Ultra-Secret Code in Poland, 1937-1938". *The Polish Review.* New York: 1978, vol. XXIII, No. 3, pp. 79-85; Anthony Cave Brown, *Bodyguard of Lies.* New York: Harper and Row, 1975; Frederick W. Winterbttom, *The Ultra Secret.* London: Futura, 1975; Józef Garliński's *The Enigma War: the Inside Story of the German Enigma Codes and How the Allies Broke Them.* New York: Charles Scribner's Sons, 1979; and especially Władysław Kozaczuk's *Enigma: How the German Machine Cipher Was Broken, and How It Was Read by the Allies in World War Two.* University Publications of America, Inc., 1984.

[13] For complete lists of Polish paratroopers trained by British Special Operation Executives see Józef Garliński, *Politycy i Żołnierze* (Politicians and Soldiers). London: Odnowa, 1971, pp. 247-279. The book was also published in 1969 in England under the title *Poland, S.O.E. and the Allies.* London: George Allen & Unwin Ltd., 1969.

[14] Cf. Janusz Zawodny's definitive work on the massacre of Polish officers by the Soviets in Katyń, *Death in the Forest.* South Bend: Notre Dame University Press, 1980; also highly recommended for its literary value is Józef Czapski's *The Inhuman Land.* The author, a prominent painter, was in charge of on the spot investigations as cavalry major serving under General Anders.

[15] See Anders, *op. cit.*, pp. 38-60.

[16] The differentiation between "emissary" and "courier" was defined in 1940 by the underground headquarters of ZWZ (Union of the Armed Struggle, the Home Army's predecessor). According to that instruction found in the Sikorski Institution in London (MS L. dz. 3152/og. tjn. 40, L. ew. I/A).
An Emissary serves the purpose of liaison for the higher echelons of the Movement... Only very important missions are assigned to him; therefore, he must be well-acquainted with the general military and political situation and also be aware of the entire scope of activities of the sending organization... he has to know the content of the documents which he carries, and be able to reach the very sources of the organization by having the clandestine addresses or direct contacts.

[17] Karski, *op. cit.*, pp. 140-190.

[18] Władysław Bartoszewski and Zofia Lewin, eds., *Ten jest z Ojczyzny mojej: Polacy z Pomocą Żydom, 1939-1945* (That One Is From My Fatherland: Poles Who Aided the Jews, 1939-1945). Kraków: Wydanie drugie, Znak, 1969, pp. 321-335. Cf. footnote on p. 334. The same book has been published in New York by Twayne Publishers in 1970, under the title, *The Samaritans: Heroes of the Holocaust.*

[19] MS "Notatka dla Rząd Polskiego przesłana Gen. Sikorskiemu w Londynie przez Jana Karskiego. Dotyczy misji ppor. Jerzego Lerskiego" (The Note for Polish Government sent to Gen. Sikorski in London by Jan Karski on February 5, 1943 (see Appendix, Doc. No. 1, dealing with Second Lt. Jerzy Lerski's Mission). Collection: J. Karski #46033-8 M.30, Box #2. Stanford University: Hoover Institution on War, Revolution and Peace.

[20] Cf. Michał Sokolnicki, *Dziennik Ankarski, 1939-1943* (Ankara Diary, 1939-1943). London: Gryf, 1965, pp. 450-454; and Marian Kukiel, *Generał Sikorski: Żołnierz i Mąż Stanu Polski Walczącej* (General Sikorski: Soldier and Statesman of Fighting Poland). London: Instytut Polski i Muzeum im. Gen. Sikorskiego, 1970, pp. 215-216.

254

21 MS. "Dziennik Czynności Naczelnego Wodza" (Calendarium of the Commander-in-Chief's Activities). London: Instytut Polski i Muzeum im. Gen. Sikorskiego.

22 MS. Instytut Polski i Muzeum im. Generała Sikorskiego, Zespół ministerstwa Spraw Wewn. Depesze do Kraju. Poczta Nr. XIII, Lonyn, 11 Luty, 1943. Collection of the Ministry of the Interior. Cables to Poland. Mail No. XIII, London, Feb. 11, 1943.

23 For animosity towards civil couriers see Jan Erdman, *Droga do Ostrej Bramy* (The Way to Ostgra Brama). London: Odnowa, 1984, pp. 168 *et* 171.

24 *Unseen and Silent: Advantures from the Underground Movement, narrated by Paratroopers of the Polish Home Army.* London & New York: Sheed and Ward, 1955, pp. 26-30. This book is an English translation of Drogi Cichociemnych; Opowiadania zebrane i opracowane przez koło spadochroniarzy Armii Krajowej. London: Veritas, 1954, mianly edited by the author. Also see Józef Garliński's thorough study of the problem, *Politycy i Żołnierze*, pp. 258-259. The author makes a mistake, however, in his description of our flight — the reception unit "Pies" (Dog) was not near the town of Nałęczów, but near Opoczno on the other side of the Vistula River.

25 Józef Zabielski "Żbik", autobiographical *First to Return.* London: Garby Publications, 1976.

26 Stefan Korboński, *Fighting Warsaw: Story of the Polish Underground State.* London: Minerva Press, 1968, p. 41. Also see his *Polskie Państwo Podziemne; Przewodnik po Podziemiu z lat 1939-1945* (The Polish Underground State: the Guide to the Underground for 1939-1945). Paris: Instytut Literacki, 1975, p. 65.

27 Cf. Lerski, "Lwowska Młodzież...", *loc. cit.*, pp. 163-167.

28 See Leon Chajn, ed., *Materiały do historii Klubów Demokratycznych i Stronnictwa Demokratycznego w latach 1937-1939* (Materials to the History of Democratic Clubs and the Democratic Party for the years 1937-1939). Warsaw: Epoka, 1964, p. 368.

29 Cf. Wieńczysław Wagner, "Sprawy zagraniczne w Delegaturze Rządu (1943-1944)" (Foreign Affairs in the Governments Delegate's Office, 1943-1944). Zeszty Historyczne Vol. 73. Paris, 1985, pp. 229-233.

30 Report on my mission to General Grot was first published in the 1947 issue of *Trybuna* (No. 9), London's organ of the Polish Freedom Movement, "Independence and Democracy" (NID), and reprinted in No. 50 of *Biuletyn Informatyjny Koła A.K.* (Information Bulletin of the Home Army's Veteran Association). London: Sept. 1973.

31 Cf. Jan Erdman's fascinating biography of his brother-in-law Lt. Col. Maciej Kalenkiewicz, *Droga do Ostrej Bramy*, p. 213.

32 It was difficult and extremely expensive to free by bribery those who were incarcerated in the German camps. We were able, through the Socialist organization, to help Mrs. Grosfeld, the wife of the Socialist Minister of Finance, and her daughter, to escape from Przemyśl Ghetto to live under Aryan papers in the Bielany suburb of Warsaw where I visited with them. For Polish attempts to save the Jews see Bartoszewski, *The Samaritans;* Kazimierz Iranek-Osmekci, *He Who Saves One Life.* New York: Crown Publishers, 1971; Philip Friedman, *Their Brothers' Keepers.* New York: Crown Publishers, 1957; Andrzej Chciuk. *Saving Jews in War-Torn Poland, 1939-1945.* Melbourne, 1969.

33 Soon after the war I married in London Lieutenant Hanna Hryniewiecka, decorated with a Cross of Valor for her six years liaison service in the headquarters of the Home Army (A.K.), and her heroic performance in the Warsaw Uprising.

[34] Cf. Jan Nowak, *Courier from Warsaw*. Detroit: Wayne State University Press, 1982, p. 173.

[35] Apparently there is a "Lerski plaque" installed after the war on the Kościelec Ridge near the Mylna Pass. Cf. Father Andrew Woźnicki, in San Francisco's *Boży Siew* parish monthly, "Płyta Lerskiego", Vol. VI, Nr. 1/59 (January 1981), p. 55-57.

[36] Many years after the war a Kraków Univeristy art historian, Professor Karol Estreicher, told us at a lecture in San Francisco that, on the basis of that list obtained by me in Krakow in the summer of 1943, he was able to recover most of the illuminated manuscripts which the Nazis had stolen from the Jagiellonian Library.

[37] Włodzimierz Wnuk, *Byłem z Wami* (I Was With You). Warsaw: Pax, 1972, pp. 200-223. It is rather sad that in his autobiography, Wnuk was afraid to mention my name while describing all the underground contacts with "Ojczyzna" and the Department of Information where I was his immediate supervisor and close friend at the time. Remaining a non-person for "Pax" publishers I also became a victim of a typical self-sensorship.

[38] See Zawodny, *Death in the Forest*, as quoted in Footnote 14.

[39] According to Sarah Meiklejohn Terry's *Poland's Place in Europe*, the Soviet agent Colonel Philby was in charge of the British intelligence operations in Gibraltgar during the accident.

[40] For the full text of the corrected PPS-WRN letter to the Labour Party, see Appendix, Doc. No. 2.

[41] Cf. Kazimierz Koźniewski, *Zamknięte Koła* (Closed Circles). Warsaw: Iskry, 1967, pp. 109-110; also see W.L. Evert, *et. al.*, *Leszek Raabe: We wspomnieniach przyjaciół* (Leszek Raabe: In His Friends Remembrances). Warsaw: Iskry, 1969. This otherwise fine book does not mention the communist involvement in Raabe's disappearance. After all, it was published in captive Poland.

[42] The Soviet version of the trial is given in *Trial of the Organizers, Leaders and Members of the Polish Diversionist Organizations in the Rear of the Red Army on the Territory of Poland, Lithuania, and the Western Regions of Byelorussia and the Ukraine*. Moscow: Hutchinson & Co., 1945. For the Polish version see Zbigniew Stypułkowski's *Invitation to Moscow*. London: Macmillan Press; and Bronsiław Kuśnierz's Stalin and the Poles; an Indictment of the Sovit Leaders, London: Holls & Carter, 1949, pp. 228-235.

[43] Cf. Stanisław Broniewski, *Całym życiem* (With Whole Life). Warsaw: 1983, pp. 251-252.

[44] The Polish text of the Appeal was recently published in a collection of saved war documents under the title *Szare Szeregi Związek Harcerstwa Polskiego w czasie II Wojny Światowej: Główna Kwatera Harcerzy "Pasieka": Ocalałe dokumenty* (The Gray Rows: The Union of Polish Scouting During World War II; The Headquarters of the Scouts "Apiary"; surviving documents). London: Polonia Book Fund, Ltd., 1982, pp. 231-232. For the full English text see Appendix, Doc. 3.

[45] As anticipated, that wretched pencil was to cause me much trouble after the war as part of "Dołęga's" vengeance for what he dared to call my "breach of trust". However. I was fully exonerated in a special court presided over by General "Bór" (Komorowski) in 1947.

[46] For cables texts pretaining to my return trip via France and Spain see Appendix. Doc. No. 4, 5, and 6.

47 The three Frnech families who helped me during a one month stay in Paris in the winter of 1944, were, soon after my departure, caught by the Gestapo, being involved with sheltering a British agent of high military rank. Messrs. De Corta, Lecomte, and Robin were deported to Dachau; their wives were sent to Ravensbruck. Only M. Robin and his common law wife, Mme. Menard, and Mme. Lecomte survived the war, being awarded on my initiative the Cross of Merit by the Polish Government in Exile.

48 On October 2, 1945 I was duly honored by the Defense Minister's generous award, on his own initiative, of the Cross of Valor (Krzyż Walecznych Nr. 6831). This was before our services were recognized by his Majesty's Government, which decorated most of the SOE-trained secret couriers with the King's Medal for Courage in the Cause of Freedom — a special medal for foreigners. This award, in my case, was presented in 1950, in the British Embassy in Washington, D.C. by the military attache Colonel Peter A. Wilkinson. At the time of the Postwar demobilization, I was gratified to receive a fine assessment from the Chief of Staff, General Stanisław Kopański, the heroic commander of the Carpathian Brigade at the Battle of Tobruk. See Appendix, Doc. No. 7. As late as May 8, 1985 I was recognized by the Yad Vashem Institute in Jerusalem for the services rendered to aid the Polish Jews during the war. See Appendix, Doc. No. 8.

49 MS. President Raczkiewicz's Diary by his *aide de camp*. London: Sikorski Institute.

50 For the front page article in *Dziennik Polski* see Appendix, Doc. No. 9.

51 For translation of Karol Wagner's statement, see Appendix, Doc. No. 10.

52 For the text of General Bór's cable, see Appendix, Doc. No. 11.

53 Cf. Nowak, *op. cit.*, p. 249.

54 See Karski, *op. cit.*, pp. 100-103, *et.* 119.

55 Minutes of the Polish National Council Meeting are available in the Archives of the Polish Institute and Sikorski Museum in London, and in the Archives at the Hoover Institute for War, Revolution and Peace. A copy is also in the author's possession.

56 Cf. WRN letter to PPS received in London on March 4, 1944. It stipulates the following: "Simultaneously we send you our letter to the Executive Committee of the Labour Party with the request that you deliver it to the addressee. We think it would be advisable to take Jerzy with you to provide a commentary on the letter..." Also see J. Lerski, "Socjaliści polscy do brytyjskich," *Zeszyty Historyczne*, Paris (1986): 75, pp. 122-139.

57 For the Foreign Office documents pertaining to my reports, see Appendix, Doc. No 12 and 13; these documents were kindly provided by Mr. Jan Nowak after his research in London's Public Records Office.

58 Cf. Władysław Pobóg-Malinwoski, *Najnowsza Historia Polityczna Polski 1864-1945: Tom Trzeci (1939-1945)* (Recent Political History of Poland, 1864-1945, Third volume: 1939-1945). London: Veritas, 1951, pp. 200-202. The main source for the Home Army's (A.K.) operations *Polskie Siły Zbrojne w Drugiej Wojnie Światowej, Tom III: Armia Krajowa* (Polish Armed Froces During World War II, vol. III: Home Army) should also be consulted, in this particular case pp. 496-512. This major owrk was done by the Historical Commission of the Polish General Staff in London and published by the General Sikorski Historical Institute in 1950.

59 *The Edinburgh Scotsman* published the photograph of my brother and me. For the text see Appendix, Doc. No. 14.

[60] See Nowak *op. cit.*. 287-288.

[61] Cf. Henryk Kątny. ed. *1 Pułk Artylerii Przeciwlotniczej 1 Dywizji Pancernej: Zarys Historii. 1939-1984* (Historical Outline of the First Anti-aircraft Artillery Regiment of the First Armored Division. 1939-1984). London: 1984. p. 33.

[62] "Makary" (Kazimierz Iranek-Osmecki). "The Capture of V-Weapon Secrets" in *The Unseen and Silent*. pp. 159-171.

[63] Jan Kwapiński. *(1939-1945) (Z Pamiętnika)* (From Memoirs. 1939-1945). London: Światpol. 1947. pp. 162-163.

[64] These documents were purchased in 1980. on my inititive. by the Hoover Institution on War. Revolution and Peace from Marian Mikołajczyk. son of the late Prime Minister.

[65] Włodzimierz T. Kowalski. *Walka Dyplomatyczna o miejsce Polski w Europie. 1939-1945* (Diplomatic Struggle for Poland's Place in Europe. 1939-1945). Warsaw: Książka i Wiedza. 1972. p. 576: cf. also *The London Sunday Times* of December 17. 1944.

[66] Adam Pragier. *Czas Przeszły Dokonany* (Past Tense). London: B. Świderski. 1966. pp. 799-800.

[67] Tomasz Arciszewski. "Nieznane expose" (Unknown Expose). In *Zeszyty Historyczne*. Paris: Instytut Literacki. 1962. no. 1. pp. 9-24.

[68] *Dziennik Polski i Dziennik Żołnierza. London: Jan. 8. 1945.*

[69] Jerzy "Jur" Lerski. "Tragedia Żydowska i Dywersje Komunistyczne" *(Jewish Tragedy and Communist Diversion). In Orzeł Biały.* London: Feb.. 1978. pp. 9-10.

[70] *New York Times.* Jan. 5. 1945

[71] *Dziennik Polski.* Jan. 20. 1945.

[72] *Ibid..* Feb. 15. 1945.

[73] Wacław Jędrzejewicz. *Polonia Amerykańska w Polityce Polskiej: Historia Komitetu Narodowego Amerykanów Polskiego Pochodzenia* (American Polonia in Polish Politics: History of the National Committee of Americans of Polish Descent). New York: National Committee of Americans of Polish Descent. 1954. pp. 127-132.

[74] Jerzy R. Krzyżanowski. *Generał.* London: Odnowa. 1980. p. 173.

[75] Jan Karski's *opus magnum. The Great Powers and Polnad. 1919-1945: from Versailles to Yalta.* New York: University Press of America. 1985. in the last five chapters of the book exposes well the duplicity of Western policy towards Poland during the Teheran and Yalta conferences. Another important source is Edward J. Rożek's *Allied Wartime Diplomacy: A Pattern in Poland.* New York: John Wiley & Sons. 1958. Excellent accounts of the entire problem were given by the Polish Ambassador in Washington. D.C.. Jan Ciechanowski. in his *Defeat in Victory.* Garden City. N.Y.: Doubleday & Co.. 1947: and last but not least by a noble U.S. ambassador to Poland. Arthur Bliss Lane's *I Saw Poland Betrayed.* New York: The Bobbs-Merrill Co.. 1948. All four books are important to understanding that phase of diplomatic history.

[76] Cf. "Historyczny protest" (Historical protest). In my own *Emisariusz "Jur".* London: Polska Fundacja Kulturalna. 1984. p. 207-210.

258

[77] Pragier, *op. cit.*, pp. 879-881.

[78] Jerzy Lerski, "Konferencja PPS z Labour Paty" (Polish Socialist Party Conference with Parliamentary Labour Party). In *Orzeł Biały*, Dec. 1975, pp. 3-5. The minutes of the meeting prepared by me were preserved in Adam Ciołkosz's private archives and kindly handed to me in March 1975, during by sabbatical visit to London.

[79] J.D. Thackrah, "Aspects of American and British Policy Towards Poland from the Yalta to the Potsdam Conference, 1945." In *The Polish Review*, 1976, vol. XXI, no. 4, pp. 3-34.

[80] Anders, *op. cit.*, pp. 255-257.

[81] Wacław Jędrzejewicz, ed. *Poland in the British Parliament: 1939-1946.* New York: Józef Piłsudski Institute of America, 1963, vol. III, pp.379-561.

[82] Winston Churchill, *Triumph and Tragedy.* Boston: Houghton Mifflin Co., 1953, pp. 399-402.

[83] Jędrzejewicz, *op. cit.*, pp. 542, 588, et 589-601.

[84] Lerski, *op. cit.*, pp. 220-222.

[85] Tadeusz Kochanowicz, *Na wojennej emigracji: Wspomnienia z lat 1942-1944* (On the War Emigration: Memoirs for the years 1942-1044). Warsaw: Książka i Wiedza, 1975, pp. 292-293.

[86] *Polscy Spadochroniarze-Pamiętnik Żołnierzy* (Polish Paratroopers soldiers' Memoirs). London: Fundusz Wydawniczy Plutonu Opieki I. Samodzielnej Brygady. Spadochronowej, 1949, p. 358.

[87] "Premier Arciszewski wśród żołnierzy w Szkocji" (Prime Minister Arciszewski Among Soldiers in Scotland). In *Dziennik Polski*, June 12, 1945.

[88] It should be noted that the cable, despite its tone of politeness and respect, was addressed to "His Excellency" and not the Prime Minister of Poland.

[89] The other vice-chairman was Jan Jankowski, and the chairman since 1945, Rowmund Piłsudski. Among the original leaders of NiD also were: Stefan Gacki, Stanisław Grocholski, Dr. Bronisław Jedlewski, Dr. Zbigniew Jordan, Bolesław Łaszewski, Zygmunt Nagórski, Jr., Andrzej Pomian, Adam Rudzki, Franciszek Skrzeszewski, Zygmunt Szempliński, Dr. Tymon Terlecki, and Bolesław Wierzbiański.

[90] Edward Raczyński, *W sojuszniczym Londynie* (In Allied London). London: Widenfeld and Nicholson, 1962, p. 366.

[91] Cf. Aleksander Bergman's sober account of the San Francisco Conference *Dzieje Pustego Fotela: Konferencja w San Francisco i Sprawa Polska* (The Story of an Empty Chair; the San Francisco Conference in the Cause of Poland). London: 1948.

[92] Karl Marx, "Poland's European Mission." In Paul W. Blackstock's and Bert F. Hosellize's Collection of Articles. Speeches, Letters and New Dispatches, *The Russian Menace to Europe, by Karl Marx and Friedrich Engels.* Glencoe, IL: The Free Press, 1952, pp. 104-108. This particular speech of Marx, delivered in London for the Meeting of the International Working Men Association, (the First International) in 1864, is of course missing in the so-called Complete Works of Karl Marx, published in the Soviet Union.

INDEX OF NAMES

Fisher, H.A.L., 202
Fiszer, Czeslaw, 113
Folkierski, Władysław, 97, 198
Frank, Hans, 121, 233
Freyd, Emanuel, 207

G

Gacki, Stefan, 223, 259
Gamble, Sandra, 8
Gargulińska, Murka, 121-122
Gawlina, Józef, 142
Gaworski, Tadeusz ("Lawa"), 24, 148
Geekie, Ian, 47
Geekies, Mr. & Mrs., 47
George VI, King, 226
Gieysztor, Aleksander ("Olicki"), 116
Glabisz, Kazimierz, 219
Głuchowski, Janusz, 186, 219
Godfrey, Archb., 194
Godunow, Borys, 48, 151
Goebbels, Joseph, 38, 127, 128, 149
Goldstein, Lt., 159
Gomułka, Władysław, 214
Gorbaty, Jan, 112
Goring, Herman, 153
Gotesman, Gustaw, 180
Gotesman, Patricia, 180
Grabowski, 161
Grabski, Stanisław, 67
Graham, Alan, 206
Graliński, Zygmunt, 32
Green, William, 176
Greenwood, Arthur, 181, 207, 211
Griffin, Archb., 194
Grocholski, Stanisław, 259
Grochowski, Józef, 195
Grosfeld, Ludwig, 197, 216
Grosfeld, Mrs., 255
Grudziński, Józef, 135

265

Grycko. Stanisław. 80
Gryziewicz. Stanisław. 223

H

Halecki. Oskar. 33
Haller. Józef. 224
Handelsman. Marceli. 137.
Harriman. Averell. 189. 210
Hartman. Józef. 81
Hazell. Ronald. 61
Herceliński. Wacława. 123
Hertz. Jadwiga. 127
Hess. Rudolf. 41
Himmler. Heinrich. 23
Hitler. Adolf. 30. 35-36. 38.
   41. 44. 47. 52. 55.
   135. 151-153. 167. 236. 237
Hlond. August. 141
Hopkins. Austin. 212
Horko. Tadeusz. 226
Hryniewiecka. Hanna. 255
Hubert. Stanisław. 204
Hulewicz. Witold. 67
Huysmans. Camille. 157

I

Ismay. Hastins. 170

J

Jabłonski. Tadeusz ("Jan").
   146-147. 149. 150. 153
Jakubowski. Zbigniew. 111
Janik brothers. 82. 82
Jankowski. Jan B. 259
Jankowski. Jan S. ("Doktór"). 91.
   93. 129. 132. 139-140.
   167. 172-173. 228
Januszewskik. Maksymilian. 201
Jarema. Stefan. 131
Jarosz. Janusz. 30

266

Jasiukowicz, Stanisław, 134
Jastrzebski, Antoni ("Ugor"),
  56-57
Jaworski, Władysław, 134
Jedlewski, Bronisław, 187, 222,
  259
Johnson, Charles, 207
Jordan, Zbigniew, 259
Jurecki, Marian, 54

K

Kaczyński, Zygmunt, 71, 77, 113
Kalenkiewicz, Maciej
  ("Kotwicz"), 109-110, 255
Kamiński, Aleksander
  ("Hubert") and ("J.
  Górecki"), 142
Kann, Maria ("Murka"), 110,
  116
Karaś, Janina ("Mrs. Berg"),
  103-104, 109
Karaszewicz-Tokarzewski,
  Michał, 65, 108
Karolus, Sylwester, 196
Karpińska, Zofia, 122-123
Karski (Kozielewski), Jan, 33-34,
  56, 63, 65-66, 70, 72, 74-
  76, 103-104, 117, 175, 177,
  181, 231

Kasprzykowski, Konstanty, 32
Kaszyński, Eugeniusz ("Nurt"),
  114
Katz-Suchy, Juliusz, 223
Kauzik, Stanisław ("Dołęga"),
  94, 119, 144-145, 147
Kerr, A. Clark, 210
Ketling-Prugar, Bronisław, 36
Khrushchev, Nikita, 18
Kisielewski, Józef, 43

Knoll, Roman, 76, 94, 101-102,
  137, 168
Kobielski, Ireneusz, 31

Kuntz, 121
Kutrzeba, Hanka, 121
Kutrzeba, Stanisław, 121
Kuźmicki, Mieczysław, 82-85
Kwapiński, Jan, 79, 175-176,
189, 207, 218
Kwiatkowski, Michał, 71

L

Lalewicz, Stanisław, 80
Langrod, Witold, 216
Lapter, Karol, 223
Lawrence, Pethick, 187
Laskowski, Otton, 33
Lasocka, Anna, 101, 116
Lech, Jan, 20-21
Lecomte, M. and Mne., 154-155
257
Lelech, Władysława, 91, 93, 119
Lenin, Vladimir, 115, 202
Lerski, Jan, 34, 65, 180, 181
Lerski, Mieczysław, 13, 72, 118,
256
Lerski, Thomas, 127
Leśniewski, Andrzej, 101
Leśniowska, Zofia, 128
Librach, Jan, 66
Limanowski, Bolesław, 95
Lipiński, Karol, 97
Lipski, Józef, 32
Litauer, Stefan, 77, 140, 170,
172, 174
Low, David, 194
Lutosławski, Tadeusz, 192
Luxemburg, Rosa, 194
Lyon, Percy, 184

Ł

Łaszewski, Bolesław, 8, 223, 259
Łopatniuk, Lt., 124

Łuczkiewicz, Stanisław ("Sep"),
132
Łychowski, Tadeusz, 217

M

Mack, Julius, 178
Maczek, Stanisław, 36, 48, 182,
219
Maisky, Ivan, 53, 65, 69
Makowiecki, Jerzy ("Malicki"),
104, 133, 137, 145
Makowski, Wacław, 82
Malessa, Emilia ("Marcysia"),
146
Malicki, 104
Małcużynski, Karol, 131
Małecki, Zbigniew, 12
Mara-Meyer, Jerzy ("Filip"), 90
Markowska, Jadwiga, 95
Markowski, Wincenty ("Paweł"),
95
Martin, Kingsley, 194
Marx, Karl, 115, 229
Masaryk, Jan, 217
Mazalon, 92
Mazur, Judge, 189
McClure, Robert, 80
McLaren, Morray, 177
Menard, Mme., 156, 257
Meysztowicz, Jan, 174
Męclewski, Alojzy W., 132
Mickiewicz, Adam, 16, 33, 138
Mikołajczyk, Jan, 86-87, 114,
127
Mikołajczyk, Maria, 87, 113
Mikołajczyk, Marian, 258
Mikołajczyk, Stanisław, 55-56,
61, 63, 69-70, 75, 79, 91,
128, 134-135, 166-169, 174-
175, 178-179, 186-187, 191,
193, 197-198, 208, 213-216,
220, 224, 228
Miłosz, Czeslaw, 5, 131
Miszewska, Ewa, 26

270

S

T

U

V

W

278

PHOTOGRAPHS

The author after his return to London in 1944.

New Year's Day, 1940; on the Daube River in Budapest on his way to France. Aut ior is the second from left.

After joining his anti-aircraft Artillery Unit in Les Forges de Paimpont (Brittany, France). Author in the center of the last row.

Early Spring in Pontchateau, 1940. Author as Second Lt. of the anti-circraft artillery unit.

May, 1940 in Pontchateau. Author in the center with his fellow officers of the anti-aircraft artillery unit.

Author's unit in Toulouse after the fall of France prior to evacuation to Great Britain.

On the way to Great Britain on the Polish S.S. Sobieski. Author in center.

July, 1940 in the Scottish camp in Crawford (Lanarkshire).
Author second from right.

Summer, 1940 in Crawford among proponents of the West-
Slavic Federation. *Standing from the left: Zygmunt Sławiński,*
Bronisław Ajdukiewicz, Prof. Tadeusz Sulimirski, the author,
and Kazimierz Czerwiński.

August, 1940. Commander-in-Chief Gen. Władysław Sikorski on his inspection of Crawford Camp.

Author on the left reports as educational officer of the Crawford Camp to Gen. Sikorski in presence of the President of the Republic, Władysław Raczkiewicz, Lady Norton and the Carson Sisters, Church of Scotland helpers.

Author explains to President Raczkiewicz, Chief-of-Staff Col. Klimecki, and Gen. Sikorski the future borders of the proposed Federation of East-Central Europe. In the center background, the author of the map, Second Lt. Stanisław Połujan.

December, 1941. Ringway Airport near Manchester (Lancashire). Training of the paratroopers.

Winter, 1942-43. Audley End, Essex Station No. 20 for the secret paratroopers before their flight to occupied Poland.

August, 1967. Radzice Duże, Poland. The survivors of the regional Home Army (A.K.) receiving unit of 1943 Secret Paratroopers Operation from England. Among them in the center, one of the secret couriers, Piotr Nowak ("Oko"), who jumped on the night of February 19, 1943 with the author. Mrs. Irena Rakoczy in the white blouse who accompanied us to Warsaw, and Stanisław Kiszyta in striped shirt, who was in charge of the "Pies" (Dog) Special Unit.

August, 1944. Minister of National Defense, Gen. Marian Kukiel decorates the author with the Cross of Valour for performing the secret envoy mission to Poland.

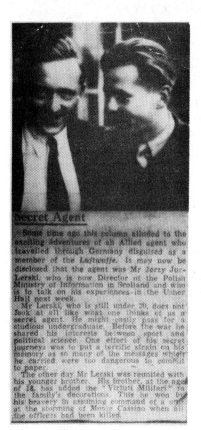

August, 1944. The author's reunion with his half-brother, Jar Sołtysik in London after the latter's Monte Cassino assault under Gen. Anders.

December 1944. President of Poland Władysław Raczkiewicz and Prime Minister Tomasz Arciszewski under the portrait of King John III Sobieski in the President's office at George Street, London.

Jur-Lerski after press conference in London. Standing from the left: Dr. Ludwik Rubel, press officer of the II Polish Corps in Italy, Boleslaw Wierzbianski editor of the Polish Press Agency in London, Jur-Lerski and Zbigniew Raciéski Polish Union of Journalists in London.

Prime Minister Tomasz Arciszewski's photo portrait, with personal dedication from the author's name day of April 24, 1945.

May, 1945. Prime Minister Arciszewski with three Cabinet members: from the left, Prof. Adam Pragier (Information and Documentation); Prof. Władysław Folkierski (Education and Congressional Affairs); Stanisław Sopicki (Minister of Public Administration and Reconstruction) — in Prime Minister's office, 18 Kensington Palace Gardens, London.

June, 1945. Premier Tomasz Arciszewski and the author as his Private Secretary in Forfar (Angus) in Scotland during the inspection of the Fourth Grenadiers Division.

The author after his retirement as professor Emeritus of Modern European History at the University of San Francisco.

London, 1945. Drawing by Zofia Wiśniewska. The attorney Jan Jankowski and the autor as vice-chairmen of the Polish Freedom Movement "Independence and Democracy" (NiD).

TABLE OF CONTENTS